The Ascendancy of the Congress in Uttar Pradesh

Class, Community and Nation in Northern India, 1920–1940

GW00722608

The Ascendancy of the Congress in Uttar Pradesh

Class, Community and Nation in
Northern India, 1920–1940

By

GYANENDRA PANDEY

Anthem Press
London

Anthem Press is an imprint of
Wimbledon Publishing Company
PO Box 9779, London, SW19 7QA

This edition first published by Wimbledon Publishing Company 2002

© Gyanendra Pandey

British Library Cataloguing in Publication Data
Data available

Library of Congress in Publication Data
A catalogue record has been applied for

ISBN Hb 1 84331 056 2
Pb 1 84331 057 0

To my mother

and

to the memory of my father

Contents

Preface to the second edition

All the histories of Indian nationalism that I had come across in my years in school and college were preoccupied with the matter of how the nation achieved its independence. There was never any question of how the idea of the 'nation' itself came into existence, or how this particular nation came to be thought. For these were taken to be natural, given conditions - with their roots lying very far back in history, in a dimly perceived and distant past. The historical investigation was limited to the way in which the people of India struggled to realize this readymade conception, how they worked for freedom and the right to determine their own conditions of corporate life.

Based on a doctoral dissertation that was researched in the 1970s, this book was another attempt to study the process of mobilization in the Indian national movement, yet one that marked something of a departure from the perspective outlined above, as I trust the following pages will show. The anti-colonial struggle in India was one of the two or three great mass movements of the first half of the twentieth century. By 1939, it was possible for Jawaharlal Nehru to claim that the frontiers of the Indian national movement lay in China on the east and Spain in the west, reflecting the international aspect of the struggle against colonialism and imperialism. By that time, too, the demand for social transformation and economic justice was a feature of the anti-colonial and nationalist struggle, the "workers' and peasants' state" in Russia was being hailed as a beacon light, and working people all over British India were beginning to demand the rights of full citizens.

The struggle against colonialism in the subcontinent began of course in a far more scattered and tentative form. In the later nineteenth century, urban professionals and notables had formed diverse public associations that held occasional meetings and produced moderate manifestos and appeals. Even these associations had to reckon with the conditions and difficulties of arbitrary colonial rule; some spawned more radical splinters in time; and some saw their concerns overlapping with the concerns of wider sections of the population as expressed in episodic (but significant) local protests and risings. It was not until after the First World War, however, that these different streams of politics came together more fully to generate the mass struggle that is remembered as the Indian national movement.

For a long time, Indian nationalist historiography explained this transformation in terms of the thought and actions of an extraordinary leadership, unmatched in its vision and commitment. British colonialist (and neo-colonialist) historiography, in its turn, argued that this leadership itself, and consequently the Indian struggle as a whole, was a product of colonial education and reform, and more specifically (in a version that came to have considerable influence in the 1970s) that the character and power of the movement flowed from the constitutional arrangements and opportunities offered by this reforming colonial regime. The argument put forward in this book was - and is - that both the Indian national movement and its achievements were more layered than either of these perspectives allowed; that behind its achievements lay not only the initiatives and sacrifices of an enlightened leadership, but also the initiatives and struggles of masses of people in diverse economic and cultural situations with diverse claims on liberation; and that the achievement too was more incomplete, and (for many) more uncertain than had been made out.

Today, over two decades after the first publication of this work, these propositions may seem so obvious to some people as to be taken for granted. Perhaps it bears reiterating that they were not quite so readily accepted when they were first advance by a whole new crop of historians in the late 1970s and 1980s. Nor does their acceptance, which is far from being universal even today, detract from the need to examine the diverse forces, the many-sited initiatives and the multiple contests that went into the making of the Indian national movement.

Conceived at a time when the Naxalite movement had raised important questions about the extent of the bourgeois democratic revolution in India and the way forward to a more just and egalitarian social arrangement, this book was centrally concerned with the part that workers and peasants and other 'ordinary' people had played in the recent history of India. It raised questions about the contest over the national idea, as much as over how that idea - or those ideas - were to be realized. It attempted to underline the historicity, or historical character, of nationhood and nationalism; and stressed the importance of studying the *process* whereby that sense of nationhood and that feeling of nationalism came into being, as well as examining the divisions and contradictions that remained. It spoke to the problem of agency.

Some of these arguments were more implicit than explicit in 1978. Many of them have been more fully worked out since then, and numerous scholars have asked the same kinds of questions. What constituted the goal of *swaraj*, or self-rule, for diverse castes, classes and communities in a country such as India? How widely were particular senses of nationhood, and nationalism, shared; how differently were they interpreted? What were the contests that resulted? What was the distribution of power between different classes, castes, communities, sexes in this newly imagined political community - in the 1920s, in 1942, or in 1947? What were the contradictions *within* the Indian national movement? What were its compromises?

I wrote in the preface to the first edition:

> What began in the author's mind as a somewhat idealized history of 'the people' in isolation has emerged, after research, more as an account of the people's experiences at the hands of the privileged classes - British and Indian. This is in part a function of the archival records; quite simply, the writings of the period have far more to say about the British rulers and the Indian elites than about the Indian masses. A more complete account of the conditions, aspirations and political activities of the poorer classes requires a closer study of other sources - popular literature, oral tradition, judicial records (especially the detailed proceedings of criminal courts) - than I was able to make in the course of this investigation, and a greater effort to 'soak up' their society and culture through time actually spent among them in the towns and villages. Yet, I would emphasize that both the elites and the masses appear as active agents in the story that follows, that in this experience of mass politics there were distinct influences flowing either way....

The work pointed in this way to the existence of different streams of politics within the anti-colonial struggle, diverse strands whose braiding and interweaving and pulling in several directions at once made up the tapestry of Indian nationalism.

Both Sumit Sarkar and Partha Chatterjee have, in later writings, characterized national liberation in India as a particular form of what Gramsci had called the 'passive revolution of capital', involving a 'molecular transformation' that accommodated the dominant classes as partners in a new historical bloc while necessitating no more than a partial incorporation of the popular classes. This book may be seen, in retrospect, as an early attempt to see how the contests that went into the making of that passive revolution were played out in northern India in the first half of the twentieth century.

Revising a first book, twenty-five years after it was first written, is probably never an easy task. Reading through this one now, I see it as the product of a very different time in the development of the society and the academy, as well as the author. It is a young person's book, and suffers - if that is the word - from the passions and the limitations of a young person's outlook. If I were to re-write it today, it would be a very different book: certainly more restrained and perhaps (since this must always remain a hope) more nuanced. But if there was merit in the book, friends have said to me, it came in part at least from its clarity of argument and directness of expression.

I have gone along with the advice of these friends and left the book substantially as it was when it was first published in 1978. What I have done for this new edition is to iron out a few of the most inelegant expressions and passages, update the bibliographical references, and add some material in different chapters to show that the argument stands for the period 1920 to 1940 as a whole. I should add that neither the bibliographical revisions, nor the additional materials on the early 1920s and the late 1930s, are intended to make this a comprehensive account of the anti-colonial struggle in Uttar Pradesh for the years under study. In regard to the new historical literature, I have simply sign-posted some of this, while pointing readers to other books where more comprehensive bibliographies may be found. As to comprehensiveness of historical detail, this work was never intended to be a blow-by-blow account, a definitive statement on all aspects of the national movement in the UP of the inter-War period. I presented it rather as a hypothesis, an intervention in a debate, and an invitation to further research and deliberation. I hope it may still fulfill something of that function.

Several of the acknowledgements made in the first edition of this book need to be reiterated. I owe thanks to the Rhodes Trust, the Beit Foundation and Nuffield College, Oxford, for providing the scholarships and funds that made this research possible; and to Wolfson College and Lincoln College, Oxford, for electing me to Fellowships that gave me the leisure and stimulus to complete the writing of the book in its initial form. Also to the staff of the archives and libraries where most of the research for this book was done: the Indian Institute Library, Oxford; the India Office Library and Records, London; the National Archives of India and the Nehru Memorial Museum and Library, New Delhi; the UP State Archives, Secretariat Record Room and Criminal Investigation Department Office, Lucknow; the Collectorate Record Rooms in Agra, Allahabad, Azamgarh and Rae Bareli; the Shibli Manzil, Azamgarh; and the Kashi Nagri Pracharni Sabha, Varanasi.

Among individuals, I wish to express my gratitude, once more, to the numerous old Congressmen, peasant leaders, revolutionary-terrorists and 'sympathizers' – many of them, unfortunately now dead – who talked to me about their activities and experiences: among them, Pandit Padma Kant Malaviya and Thakur Srinath Singh of Allahabad; Pandit Rup Narain Tripathi, Thakur Sheomurti Singh and Pandit Mahabir Prasad Shukla of Jamunipur and Kotwa and Sirsa in that district; Pandit Anjani Kumar Tewari of Rae Bareli; Babu Satyanarain Srivastava of Bakuliha in Rae Bareli district; and Babu Jagan Prasad Rawat of Agra.

Some intellectual and personal debts also need to be re-stated: to P.S. Dwivedi and Mohammad Amin, teachers in St. Stephen's College, Delhi; Tapan Raychaudhuri, S. Gopal, David Fieldhouse, Laurence Whitehead, David Goldey, advisers and friends in Oxford; Peter Reeves and Ranajit Guha, mentors and guides beyond. Also to David Page and Bruce Cleghorn, Chris Bayly and Sumit Sarkar, Barun De, Shahid Amin and David Hardiman, friends of yester-year (and some even of today!)

And some added. I am grateful to Crispin Bates who suggested Anthem Press as the publisher for this revised edition, and to Kamaljit Sood and his colleagues at Anthem for their enthusiastic support in its production. Also to Sarah Khokhar and Lisa Emanuello for valuable technical assistance in the preparation of the manuscript.

As before, I wish to acknowledge the extraordinary personal support of my parents, and of Jayanti, Geetanjali, Gayatri, Asha and Shailendra. To them I must now add Nishad, who was not around in

1978 to ask the questions he has been asking since; Sudhir, intellectual comrade in more ways than he knows; and Ruby, intellectual comrade and more.

Gyanendra Pandey
Baltimore
January 2002

List of Maps and Tables

MAPS

TABLES

Abbreviations

AICC	All- India Congress Committee
AICC Suppl.	All- India Congress Committee Supplementary Papers
CID	Criminal Investigation Department
CSP	Congress Socialist Party
CWMG	*Collected Works of Mahatma Gandhi*
DCC	District Congress Committee
FR	Fortnightly Report for the United Provinces. (File numbers for these are given in the Bibliography. In the Notes these reports are identified simply by their month and year, with the figure 1or 2 indicating the first or second half of the given month.)
GAD	General Administration Department
GOI	Government of India
Home Poll	Home Department, Political Branch, of the Government of India
ICP	Independent Congress Party
IOL	India Office Library and Records
JN	Jawaharlal Nehru
KNPS	Kashi Nagri Pracharni Sabha, Banaras
Kw	'Keep with', an appendage to a Government file
MN	Motilal Nehru
NAI	National Archives of India, New Delhi
NML	Nehru Memorial Museum and Library, New Delhi
NOP	Note on the Press of the United Provinces of Agra and Awadh (prepared weekly by the Government Reporter)
PAI	Police Abstract of Intelligence (a weekly abstract of intelligence reports from the different districts of the United Provinces)

PCC	Provincial Congress Committee
PP	Proscribed Publication
Rs.	Rupees
SRR	Secretariat Record Room, Lucknow
TCC	Town Congress Committee
UP	The United Provinces of Agra and Awadh (after independence, Uttar Pradesh)
UPLC	The United Provinces Legislative Council
UPSA	Uttar Pradesh State Archives, Lucknow

1

Introduction

The years between the two World Wars bore witness to a radical transformation in the Indian political scene. During this time the anti-colonial struggle developed into a powerful mass movement, and its leading party, the Indian National Congress, moved from well-ordered annual meetings and polite calls for constitutional reform to the demand for 'complete (political) independence' and extensive debate on the conditions that would make for social and economic independence at the same time. By the end of this period, indeed, when, at the outbreak of the Second World War, the British colonial rulers looked for its cooperation in the pursuit of the war, the Congress was insisting on 'independence *now*'. It was by then very much the party in waiting, demonstrably ready and able to head a successor regime.

Historians of all shades of opinion have recognized this advance – or at least, some aspects of it. To many the strength and popularity of the Congress and the nationalist movement appeared as a steadily rising curve all the way from the late nineteenth century, with only occasional and negligible downward movements. The ascent was seen to be especially steep in the period after 1919. From the Hindu nationalist R C Majumdar to the secular liberal Jawaharlal Nehru and the Marxist R P Dutt, nationalist and anti-imperialist writers seemed to be at one on this point.[1] It was noted that some 60,000 satyagrahis were arrested in less than a year of civil disobedience in 1930–1, and at least 120,000 during the fifteen months from January 1932 to March 1933, compared with only 30,000 during the Non-Cooperation Movement of 1920–2. The agitations of the early 1940s apparently achieved an even greater scale. Officials estimated that over 60,000 people were arrested, 18,000 detained without trial, 940 killed and 1,630 injured in police and military firing in under five months after 8 August 1942.[2]

On the imperialist side too there were few dissenters from this view of the progress of the Indian nationalist movement. Some, in the earlier stages, had fondly clung to the opinion that the Congress was a small collection of self-seeking *babus*. By the 1920s and 1930s, however, they had to add that this coterie was capable of, and successful in, 'deluding the masses'. After the shock of the Swadeshi Movement in Bengal and the even more massive Non-Cooperation and Civil Disobedience Movements, 'it was…generally agreed,' says Spear in a review of British writing on the Indian nationalist movement, 'that Gandhi had achieved the miracle of extending the movement to the masses.'[3]

Such a view of the unilineal progress of Indian nationalism is perhaps somewhat oversimplified. For if this picture were true it would be difficult to explain the want of mass participation in the institutional politics of several parts of India and Pakistan in the years after independence. If mass involvement in Congress activities grew so distinctly and indubitably, under the guidance and encouragement of the Congress leadership, from 1885 to 1947, why is there some rather mixed evidence of it in the politics of the Congress after that date? Were the 'masses' of the sub-continent concerned solely with the removal of the British and content to retire from an active role in public affairs once this has been accomplished? R P Dutt's work provided a solitary, but extremely useful, lead towards an answer to this puzzle. There was, from the very beginning, a 'double strand' in Congress politics, he argued – 'on the one hand, the strand of cooperation with imperialism against the "menace" of the mass movement; on the other hand, the strand of leadership of the masses in the national struggle.'[4]

Again the traditional account of a triumphant, all-encompassing nationalist movement provided no real explanation for the birth of two separate 'nation-states' in 1947. Owing to this particular weakness it left unanswered some of the questions posed by the Hindu chauvinist and British colonialist theories of Indian nationhood. On the one hand we have the point of view represented by Majumdar, that the Indian nationalist movement was nothing but a movement for the self-determination of what he calls 'the Hindu nation' (which, in his view, had in fact lost its 'independence' in the thirteenth century).[5] The colonialist theory, on the other hand, denied the existence of an Indian nation, while insisting that Hindus, Muslims and indeed other communities, tribes and castes were deeply – not to say irremediably – divided. In this reading, what might follow the end of British rule in India was anybody's guess; and it would be matter for small surprise were the sub-continent to break up into two (or many more) successor states, if it did not descend into complete chaos.[6]

In addition, there was nothing in either the liberal nationalist historiography or the Hindu chauvinist and British colonialist theories mentioned above that constituted a proper explanation of the differential role of the various social groups in the mass nationalist campaigns. For those who believed that the Hindus had constituted a nation since ancient times, as much as for those who altogether denied the existence of any Indian nationhood, the development of a powerful nationalist movement could be explained only by some sort of historical force – such as a 'man of destiny'. And in yet another remarkable convergence of views the different schools of historians found in Gandhi their 'man of destiny'. Majumdar called the period 1920–47 'The Age of Gandhi', for it was 'almost wholly dominated by the personality of Mahatma Gandhi'.[7] Nehru, in his turn, expressed the liberal's sense of relief as he recalled how

'Gandhi came…like a powerful current of fresh air which made us stretch ourselves and take deep breaths…He sent us to the villages and the countryside hummed with the activity of innumerable messengers of the new gospel of action. The peasant was shaken up and he began to emerge from his quiescent shell.'[8]

Among one section of Indian historians, writing a little later, there was some recognition of the different class forces and interests encompassed by the nationalist movement. Following R P Dutt, these scholars suggested that there were two basic elements in the development of popular nationalism in India: the clash between the Indian and the British bourgeoisie, and the growing impoverishment of the peasantry, leading to mass unrest. Yet mass discontent was no recent phenomenon, and there was a need to explain how the link between the 'masses' and the bourgeoisie (or the intelligentsia representing the bourgeoisie) was forged. Here the scholars returned to a trusted argument: Gandhi remained the magician, and the great mobilizer.[9]

British observers too, barring some of the 'die-hard' imperialists who were satisfied with the 'conspiracy' theory of 'self-seeking babus' deluding 'dumb millions', came to emphasize the force of religion and the importance of Gandhi's 'saintliness'. Valentine Chirol provides a fair illustration: 'Gandhi acquired a personal hold, unexampled perhaps since Buddha, on the masses both in the congested slums of the modern cities and in the stagnant backwaters of agricultural India. For if he was a reckless agitator, the saint that was also in him was moved like the founder of Buddhism by a great compassion for the poor, the humble and the sinner.'[10]

As the nationalist movement stabilized and broadened an updated version of the same view, garnished with liberal values, came to be put forward by British historians and administrators. Indian nationalism was henceforth to be identified as a product of Indo-British cooperation. It was something that the British had encouraged all along, the new argument ran, though it may have been hastened by the 'persuasive oratory' of nationalist leaders, by the emotive power of 'OM' and 'Bande Mataram' and by 'deep forces in Hinduism of which we know little'.[11]

II

The 1960s and 1970s saw the emergence of a more detailed historiography, based on recently released government documents and collections of private papers. The notion of a giant clash between imperialism and nationalism in the sub-continent was now increasingly contested by several groups of historians. Their researches focused on the regional variations of the Indian nationalist movement and the contradictions within it.[12] Not only was the earlier vision of the unity of the movement challenged as a result; the continuity and indeed the very existence of the movement was again called into question in the writings of some of these scholars. Yet the mass of contemporary evidence, official and non-official, regarding something then perceived as a strong and lasting nationalist struggle, remained. Faced with this stubborn fact, the 'revisionist' historians found it necessary to admit that the nationalist movement was not entirely an optical illusion. However, their 'new' interpretation of its development marked a return to the stance of the post-Chirol liberal colonialists, only marginally modified by new data.

There was a revival of the view that English education produced a new 'class' that began and continued agitation for its own ends.[13] British 'beneficence' and Indian 'intrigue' were thus again wedded. Subsequently a slight shift in emphasis led to a modification of this view of the Indian nationalists as the spiritual progeny of British liberal education. English constitutional innovation rather than Macaulay's cultural crusade was what was now supposed to have made a nationalist of an Indian. Making interesting use of some modern anthropological and sociological work, this particular version suggested that it was traditional local battles that provided the stuff of Indian politics. Increasingly in the late nineteenth and twentieth centuries, it was argued, these battles were fought in modern (western) political forms, such as associations, parties, petitions and perhaps even agitations. The links between different levels of politics, different regions and different interests were provided by the formal political structure imposed on the country by the British.

Constitutional development then accounted for a lasting 'nationalist movement' and changes in constitutional structure explained changes in the intensity, scale and form of 'nationalist' struggle. In this inter-pretation, 'nationalist' agitations arose whenever constitutional change was anticipated and declined as soon as the nature of the change became clear and no further concessions could be gained by agitation. At that point, Indian 'nationalists' returned to the politics in which they thrived, the traditional politics of transaction and patronage, aimed at establishing or maintaining social position, rewarding kith and kin and associates, and pursuing old (caste and other) battles.[14]

An obvious limitation of most of these analyses was the exclusive concentration on elites and the leadership elements. Differences among 'nationalist' leaders were read as decisive divisions in the 'nationalist' movement. Links between individual leaders became the critical 'nationalist' links. The patronage of influential men was seen as being the key element in drawing large numbers of men from less privileged sections of society into the politics of agitation. Local 'connections' and patron-client relationships were somehow reproduced – on a completely altered scale – at the district, the provincial and even the national level! There was something unfathomable in the culture and the country (as the old colonialists would have had it) that enabled all this to occur. This kind of argument required another assumption, that the hundreds and thousands, indeed tens of thousands, who turned out for nationalist protests and demonstrations in town and country had no judgement, or desires, of their own. Even historians who traced the rise of new elite groups in different parts of the country as the motor of modern politics ignored the identity and the concerns of those who provided the popular following of the new social and political movements.[15]

Since the 1980s, the elitism of this historiography has been fundamentally challenged, one might even say overturned, by *Subaltern Studies*, by Sumit Sarkar's summation of new trends in the under-standing of modern nationalism and politics in India, by the emergence of a distinct feminist historiography, and by a host of other writings foregrounding questions of difference and perspective, of marginalized groups and peoples, of lower castes and classes.[16] What these interventions have done collectively is to banish once and for all any notion of the nation and nationalism as something eternal, homogenous, ready to be awakened by the first calls of a 'modern' (that is, Western educated) leadership. The new historiography has laid stress on the *process* of nation-formation, on the contradictions that marked this process reflecting both old and new contradictions within a changing Indian society, on the struggle to imagine the political community of the future, as well as the struggle between different imaginations and different visions of how these imaginations were to be realized. The national movement thus appears far more variegated, far richer, and – not to put too fine a point on it – far more *historical* than ever before.

III

The present work was one of the first of this new crop of studies that sought to analyze the differentiated character of the Indian national movement, stressing its multiple layers and points of initiative, underlining its contested character, and suggesting that the particularity and strength of the movement came from the imbrication of quite different kinds of politics, political attitudes and political expectations. The question of mobilization was central to this investigation. For this purpose, it focused on one north Indian province, UP (earlier called the United Provinces of Agra and Awadh, after independence Uttar Pradesh), and on a comparatively limited period of mobilization, organization and agitation, the decades between 1920 and 1940, which marked perhaps the most crucial advance in the popular phase of the national movement. It examined for that period the state of the movement and the factors responsible for its manifest strength and its equally obvious limitations.

The Indian National Congress occupied a central place in this study. Chapter 3 contains a detailed discussion of its organization and leadership in UP. Chapter 4 examines the techniques of mobilization used by the Congress leaders, the manner in which they sought to establish contact with 'the masses' and the message that they sought to put out. But this study was not concerned primarily with the Congress leadership and their actions. The finer details of the decision-making process and the discussion on these in the Congress councils were peripheral to the analysis. I felt the need to turn my attention rather more to the relationship between 'leaders' and 'followers' and the activities of individuals and groups outside the formal leadership. Chapter 4 considers the contributions of the revolutionary terrorists and other groups, with their own techniques of mobilization. It deals particularly with the cumulative impact of political demonstrations and acts of political violence, on the one hand, and of 'constructive' (social reform) activities aimed at promoting cottage industry or combating some of the consequences of Untouchability, on the other.

It was my concern to investigate in some detail the context and circumstances of particular political interventions by individuals as well as groups – the political climate of the time, the social conditions, the immediate and often crying economic problems. Chapter 6 charts the different patterns of mass mobilization and agitation in different parts of the province during the civil disobedience campaigns of the 1920s and 30s, seeking to establish 'how it all came about'.[17] Chapter 5 deals with the very different question of why the Muslims of UP, who had responded in large numbers to the Congress and the Khilafat leaders' appeal for anti-British struggle at the beginning of the 1920s, took so little part in civil disobedience in the 1930s. All this allowed me to ask a further question about where the political initiative lay: in far-sighted and powerful urban leaders mobilizing the 'masses' at will; or also in the hands of little known men and women, scarcely distinguishable from the 'masses', who interpreted nationalist goals and demands in their own way and sometimes carried the 'leaders' along with them.

Any region of India could have served for a study of this kind. The choice of UP had the advantage that it was to the fore in the nationalist agitations of the last three decades of British rule. In the 1920s the province came to be regarded as a considerable thorn in the side of the British Government of India. By the 1930s the Congress in UP was clearly in control of wide-ranging forces of protest, and each of the contending parties – the Congress and the Government – was well aware of the other's strength and objectives. The Government frankly acknowledged the potency of the opposition that it faced. Malcolm Hailey, governor of the Punjab and UP successively in the 1920s and 1930s, affirmed that in UP, unlike in the Punjab, his task was 'to maintain the position of Government in view of the growing influence of the Congress'.[18] Another letter, written to a Congress leader by another official who was acting Governor of the province in 1928, conveys a sense of the unusual respect with which the British rulers had come to view the leading nationalist party. 'You have...undertaken a tall order,' it read. 'We are keeping a close eye on agricultural developments, and *can compete with you* by having our own staff not only in every district but in every tahsil and parganah.'[19]

Part of the reason for the prominence of UP at this time, and another point in favour of its choice for this study, is that it mirrored in a particularly acute form some of the principal opportunities and problems facing the national movement in the country as a whole. The most obvious of the problems was that of 'communalism'. 'UP Muslims were at the heart of Muslim separatism', as several analysts of the question have noted.[20] The agrarian question was at least as significant. 'For the Congress,' Nehru wrote in 1945, 'the agrarian question was the dominating social issue and much time had been given to its study and the formulation of policy. The United Provinces Congress was in this respect the most advanced and it had reached the conclusion that the Zamindari (landlord) system should be abolished.'[21]

'Truthful relations between Hindus and Musalmans, bread for the masses and removal of untouchability,' Gandhi once said. That is how I would define swaraj at the present moment.'[22] It was a powerful, and radical, conception – and one that we could still usefully attend to. Each aspect of the liberation adverted to by Gandhi was a burning issue in the UP of the 1920s and 1930s. None of them has been adequately resolved even to this day. That is, unfortunately, the fate of national and democratic movements struggling with issues of this kind over many of those parts of Asia and Africa that were colonized in the nineteenth and twentieth centuries. National and international forces, and the facts of gross inequality, scarce resources and personal ambitions, have all contributed to such results. Nevertheless, the attempted resolutions, the great struggles to realize these, the many successes (partial but far from trifling) and the accompanying failures, have formed a large part of the recent – and continuing – history of the world. It is these aspirations and these struggles that this book seeks to describe for a north Indian province in the years between the two World Wars.

2

Uttar Pradesh After the First World War

The Non-Cooperation Movement makes for an intricate mosaic of politics in UP. To interpret it in undifferentiated terms would be altogether misleading. It was not a case of one clean sweep by a mass upsurge with no fissures in it. Nor was it a case of a unified will emanating from a single charismatic individual or a monolithic high command switching patriotic currents on or off by pushing a spiritual or organizational button. The upsurge, the charisma and the high command were all there, but only as the generalized expressions of a multitude of crosscurrents and conflicts, of motivations and actions pulling in different directions. It is these contradictions that make up the concreteness of UP politics in the 1920s, and it is out of their interactions that the broad parallelograms of the nationalist movement eventually emerged.

It has been my aim in this study to grasp the concrete character of nationalism in UP by acknowledging and analysing the diversity of the social composition of its protagonists as well as of their regional distribution. In the 1920s, for the first time in the history of the province, new classes, groups, communities, castes and professions entered an arena that had been more or less the preserve of a few administrators, landlords, bankers and lawyers – linking up, only in rare cases, with groups in the middle and lower ranks of society.[1] The fact that many of the new elements forced their way into 'politics' in large numbers and gave it a mass character contributes directly to the differentiation of ideas, interests, objectives and styles of action within the nationalist movement, making it infinitely more complex than before.

The degree of this complexity can be appreciated at one critical level by considering the regional distribution of the Non-Cooperation Movement in UP. Here, as elsewhere, this was primarily an urban campaign. In the cities large numbers of people from widely varying social backgrounds were caught up in it. But the category of 'urban' in this instance extended beyond the big city and even the district headquarters. It covered the small market towns and distributing centres, which had sprouted along the railway lines and major roads. It included also older *qasbas* of this kind, along the riverine tracks and other traditional routes, and many declining but persistent centres of handicraft industry, which survived owing to the imperfect character of the advance of the capitalist system or, sometimes, on account of administrative convenience. In these 'urban' areas, barely distinguishable from their rural surroundings, teachers and journalists from petty landholding families who had sought alternative employment, either to supplement their agricultural incomes or simply because they would not touch the plough, small time lawyers, students and other men of rural background provided a good number of non-cooperators. In one area of UP, roughly the districts of southern and eastern Awadh, rural involvement in the Non-Cooperation Movement was greater still on account of a fairly powerful and prolonged agitation of poor and middle peasants, although this agitation had begun independently of, and prior to, organized Non-Cooperation.

Complexities of this kind and the factors that generate them can hardly be understood as isolated phenomena. Their meaning lies in the context of UP society as a whole. The following outline of some of the basic facts of economic life and social structure in the province might help the reader to appreciate this context and relate it to the historical narrative in the rest of this work.

II

Of the 46 million people in UP in 1921, 89 per cent lived in rural areas.[2] Throughout the first half of this century agriculture accounted for 74–6 per cent of the province's workforce, although its distribution was by no means uniform in all districts.

The divisions of western UP and the *doab*[3] had a relatively low share of agriculture in the work force, rarely over 66 or 67 per cent, and a relatively high share of manufacturing, generally over 9 per cent. By contrast, the divisions of eastern UP and Awadh generally had some 80 per cent of their work force in agriculture (around 70 per cent in Banaras, the most 'industrialized' of these divisions) and only 4–6 per cent in manufacturing (except in Banaras where the figure was nearer 10 per cent). In Meerut, on the western extreme of the province, 53 per cent of the work force was in agriculture and as much as 13 per cent in manufacturing. In Gorakhpur, at the other end, the figures were 85 per cent and less than 5 per cent respectively. Krishnamurty puts it succinctly: 'Meerut is the Gujarat of Uttar Pradesh, Gorakhpur...its Orissa.'[4]

The western divisions of the province, particularly Meerut and Agra, advanced in terms of 'urbanization' and 'industrialization' since Mughal times, had been especially affected by the coming of the railways and improvement in communications, the influx of factory-made goods and the general increase in commercial activity. So had the districts along the Grand Trunk Road and the main railway line between Delhi and Calcutta. Kanpur, which lay on this track, became the industrial and commercial centre of this part of the country. In UP, Agra was the only other city with a significant modern industrial sector until well into the twentieth century.

There was a fairly rapid advance in industry after the First World War and, even more, after the coming of protection – to a limited extent in the 1920s, more definitely from the early 1930s. The number of factories registered under the Factories Act in UP rose from 222 in 1916 to 332 in 1927. The average number of daily workers employed in them increased concurrently from 68,172 to 88,319.[5] An index of the expansion was the volume of goods traffic carried in and out of Kanpur by the Great Indian Peninsula Railway that connected the city with Bombay. In 1902 this traffic amounted to 280,800 tons. In the year ending 31 March 1922 it was 310,000 tons. Five years later it had risen to 436,900 tons.[6]

For all this development UP remained an overwhelmingly agricultural province, and an analysis of its agrarian structure and circumstances is central to any understanding of its social and political condition. UP comprised the two provinces of Agra and Awadh. Annexed piecemeal by the British, the province came to have at least three distinct tenurial arrangements. In the district of Banaras and small areas adjacent to it a permanent settlement of the Bengal type was made with individual landowners called *zamindars*. In the rest of Agra province, acquired mainly between 1801 and 1817, the *mahal* (estate) rather than any individual was taken as the unit of settlement. Theoretically the settlement was with village communities who undertook cultivation themselves, and some of the *zamindars* who had established their dominance over large areas in the confused period leading up to British annexation were displaced.

UP, 1920–40: Administrative Divisions

Finally in Awadh, after the scare of the 1857 uprising, the British returned to 'the natural leaders of the people' and settled with the great *taluqdars*, the Awadh equivalent of the *zamindars*. Indeed the *taluqdars* gained an extremely privileged position. They were granted *sanads*, or bills of rights. The Talukdars' Relief Act of 1870 guaranteed the rescue of any *taluqdari* estate that got deeply indebted through mismanagement or bad luck. The Government encouraged the formation of a *taluqdars's* association, modelled on the British Indian Association of Calcutta and named after it, and came ultimately to collect the subscription for this body along with the land revenue.[7]

Whatever the nature of the original settlement, the structure of agrarian society was fundamentally the same throughout UP in the 1920s and 1930s. Apart from the Government and those who contracted to pay the land revenue to it, there were generally one or more subordinate layers of holders of rights in land, paying rents to their immediate superiors for the land they held and often cultivated, as tenants, sub-tenants or worse. In addition to these groups, there were the landless or near-landless labourers and various marginal groups whose rights were not at all clear – such as the intriguing categories described in the *khatauni* (village accountant's register of rights in land) as 'occupiers of land without title' or 'occupiers without proper consent'.

The subordinate tenant layers did not exist in all villages. Sometimes the village co-sharers (*pattidars*) or brotherhood (*bhaiyachara*), who paid the revenue, themselves cultivated the land. But even in the *mahalwari* settlement area, possibly because of defects in the original settlement and because the richer and stronger landowners tended in any case to buy up or otherwise acquire the rights of weaker communities and individuals, the non-cultivating, rent-collecting landowner soon became a common figure.

When the Wisers visited Karimpur village in Agra district in 1925, they found two absentee landowners controlling all its property.[8] Mahewa in Etawah district was in a similar position; the Thakur peasant proprietors of the place spoke in the 1950s of how independence and Zamindari Abolition had removed 'the elephants', the British and the landlord.[9] More striking still is the evidence of the 1931 census, which suggests that the proportion of cultivating proprietors was not everywhere greater in Agra province than in Awadh. Excluding Kumaun, a sparsely-populated, mountainous tract which was exceptional, only in Meerut and Gorakhpur divisions was there a significantly higher proportion of peasant proprietors than in Faizabad division; and in three Agra divisions, Rohilkhand, Allahabad and Agra, the proportion was actually lower than in this part of Awadh.[10]

What is indisputable is that the status and wealth of landowners, whether *taluqdars, zamindars* or *pattidars*, varied enormously. There was practically nothing in common between Raja Sir Rampal Singh, Knight Commander of the Indian Empire, *taluqdar* of the Kurri Sidhauli estate in Rae Bareli, head of the Naihasta branch of the Bais Rajputs, who paid an annual revenue of Rs 34,271 and earned almost Rs 500,000 a year from money-lending alone, and the small proprietor in Meerut district who had to rent his own land from his own occupancy tenant at twice the rental he received for it.[11]

But, even here, the impression that any part of UP had a monopoly of the great landlords is incorrect. Awadh did have a heavy concentration of huge estates, meeting a very high proportion of the revenue demand. Thus in Rae Bareli 27 landowners paying a revenue of over Rs 100,000 each met 62.4 per cent of the total revenue demand of the district. On the other hand several districts in Agra, such as Azamgarh, Agra and Meerut, had few large estates, an enormous number of petty proprietors and a substantial number of middling revenue-payers. But there were others, such as Aligarh and Allahabad, where the number of large landowners was comparable to that in Awadh districts. Allahabad had 24 paying an annual revenue of more than Rs 10,000 each. Together they accounted for 35.6 per cent of the Rs 2.6 million revenue due from the district, proportionately not as much as the major *taluqdars* of Rae Bareli but still very substantial.[12]

For UP as a whole, then, we have a picture of a few great landlords dispersed over many districts – men possessing a good deal of land and living almost completely on rents, other cesses and usury. There was a much larger number of small landlords and rich peasants, and these were to be found all over the province. They held fairly substantial and secure holdings, either as *zamindars* or as tenants, and sufficient land to rent out or have worked by wage labour. The supervision of agricultural operations was the closest they got to the plough. Below these categories were the middle peasants, who lived primarily on the produce of their own land and on family labour, employing only seasonal, part-time labour; the poor peasants, whose little land and other resources were insufficient to feed their families and who needed to hire themselves out as labourers; and of course the landless rural proletariat.[13]

How vast the size of these lower classes was in rural society may be judged from the fact that in 1944–5 nearly ten million people, that is over 81 per cent of the 'agriculturists' listed in Part I of the *khataunis*[14] in UP, cultivated or otherwise occupied holdings of less than five acres. This is remarkable when one observes that the UP Banking Enquiry Committee reported in 1930 that an 'economic' holding for a cultivator and his family was 4.6 acres for a life tenant in Meerut division and four acres for any tenant in Gorakhpur division, both among the more productive parts of the province.[15] Even if one argues that this calculation of minimum requirements was inflated by the conditions of the World Depression – an argument that is not really tenable since the slump did not seriously affect UP until the latter part of 1930 after the Banking Committee had finished its enquiries – there can be no doubt that the 4.6 million people, a very large number of them in Gorakhpur division, who held less than one acre each, were in no position to support their families on the proceeds of their holdings. This statement applies with equal force to tenants on *sir* and *khudkasht* (holdings reserved by landowners for their personal cultivation), and to sub-tenants of all kinds, who usually paid steep rents and very often held tiny plots: in Azamgarh, in 1944–5, the average was well under half an acre.

There is rarely a sharp distinction between one class and the next in rural society, but in UP the distinction between poor peasants and landless labourers was especially blurred. Caste was a factor of some importance here in that the untouchable castes were traditionally debarred from holding land. But even this was not a rule without exception, and certainly, apart from this, there was little way of distinguishing one category from the other. The poor peasant with a small holding almost invariably needed to find work as an agricultural labourer. The man who lived almost entirely by selling his labour might still have some remote right of holding in a minute piece of land.

In one of the most crowded and backward parts of UP, western Gorakhpur, it was estimated in 1919 that only 11 per cent of the people were purely agricultural labourers, and that 'the vast bulk of the rural poor crowded into the ranks of the lower tenantry'.[16] On the other hand, the 1931 census counted over 3.4 million agricultural labourers in UP, that is over 19 per cent of all 'agriculturists', and a further 580,000 'general labourers', many of whom worked as agricultural or general labourers 'as occasion offers'.[17] The census was of course concerned to classify men by their 'principal occupation' or by the manner in which they earned the major part of their incomes. It noted that a large proportion of 'tenants' had passed since 1911 into the category of 'agricultural labourers', 'either having lost their holdings altogether or deriving more income from labouring than from their own cultivation. They number somewhere about 400,000 or 3 per cent of the tenants returned 20 years ago'.[18] This explains the apparent discrepancy between the 1919 estimate and the 1931 figures. What it confirms is that there was a very large body of workers and poor peasants living at the very bottom of the agrarian hierarchy.

Conditions at the lower levels of this hierarchy were hard and the masses of people who were clustered here lived at a very low level of subsistence. There has been a return recently to the British administrator's argument that the kind of analysis of agrarian society made above is an undue simplification and the statement of depressed conditions greatly exaggerated. Such an analysis, it is alleged, ignores the multiplicity of resources available to everyone in the countryside – the variety of patrons from whom an artisan or labourer might choose, for example, a multiplicity that was heightened by the extension of trade and money-lending, bureaucratic intervention and 'modern' politics under the British. Take these factors into account, the argument goes, and the position of the poorer classes in rural society seems much less hopeless.[19]

Any such objection has to contend, however, with the weighty evidence of contemporary British officials and other observers who held the contrary view. 'The average villager who relies on agriculture for a livelihood for himself and numerous dependents, usually lives from hand to mouth, with little or no reserve for lean times', wrote S S Nehru, a senior ICS official, after his survey of 54 villages in Rae Bareli district on behalf of the Banking Enquiry Committee in 1929–30.[20] To take another example, UP's Settlement Commissioner wrote as follows of the Agra district in April 1930: 'In years of scarcity there must be serious underfeeding and this is bound to leave a proportion of the population in no condition to resist the attack of fever or influenza.'[21]

The factor of new sources of credit in the form of a growing number of money-lending rural notables and city *mahajans* (private bankers and money-lenders) and, later, cooperative societies made no real difference. In credit and other matters, as Whitcombe notes, 'Only that minority of the rural population already in a position of prosperity and sufficient power to maintain some independence of action had access to the benefits of innovation.'[22] The poorer sections of rural society were certainly involved in new kinds of money transactions and with some of the new sources of credit, but not to their advantage. Research has shown that the subsistence element in the peasant economy was reduced, and monetization extended, not on account of a surplus but because the peasant was often forced to sell even his food and stock in order to pay instalments of rent and revenue.[23]

The essential point is that the effects of Pax Brittanica varied within UP, as outside. Premchand's *Godan* captures something of the situation of the poor peasant and labourer in Awadh, exploited by local official, landlord and money-lenders alike, after three-quarters of a century of British rule – the desperation he felt and the fatalism that sometimes flowed from it.[24] The position of agricultural labourers in the extreme eastern divisions of UP was even worse. Among untouchable labourers in Basti district, it was observed in the 1950s, 'the practice of eating *gobraha* (grains collected from animal excreta and cleaned) is common. Eating of carrion is also common. Almost a fifth of the population of the district is compelled to resort to these abnormal practices.'[25] In other parts of UP, where the density of population was not so great, as in Kumaun and Bundelkhand, or where some alternative avenues of employment existed, as in western UP, abject poverty was not encountered on this scale. Nevertheless, the idea that all men were *jajmans* in a relatively egalitarian agrarian order, with new resources in the nineteenth and twentieth centuries strengthening the poorer and weaker *jajmans* against the richer and stronger, is as illusory as the picture of the self-sufficient, non-violent and happy Indian village republic.[26]

Generally speaking, conditions in the UP villages were worse than in many other parts of India. The area was more densely populated than southern or central India. It was less developed in terms of irrigation facilities and urban employment opportunities than Punjab and western India. To make matters worse, the weight of the rental demand on the subordinate sections of agrarian society in the province was far heavier than in other regions. The Commission of Enquiry into the Bengal famine of 1943 found that:

> In relation to the value of the gross produce, the rent paid by ryots in Bengal was, subject to certain exceptions, smaller than the revenue paid by ryots in Madras and the Punjab, and much smaller than the rent paid by tenants of temporarily settled estates in the United Provinces.[27]

Within UP, the eastern divisions of Banaras and Gorakhpur were the most overcrowded and suffered most from the subdivision and fragmentation of holdings. But Awadh was the area worst off in terms of the rack-renting and exploitation of the subordinate classes by the superior ones. This was chiefly because of the specially favoured position of the Awadh *taluqdar*, reflected in the poor legal protection available to the majority of his tenants.

The Rent Act of 1886 had granted to all tenants-at-will in Awadh the right to hold their land undisturbed, at an unchanged rental, for seven years. After that period, however, the tenant could be ejected and the rent enhanced up to a specified limit. In 1921, after the fierce agrarian agitation in parts of Awadh, a new category of 'statutory tenants' was created by the Oudh Rent (Amendment) Act. (The Agra Tenancy Act of 1926 adopted the category for Agra.) Statutory tenants had security of tenure for life, their rents could be enhanced only once in ten years at rates agreed upon by landowner and tenant or in court, and the heir of such a tenant continued to hold the land on the same terms for five years after his death. Most of the former tenants-at-will in Awadh qualified for these rights. Even so, in the 1920s and 1930s some 10 per cent of the cultivated area in Awadh was in the hands of tenants without such rights, and the extension of protection to the statutory tenants, who now cultivated 70 per cent of the area, was far from complete. The Awadh landlords overcame the new legal hurdles from the late nineteenth century onwards not only by ignoring the law to a large extent but by skirting the rental issue and instituting a new system of unofficial taxation. This was the *nazrana*, or premium paid by a tenant to be admitted or re-admitted to a holding. In Rae Bareli, it was observed, *nazranas* were taken in some estates immediately after the settlement of 1898 'in order to make good wholly or partly the increased revenue assessed'.[28] By 1920 in many districts landlords had 'ceased to trouble themselves about the raising of the rent, taking their enhancements by means of premia on re-letting'.[29]

In Agra province, by contrast, an 'occupancy' right, heritable though not transferable, with rents at customary rates and certain statutory controls on enhancement, had been long recognized for some categories of tenants. Act X of 1859 first formalized the position, laying down that continuous possession and cultivation of a holding for 12 years entitled the holder to occupancy rights. Since then, a substantial proportion of the Agra tenantry was in a stronger situation legally.

The first three decades of this century indicated this clearly. The area held by occupancy tenants increased (table 2.1). Moreover there was considerable improvement in the economic position of stable tenants. While prices rose by more than 100 per cent between 1900 and the late 1920s, the rents of occupancy tenants rose by only 20–5 per cent. For non-occupancy tenants, on the other hand, the registered rent (taking no account of illegal dues and cesses) rose by about 70 per cent over this period. In Agra alone, where unwritten and illegal demands were rarer than in Awadh, such tenants were paying 110 per cent more in 1930 than they had paid in 1900. In 1928 the occupancy rent in Agra was said to represent only 10 per cent of the produce value while that of non-occupancy tenants was 20 per cent.[30] The position of the ordinary tenant in Awadh was certainly worse – unless he or she were protected by ties of kinship, or of service, with his or her superiors, in which case the burden was slightly reduced whatever the tenant's legal position.[31]

Table 2.1
Pattern of Holdings under Different Categories of Tenants in Agra and Awadh,
1899–1900 to 1935–6

		Percentage of Total Holdings area under		
		Occupancy and other tenants with hereditary rights	Statutory and heirs of statutory tenants	Other non-occupancy tenants, including grove-holders, rent-free, etc.
Awadh	1899–1900	5.6	–	82.2
	1926–7	6.5	71.4	10.5
	1935–6	6.8	69.9	11.9
Agra	1899–1900	35.9	21.0	41.9
	1926–7	54.8	–	4.0
	1935–6	49.0	23.7	6.2

Source. **Report of the United Provinces Zamindari Abolition Committee. Volume II. Statistics**
(Allahabad 1948), p. 91.

III

In the years immediately after the First World War the people of UP came under severe economic pressure. First there was a cutback in economic opportunities with the end of the war. Nearly half a million soldiers from UP, mostly from the rural areas, who had been recruited as combatants or non-combatants were now demobilized. There was also considerable industrial retrenchment with the closure of several mills and factories, especially tanneries and glass-works.[32]

The prices of certain commodities, such as cloth, salt and kerosene oil, had been rising throughout the War years. Then came a disastrous failure of the monsoon in 1918 and in its wake the worldwide epidemic of pneumonic influenza. Food-grain prices shot up, reaching an unprecedented height and declining only slightly over the next few years. The inferior grains were particularly affected.[33] The result was great suffering among the rural as well as the urban poor, for, as we have observed above, even the former had to enter into market relations, selling cheap and buying dear, in order to pay off rents, revenue and debt.

These conditions of hardship considerably debilitated the poorer sections of UP society. Then epidemic disease took an enormous toll. Over 3 million people, that is 6 per cent of the province's population, succumbed to fever (mainly influenza) in 1918 alone; and the state of the province remained 'unhealthy' (to use the government phrase) for some years thereafter.[34]

Some people of course did well out of the conditions of scarcity and high prices. Big traders, hoarders and moneylenders had a field day. The landlords of UP were able to exact larger dues than ever before. The rents of unprotected tenants rose rapidly, and in Awadh the practice of taking *nazrana*, and of evicting tenants who failed to satisfy the landowner's demands, was greatly extended.

It was against these miserable conditions and this oppression that large numbers of unprotected tenants and labourers in southern and eastern Awadh and some neighbouring districts rose in protest in 1920–1. They protested against the immediate oppressor, the landlord and the rich peasant. But they protested also, by implication and to some extent consciously, against the oppressor's protector, the British Raj. One demonstration of their grievances took the form of a 50-mile march by 200 peasants from Pratapgarh district to the city of Allahabad to seek the support of Gandhi and other nationalist leaders.[35]

In the cities and towns of UP, the economic dislocation after the end of the war and the sharp rise in food prices affected not only the poorest – slum-dwellers and beggars, petty vendors and errand runners, transport workers and mill-hands – but also the lower middle classes in general and those, in particular, with inelastic incomes. Thus people from several sectors were ready to respond to nationalist messages and appeals, which were in any case far more widely propagated in the towns than in the rural areas.[36]

Another factor of importance in the rise of popular political agitation in UP at the beginning of the 1920s was the presence of a substantial Muslim population in UP towns. This was a relic of Muslim rule in northern India, when Muslims had congregated at the administrative centres and others around these centres had adopted the religion of the court. In 1921, Muslims constituted 14.5 per cent of the population in UP. Their proportion among urban dwellers was however much higher, over 37 per cent. In Rohilkhand division they were actually in a majority in the urban areas.[37]

Most of the Muslim townsfolk were labourers and artisans. The Muslim weaver castes were noted for their work and are still responsible in Banaras for much of its famous silk. Other Muslims shared with untouchables work that caste Hindus considered defiling, such as leather curing and tanning. There was also a significant number of Muslim shopkeepers, vendors, accountants, clerks, managers of many kinds, lawyers, teachers and journalists, and the important group of *ulema* (learned men or religious authorities) who exercised a considerable influence on the Muslims at large and who had, in the mosque and the Jumah (Friday noon) prayer, a convenient platform for the propagation of their ideas.

The Muslims shared with their Hindu counterparts the hardship caused by high prices, retrenchment and the like. Common, too, to the politically advanced sections of Muslims and Hindus was their hostility to the Rowlatt Acts, sorrow and anger at the enormity of Jallianwala Bagh and disappointment over the nature of the 1919 reforms. But the Muslims, and especially those in the urban areas, were particularly incensed by the additional issue of the treatment of the Khalifa, depicted by the *ulema* and by major Muslim political leaders as an attack by the British upon their religion. Consequently the Non-Cooperation-Khilafat Movement of 1920–2 saw Muslims in the lead in several arenas of struggle in UP.[38]

IV

Such were the circumstances of political mobilization in UP in the years immediately after the First World War, and the popular agitations that then erupted made an indelible impression on the society. Before considering these developments, however, it is necessary to refer to certain other changes, in terms of constitutional innovation and educational advance, which also had some effect on the politics of the period that followed.

During and after the First World War there were important developments in local government. The UP Municipalities' Act of 1916, 'the first Indian measure to be substantially modified under non-official pressure',[39] introduced the feature of 'weighted' Muslim representation in addition to separate Hindu and Muslim electoral rolls. It also provided for a 75 per cent elected membership, with no more than two members on any board to be nominated by the Government. A private bill in 1922 lowered the qualification for franchise in municipal elections to the same level as that for voting in urban constituencies for the provincial council under the Government of India Act of 1919, thus creating about 120,000 voters in the municipalities in 1923: that number rose to over 150,000 in 1926.[40]

In 1922, again, the UP District Boards Act was passed. The voting qualification was the same as that laid down for provincial elections by the 1919 Act. Muslims obtained especially generous representation, being assured a voice on every district board. Where they constituted less than 1 per cent of the population they received 10 per cent of the seats; where they numbered 1–5 per cent they got 15 per cent; if 5–15 per cent they got 25 per cent of the seats; if 15–30 per cent, 30 per cent. Only in Moradabad, Bijnor and Saharanpur districts, where they constituted more than 30 per cent of the total, was their representation proportionate to their numerical strength. Another feature of the Act was the provision for elected non-official chairmen, and the complete exclusion of the official element, even that of the district officers as chief executive of the boards. 'Real local self-government in the rural areas of the United Provinces may with some justice be claimed to have been born in 1923', wrote the Government of the province,[41] though one must add that the district boards remained heavily dependent on the Government for funds and subject to official control in any 'emergency' situation.

The more spectacular changes in provincial government introduced by the Montagu-Chelmsford constitution of 1919 are well known. In UP the legislative council was to consist of 123 members, 100 of them elected with 30 from Muslim constituencies. Direct elections to the provincial legislature were a new departure, except in the case of a few Muslim seats filled in this way under the 1909 Morley-Minto constitution. The franchise was also considerably extended, giving a total of over 1.3 million voters in 1920 and 1.6 million by 1926. But the administration was careful about how it played its cards. The constitution was biased heavily in favour of landowning classes and the return of a safe majority of the traditionally loyal landlord element was ensured.[42]

Educational facilities in UP improved substantially during these years. The number of recognized educational institutions rose from 12,912 in 1917 to 18,559 in 1922, an increase of nearly 44 per cent, and by a further 19 per cent to 22,068 in 1927. The number of pupils at these institutions increased from 805,420 to 965,059 to 1,280,450 over the same period, a rise of over 50 per cent altogether.[43]

The expansion at the university level was striking. At the beginning of this period UP had only one university – that of Allahabad, established in 1887. In 1915 the Banaras Hindu University came into being. Five years later the Muslim College at Aligarh was raised to the status of a university, and another university was opened at Lucknow. In 1927 Agra got its own university, thereby transforming Allahabad into a unitary, teaching university. The establishment of a university at Delhi in 1922 also had an importance for UP. Between 1917 and 1927 the number of students at universities and affiliated colleges in the province almost doubled from somewhat over six thousand to around twelve thousand.[44] The demand for higher education was so great that in 1927–8 the Banaras Hindu University had to turn down a thousand applicants.[45] Yet the prospects for those who found university places and obtained degrees were not always very good. The provincial government reported in 1929 that there were an increasing number of graduates every year for whom employment could not be found.[46]

The political significance of these changes is not easy to assess. Certainly the growth of literacy and education helped to spread political consciousness, and young men and women with some English or vernacular education provided most of the active cadres of the Congress and other parties in the 1920s and later. It might also be argued that the rise in the incidence of unemployment among the educated youth made more people available for political work. Equally, the constitutional revisions noted above added to some extent to the range of political opportunities. The triennial elections to the local boards and the provincial and central legislatures became an important focus for the mobilization and organization of various political groups. The expanded assemblies also provided new and valuable platforms for political propaganda and agitation.

However, the overall impact of these developments must be viewed in perspective. If institutional changes and the Non-Cooperation Movement are seen as two independent points of departure for a study of the political scene in UP in the 1920s, it is fairly certain that the second was the more significant. It was not the long-promised 'representative' institutions (nor the new universities), but Gandhi and Non-Cooperation that captured the historical imagination of the times.

The phenomenon of the landlord with a liberal tail, which became widespread in the UP of the 1920s, was a product of Non-Cooperation and the peasant agitations that accompanied it rather than of any changes in constitutional structure. The figure of the landlord with Gandhian, or Tolstoyan, leanings was to become fairly common: Premchand depicted him in one of his early novels, *Premashram* (1921).

Premchand himself, the 'story-teller of the independence movement', was deeply influenced – one might even say moulded – by the Non-Cooperation Movement. He relinquished government employment in response to Gandhi's call and his subsequent writing shows the extent to which the movement had an impact on his mind. His most successful novel of the 1920s, *Rangbhumi* (1925), is built around the character of Surdas, a blind beggar with Gandhian ideals. Surdas wages a prolonged, non-violent struggle to prevent his little piece of land from being sold to an Anglo-Indian entrepreneur; he himself does not use the land but he does not wish it to be used for the establishment of a cigarette factory, for this would not only promote immoral 'Western' habits, but also deprive the *mohalla's*[47] cattle of their one free grazing ground.

Premchand was only the most famous of a host of writers and poets and storytellers who were powerfully affected by Gandhi and his *satyagraha*. From all the vernacular newspapers and journals, pamphlets and leaflets that survive from the 1920s, from the popular poetry of the time and accounts of the new political imagery introduced into religious festivals and other public occasions, it is clear that the Mahatma and his method had left their mark.[48] By the mid-1920s even long-established and very traditional journals, run by orthodox caste associations and individuals, were having to make concessions to the new spirit of nationalism which, of course, they twisted to suit their own ideological stances. Thus the *Brahmana-sarvasva* of Etawah, staunchly devoted to Sanatan Dharma, wrote that true *acchutoddhar*, that is, uplift of untouchables, lay not so much in bringing the latter into contact with caste Hindus as in improving their economic conditions and in preaching religion to them so that they might lead righteous lives.[49]

Yet there were many – among the poorer peasants and working people and, more clearly still, among urban youth and students from diverse backgrounds – who felt in the 1920s and 1930s that the Gandhian way was not enough, that something more daring and more direct was required to attain freedom and a better life.[50] There were others – and their number perceptibly increased through these decades – who felt that the Gandhian way, whether or not it was sufficient for Gandhi's purposes, was a negation of their very religion and culture. These men and women, as much as the sympathizers and followers of Gandhi, form the subject of the chapters that follow.

The Congress Organization, 1920–40

The authors of the Montagu-Chelmsford reforms believed or wished others to believe that they were 'deliberately disturbing' the 'placid, pathetic contentment' of the Indian people and stirring them out of their 'peaceful conservatism'.[1] Serious historians writing half a century or more later have sometimes adopted a not dissimilar position, arguing that the extension of 'responsible government', and particularly of the franchise, brought about the wider scale and greater depth of Indian nationalist activities. It would have been surprising if the leaders of the Congress, which had been, until then at any rate, a fairly elitist, conservative and constitutional party, did not take any account of the Government of India Act, 1919, in the making of any new organizational arrangements. But it would have been no less surprising for even such an organization to remain indifferent to and unaffected by the popular agitations of the next three years. As it happened, the former helped the Congress organization to shape in a particular way and enhanced the significance of its provincial level. The latter, in its turn, gave to the party a core of committed workers, a whole range of branch organizations and activities and a fund of popular sympathy on which it could rely for some time to come.

The year 1920 was perhaps crucial in the development of a broad-based and more or less permanent Congress organization. A new constitution was adopted at the Nagpur Congress that year. 'Swarajya...by all legitimate and peaceful means' became the goal of the Congress. A Congress Working Committee (CWC) was created, making the national Congress an active and functioning body throughout the year. The introduction of linguistic provinces, a many-tiered organization from village level upwards and an open membership with a fee of four annas per annum, which ensured a regular income and enabled a minimum of Congress work, all helped in the establishment of a popular base. The linguistically divided Congress provinces and the national body itself were encouraged to use the local language and Hindustani respectively for Congress business.[2] This remained the basis of Congress organization for the next fifteen years, with a small but significant modification in 1929 when the Lahore Congress defined swarajya as 'complete independence'.

Organization on this basis had two major and related weaknesses. First, a completely open organization, relying on a general nationalist appeal and discouraged by the government of the time, could maintain its strength only when nationalist feeling was at a high pitch. Rapid disintegration followed the decline of the Non-Cooperation and the Civil Disobedience Movements. In March 1923 the Congress claimed a membership of 106,046 for 16 of its 20 provinces; less than two years earlier UP alone had claimed over three times that number.[3] In 1929 the General Secretary of the UP Provincial Congress Committee (PCC) wrote that, after the suspension of the Non-Cooperation Movement:

> ...propaganda and work in the villages was more or less given up; and as the natural result of this the Congress machinery could not function effectively.... Once in a while when the elections of the PCC or for the official Councils approached, interested persons enrolled some members and set up some sort of Congress committees. During the last year or two even this was not done: in more than half of the districts, the district committees have either disappeared or have existed only nominally on paper. Even the provincial office suffered from the prevailing reaction and remained only in name.[4]

In November 1933, similarly, a Congress worker touring Karchana *tahsil* of Allahabad district, one of the best organized districts for Civil Disobedience, found that the Congress organization, 'if it ever existed in this area', had collapsed leaving scarcely a trace behind.[5]

The other weakness with the organization was that it made no specific provision for the different sections of the Indian 'masses' whom the Congress sought to represent. Even Gandhi's 'constructive' programme, which did important work in town and country during the 1920s, failed to break through to classes below the richer peasants and petty bourgeoisie, with occasional exceptions in the case of the campaigns for promotion of *khadi* (hand-spun cloth) and *acchutoddhar*.

It was only in the 1930s that the Congress made some direct efforts to involve the broader masses in the organization: through the renewed and expanded *acchutoddhar* programme under the new name of Harijan uplift, through efforts to organize workers and peasants, most notably by the Congress Socialist Party (CSP) founded in 1934, and through changes in the Congress constitution. The new constitution, adopted at Wardha in 1934, sought to increase popular participation and 'direct democracy' in the Congress, while making for greater central control through a CWC to be nominated by the president. It prescribed Hindustani as the language of all Congress proceedings. It also stipu-lated a 'manual labour' qualification for membership of Congress com-mittees, fixed the proportion of urban to rural delegates at 1:3 and provided for the direct election of all Congress bodies, including the PCCs but excepting the All-India Congress Committee (AICC).[6]

These changes did not constitute a wholesale transformation. The Congress leadership itself, and even the CSP, remained ambivalent in its attitude towards the 'masses'. Many of the new 'mass' oriented branches and activities, again not excluding the CSP, became instruments of fac-tional strife, aimed at securing seats on Congress committees and thereby on elective local and provincial bodies. Consequently it is still possible to argue that it was the imminence of elections, and in this instance also of the new constitution of 1935 that was to create a much extended elector-ate, that brought an active Congress organization into being again, and that the apparent strength of this organization was merely seasonal.[7]

Yet the ups and downs in the organization of the Congress should not obscure the important advances made in 1920 and afterwards. The UP evidence certainly makes it difficult to accept the view that the post-Non-Cooperation Congress was 'reminiscent of the early Congress'.[8] What might be said, with greater reason, is that the Congress organiza-tion in the 1920s and 1930s reached out to rather limited sections of Indian society and did so sometimes with a Hindu bias which had unforeseen implications.

II

The most significant development in the UP Congress organization in 1920 was the establishment of Congress committees at various levels. In principle every village with a minimum of five Congress members was to set up a village Congress committee. There were provisions for *mandal* (circle), *tahsil* and district Congress committees (DCCs). Independently, each town with a population of 50,000 was to have a town Congress committee (TCC), and there were to be town circle committees below these. Several of these tiers – PCCs, DCCs, *tahsil* committees and TCCs – were involved in the election of delegates to the annual and special sessions of the Congress. The PCC itself represented chiefly the 45 DCCs, which elected 114 of its 150 members. 15 members were elected by the executive committees of the Allahabad, Agra, Banaras, Kanpur, Lucknow and Bareilly TCCs, two by two educational institutions, the Kashi Vidyapith, Banaras, and the Muslim University, Aligarh; and 19 by the other elected members of the PCC. A PCC executive council was set up to meet more regularly than the PCC and to transact urgent business.[9] In 1921 neither the PCC nor its executive council seems to have been fully organized. But from 1922 the executive council generally had a membership of 21: a president, four vice-presidents, four secretaries, a treasurer and 11 other members.[10]

From 1918 to 1921 UP evidently had between 30 and 45 functioning DCCs and a large number of lower-level Congress committees. A Congress report, probably incomplete, indicated the existence of 11 DCCs, 61 *tahsil* committees and 126 Congress committees at a lower level in 1922. Incomplete figures of membership quoted by Gopal Krishna suggest that, in UP as elsewhere, the Congress acquired a large mass basis in 1921. In July that year UP reported 328,966 Congress members. Only Bihar's figure was higher: it claimed a membership of 350,000 in November 1921.[11]

It was in this period that the UP Congress for the first time acquired substantial funds for its work. Apart from the income from Congress membership fees, special contributory funds were started. The largest of these in the country, the Tilak Memorial Swaraj Fund, collected Rs 10 million in three months from April to June 1921. Between January 1921 and June 1922 'backward' UP raised nearly Rs 600,000 for this fund.[12]

A powerful volunteer organization also arose parallel to the Congress organization. The earliest volunteer organizations to come to prominence were the Seva Samitis which were established in several places in UP in 1917–19. Set up first in large towns and at pilgrimage centres, the Seva Samitis spread to smaller urban and rural centres in 1918 and 1919. By December 1918 Mathura district alone had seven branch Samitis. By 1920 Seva Samitis were known to be functioning at Etmadpur and Achnera in Agra, Ghiror and Shikohabad in Mainpuri, Pura and Chawalmandi in Kanpur, Shahabad in Hardoi, and several other small centres. In Banaras there was a move to open a branch Seva Samiti under a *mukhia* (headman) in each ward of the city.[13]

Parallel to this development there began to appear, by this time, a number of other nationalist volunteer associations. While important districts such as Allahabad and Banaras probably set up separate volunteer corps independent of the Seva Samitis, it seems likely that in most districts the Seva Samitis or at any rate their members were absorbed into these other associations. In certain respects, however, there was a significant change in the volunteer movement, that is, in the growth of Muslim (Khilafat) volunteer corps, the open nationalism of both Muslim and Congress associations and the great increase in the number and strength of these volunteer bodies. Some Muslim social service associations had already come into existence in 1918 and 1919 – in Mathura, Agra and Shahjahanpur, for example. The next two years witnessed a massive expansion of this Muslim volunteer movement. By November 1921, 35 out of 41 districts for which reports were available had Khilafat volunteer associations and the Government reported a great increase in the number of Muslim volunteers, with figures as high as 1,423 for Azamgarh, 926 for Saharanpur and 387 for Aligarh.

The Congress volunteer associations expanded equally fast at the same time. In November 1921 there was a Congress volunteer corps in 36 districts, with a total of 11,494 volunteers. It is not certain that this was everywhere a great advance on the Seva Samiti organization. But it was clearly a new development in some places. For example, no Seva Samiti unit had ever existed in Azamgarh. But now in the wake of the Khilafat organization a Congress volunteer corps emerged for the first time. By November 1921 the Congress corps in Azamgarh was said to have 1,178 volunteers, among the largest number in the province. By that date too, 'a volunteer corps of some kind existed as an appanage to practically every local Congress and Khilafat organisation'.[14]

The number of Muslim and other Congress volunteers is difficult to calculate separately as there was not always a clear distinction between local Khilafat and Congress organizations. After November 1921, when the Criminal Law Amendment Act was applied to UP and volunteer associations became unlawful, there seems to have been an even closer merger of the 'two denominations' at the town and district level. This act of government gave a great fillip to the nationalist volunteer effort in general. The Government was 'disobeyed, volunteer organizations failed to dissolve and fresh enlistments under the direction of the Congress leaders were made in large numbers', the Intelligence

Department reported. 'The strength of the Congress organisation now stood revealed and was reflected by the large response to the call for volunteers in all districts.'[15]

Early in 1922, the Congress claimed that it had 72,865 volunteers in the 15 districts that had filed reports, and the Government conceded that there were 73,626 Congress volunteers in the 37 districts of which it had information.[16] This total did not include the number of volunteers for such active districts as Gorakhpur and Budaun which, according to official admission, could have been no less than 5,000 each. Thus at a very conservative estimate there were at least 90,000 volunteers under the control of the 46 district organizations of the UP Congress at this time – a remarkable achievement, on any reckoning.

Evidently, then, an advance had been made beyond the altruistic Seva Samiti type of associations to the explicitly political and nationalist organizations of 1920–1.[17] There was one problem, however. Much Seva Samiti activity was associated with Hindu religious fairs and festivals, and it was no coincidence that not a single Muslim name appeared on the lists of the office-bearers of the Samitis. When the Khilafat volunteer associations developed later they attracted Muslims exclusively. Congress volunteer corps were set up at the same time, as we have seen. With Congress and Khilafat leaders working together, for common aims but through separate organizations, a streaming of the cadres of the nationalist movement along sectarian lines almost inevitably followed. Muslims flocked to the Khilafat associations. Thus while both Hindus and Muslims participated in the observation of Dasehra or Muharram, the agencies for these demonstrations of Hindu–Muslim concord were a Muslim volunteer association and a Congress (mainly Hindu) volunteer association. Although many Muslim volunteers joined the Congress volunteer organization after November 1921, the initial separation of the volunteer associations along communal lines was likely to be divisive in the long run. The two groups of volunteers worked together while the Hindu and Muslim leaders were in agreement. When they clashed later on, the conflict between their respective followings at the level of their separate local organizations immediately took on a communal hue.[18]

In 1920–1, however, this was not yet a problem, as the nationalists rode a popular wave. At this time the claimed Congress membership for UP alone was over six times as large as the membership of the entire Chinese Communist Party in the period of the Northern Expedition (1926–7) and larger than that party's membership in the agrarian revolutionary period that followed.[19] It was also considerably larger than the membership of the Bolshevik Party on the eve of the October revolution, and larger even than the swelling Bolshevik Party membership in the first few years after the revolution.[20] Membership figures of revolutionary parties of the Chinese and Russian Bolshevik type and those of a nationalist party like the Indian National Congress are not strictly comparable since the two are organized on radically different lines, but these figures do give an idea of scale. While the claims of the UP Congress itself were very probably exaggerated, official reports of the size of its income from public donations and of its volunteer strength testify to the immense following of the Congress at this time in this and other provinces.

III

The amazing success of 1920–1 was not to be repeated in the later years of the decade, or in the early 1930s. The claimed Congress membership attained these peaks again only after the Congress formed its first ministry in UP in 1937. The Tilak Swaraj Fund too became a much-discussed miracle. Yet several developments during the years that followed indicated that the Congress organization had acquired a certain basic strength during the Non-Cooperation period that it was never to lose again.

One such development was a protracted tussle for control of the provincial Congress organization, of a kind that became common in the 1930s and endemic later. This accompanied a bitter electoral contest in 1926 between groups led by the most senior Congress leaders of UP, Madan Mohan Malaviya and Motilal Nehru.[21] As a result of this clash the provincial Congress split down the middle. Two of the PCCs' four general secretaries joined Malaviya's group, while two remained with Nehru, who retained the important links with the all-India Congress leadership as well as control of the provincial Congress office and accounts. The attempts of Malaviya's men to gain control of the latter caused the office to be transferred from Allahabad, a Malaviya stronghold, to Lucknow and then to Banaras. This 'lockout' by Nehru's party led to the setting up of a parallel PCC in an independent office.

For most of 1927 the two rival PCCs existed side by side, each claiming to be the legally constituted body. The battle was also waged at the lower levels of the Congress organization. The arbitration board appointed by the AICC to settle the UP Congress election disputes concluded that 'the Elections of the several Committees have been generally so faulty that it is impossible to say, with justice and fairness, as to which of the Committees are validly formed and which not'.[22] So great were the differences within the UP Congress that the arbitrators found it impossible to bring the two sides to any kind of a compromise. In November 1927, when the annual elections for a new PCC became due, the dispute had still not been settled. Only the elections, coming with the nationalist unity that followed the announcement of the composition of the Simon Commission, put an end to the fighting.

This extended and bitter conflict was a measure of the importance that politicians now attached to the Congress organization. There had been earlier struggles within the Congress, of course, between Moderate and Extremist wings and indeed between Malaviya and Nehru, but never before had the battle raged so violently at so many different levels and never had the opposing sides spent so much of their time trying to prove that they were the 'real Congress'.

The terminal years of the 1920s saw an astonishingly swift revival of a strong and widespread Congress organization in UP, as a further proof of its sound base and great popularity. In March 1929, only 35 of the provincial Congress's 46 districts were represented on the PCC and definite information about DCCs was available for only 30 districts. The PCC had no information about the number of town or *tahsil* or village Congress committees. According to the PCC General Secretary there was a Hindustani Seva Dal (volunteer) Board in the province on which the PCC was represented, but the exact number of Seva Dal branches and membership figures were not known.[23]

Early in that year the PCC office was reorganized. Vinayak Dandekar, the son of a retired railway stationmaster in the Central Provinces, was appointed full-time assistant secretary and inspectors were appointed to visit different districts and set up Congress committees. Much of this work was evidently soon accomplished, and 10,000 new members were enrolled by the middle of the year. Thereafter there seems to have been a distinct spurt in organizational activity. By early September 1929 the districts of Gorakhpur, Banaras, Allahabad, Kanpur, Etawah, Lucknow, Bareilly, Almora and Agra were said to have enrolled the quota of members laid down for them by the PCC. In mid-September the General Secretary of the UP PCC reported the enrolment of 65,000 members from only 35 districts.[24]

The provincial Political Conference held at Farrukhabad from 30 March to 1 April 1929 had called for the enrolment of 100,000 Congress members and 10,000 volunteers during the year. It had also appointed a committee to raise a Satyagraha Fund for the payment of volunteers, given representation to the UP Trade Union Congress on the PCC, and decided that a monthly bulletin should be issued to all Congress committees and members. A PCC meeting at Kanpur on 8 December 1929 appointed sub-committees for prohibition, the boycott of foreign cloth, *khadi* and *acchutoddhar* work, and decided to impose a one per cent levy as a compulsory subscription on the incomes of individual members of the PCC. (The minimum subscription was to be two rupees, half of which could go to the member's local Congress committee.) Another PCC meeting at Kanpur on 19 January 1930, to take a final example, appointed a sub-committee to report on the localities in the province suitable for civil disobedience, and nominated a number of people to a newly established UP National Service for continued organization and inspection of Congress committees.[25]

The result of all this effort was a more elaborate and efficient organization than had existed in Non-Cooperation times. In Allahabad city the Congress organized *mohalla* committees in every quarter. In Saharanpur it was noted that most villages of any size had their own Congress Committees, unlike in 1920–2.[26]

The 'truce' following the Gandhi-Irwin pact of March 1931 afforded an opportunity for a considerable extension of the Congress's rural organization. The UP Government complained that, as soon as the 'truce' came into force, Jawaharlal Nehru, as general secretary of the AICC, sent out a circular declaring it 'vitally necessary' that Congressmen should take

> immediate steps to consolidate the position gained by the Congress during the last year and to strengthen it still further... If we now establish firmly definite centres of work and activity in rural areas we shall strengthen our organisation and prepare the people for any contingency that might arise.[27]

In many areas Congress workers undertook propaganda and activity on the lines laid down in Nehru's directive. As a result several districts in the province – Rae Bareli, Agra and Mathura, for example – came to be dotted with village and *mandal* and *tahsil* Congress committees and the attendant camps and flags.

Satyanarain Srivastava, a leading congressman of Rae Bareli, described the process for his home circle of Bakuliha. Bakuliha village had been an important centre of Congress activity since the beginning of 1930.

Srivastava claimed that all its inhabitants had joined the Congress, a claim supported by a local magistrate who argued that the residents of Bakuliha had 'fully imbibed' seditious ideas and would naturally not come up as police witnesses in a case of alleged instigation to non-payment of rent.[28] After March 1931, a *mandal* Congress committee centered on this village was reactivated, complete with president, secretary and treasurer. A volunteer board was organized and large numbers of volunteers and Congress members enlisted from the surrounding villages. A sub-committee was formed to deal with the many disputes and complaints that villagers brought to the Congress office. Daily meetings were held, including some for untouchable labourers who, Srivastava claimed, 'unanimously' adopted resolutions declaring Gandhi and the Congress, rather than Dr Ambedkar, to be their representative.[29]

Throughout the Rae Bareli district the DCC launched a new scheme of Congress *ashramas* to act as propaganda centres. Cultivators and landowners were asked to register complaints against *taluqdars*, police and government officials at these centres. In Rae Bareli town, a general Congress office, a publicity office and a *satyagraha ashram* were re-established. There were reports also of vigorous efforts at the reorganization of *tahsil* Congress committees, the enlistment of Congress members, the setting up of *panchayats* and the enrolment of volunteers.[30] In May a separate Kisan Sangh was established in the district with Sitla Sahai, the Rae Bareli Congress leader closest to Nehru and the provincial leadership, as president. In effect this was nothing but another new branch of the Congress concerned exclusively with the problems of the *kisans*. At the Salon Tahsil Kisan Conference in May 1931, it was announced that there were in that *tahsil* alone 426 *panchayats*, 2,100 Congress members and 1,825 volunteers, in addition, it was claimed, to a Congress flag in every village! Officials in their turn observed at this time that the district as a whole had 840 *panchayats*, 32 Congress offices, 8,040 Congress members, 13,081 volunteers and 1,019 villages with Congress flags.[31]

Similar efforts were reported from other districts.[32] A later chapter will suggest that the great increase in the Congress presence and influence outside the towns in 1931 was not entirely due to the efforts of the official Congress leadership or their lieutenants.[33] But there can be no doubt about the overall extension of the Congress's rural organization in this period.

In 1934 when provincial Congress leaders set about reviving their completely battered organization for electoral purposes, their success was again remarkable and quick. From May 1934, when the AICC meeting at Patna decided that the Congress should contest that year's elections to the central Legislative Assembly, there was feverish activity in the UP Congress camp. The districts of the province were divided into a number of groups, with each division in the charge of a member of the PCC council. Congress committees were revived and reorganized at the various levels and the enrolment of new members taken up in earnest. By June regular Congress offices were functioning in 37 districts, and 17 districts reported the enrolment of between 100 and 500 new members each. By the middle of July the number was said to be as high as 1,000 and 1,100 in Banaras and Ghazipur respectively. After the 1934 elections the work of revitalizing and extending the organization continued, with an eye to the expected provincial elections under the impending Government of India Act, 1935. By September 1935 the PCC reported a total of 62,112 Congress members in UP, 38,396 from the rural areas and 23,716 from the urban. By December 1938, the reported figures were up to 1,472,456 of which 1,345,781 were members from rural areas, and 126,675 from the urban.[34]

The Viceroy's report that the Congress's success in the 1934 elections was based on its 'superior organization'[35] was only partially true. The agitation against the Simon Commission and the Civil Disobedience Movement, as well as Gandhi's parleys and pact with Irwin, left their mark on the popular imagination just as the Non-Cooperation campaign had done a decade earlier. 'A man like Patel can whip up a very big crowd in Lahore,' wrote the Viceroy of India in June 1930, 'no doubt because on popular view he figures as a hero who has courageously stood up to the British Government.'[36] It is notable that in 1934 the Congress won all the Legislative Assembly seats from UP's non-Muslim constituencies, where in the last elections it contested, in 1926, it had won only two. In the Agra rural constituency, where in 1926 the Congress candidate Kailash Nath Katju had lost to the influential Liberal, Hriday Nath Kunzru, by over 4,500 votes, Sri Krishna Dutt Paliwal, the leader of the Civil Disobedience campaign in Agra district and now the Congress candidate, defeated the same Kunzru by almost 8,000 votes.[37] Indeed, all the Congressmen elected in 1934, except for Dr Bhagavan Das, who was 65, and possibly Sardar Jogender Singh, had been to jail for civil disobedience. The vote for the Congress would thus appear to have been a vote for the heroes of *satyagraha* as much as a vote for indefatigable organizers and campaigners. Nevertheless, the Viceroy's particular explanation does indicate how impressive the Congress organization had again become by this time.

It is true that the figures of Congress membership in the early 1930s failed to match those of the Non-Cooperation period. But if this reflected a lower level of enthusiasm, it also reflected more careful organization and tighter hierarchical control. In 1930, and even in 1932, when the Government was determined to deal most firmly with the Congress, the provincial committees appear to have been in regular contact with the central headquarters as well as with their principal district centres.[38]

The greater degree of central control was evident from the fact that most rural agitation was held back in UP for months after the start of Civil Disobedience. This had indeed led the Governor, Hailey, to imagine that the regime had nothing to fear from the Congress in areas other than the hill districts where there were no landed magnates through whom it could exercise control. Yet no sooner had the authorities decided on the formation of a special force to police the hills, in order 'to dissipate the belief so sedulously propagated that Government had ceased to exercise control',[39] than they were caught unawares in other areas. Ten days after the Governor's self-assuring thoughts were put on paper, in October 1930, the PCC council decided to launch a no-tax campaign, and agitation flared up in several districts including many in Awadh, the traditional preserve of landlord power. The finger on the button was very much in evidence again when between March and December 1931 – the hiatus between the two phases of the Civil Disobedience campaign – the Congress leadership held back peasant agitation with considerable, though by no means complete, success.[40]

Centralization and control were also the hallmarks of the Congress volunteer corps – which were revived at the time of Civil Disobedience. In the country as a whole, some 100,000 volunteers participated in the first phase of the movement.[41] This was a small number compared with that in the Non-Cooperation Movement but it soon became clear that the nature and conditions of volunteer work had changed substantially since the 1920s.

In mid-1931 the CWC decided to establish an expert and trained body which was to devote itself to certain activities specified in a newly drafted set of rules. It was resolved that the Hindustani Seva Dal would be the central volunteer organization of the Congress, to be called the Congress Seva Dal. Each province would appoint a general officer commanding its provincial Seva Dal. The Dals would consist of three sections: children (*bal*), boys and girls (*kumars* and *kumaris*) and adults (*proudhas*). The Seva Dals were to take a pledge laid down by the CWC to hold aloof from all party politics within the Congress. Elaborate rules and a training programme were drawn up.[42] In UP a training scheme was prepared by the Kashi Vidyapith and provincial Seva Dal together, and in August a six-month training camp began in Banaras. The course included a series of over a hundred lectures on subjects as varied as Indian history, the labour movement, cleanliness and health. Some of the Congress's best-known intellectuals participated as teachers. Volunteers were also given physical training and education in spinning and propaganda techniques. To begin with, one worker from every DCC in the province took the course.[43]

Another notable development in the organization of volunteers at this time was the waiving of fees due from village volunteers who were facing serious financial difficulties on account of the Depression. Provincial volunteer boards were allowed the discretion to remit the membership fees of such volunteers in any given area or even in a whole province. Thus while the organization of volunteer corps was tightened and centralized, an attempt was made to extend their social base. How effective the volunteer force proved to be during the second phase of the Civil Disobedience Movement in UP may be judged from the fact that in 1934, when Civil Disobedience was over and the Government lifted the ban on the Congress and its associate organizations, the Seva Dal was regarded as still too dangerous to be restored to legality.[44]

IV

The repeated resurgence of a strong Congress organization as described above was made possible by the establishment of a firm infrastructure in 1920–2, a network of Congress branches and offices run by a nucleus of active workers, and the presence of widespread sympathy and support for the Congress after those years. This could be seen in the continuity of the Congress leadership during the 1920s and 1930s, and in the availability of substantial funds for the organization throughout that period.

The bulk of the Non-Cooperation leadership in UP stayed on to run the Congress organization in the years that followed. All six presidents of the PCC in the latter half of the 1920s[45] – Shaukat Ali, Shiva Prasad Gupta, Purushottam Das Tandon, Govind Ballabh Pant, Jawaharlal Nehru and Ganesh Shankar Vidyarthi – were men who came to prominence during the Non-Cooperation Movement or the Home Rule agitation that preceded and merged with it.[46]

Of the two still more senior Congress leaders in the province, Madan Mohan Malaviya and Motilal Nehru, the former had held aloof from Non-Cooperation. This had only served to strengthen Motilal Nehru's claims to provincial leadership and Malaviya quickly moved to make up some of the lost ground. In 1922 he defended the Chauri Chaura rioters in their appeal before the Allahabad High Court. From 1923 onwards both he and Nehru turned their attention to the legislatures. Both worked to gain wider acceptance of their different approaches to nationalism and sought for electoral purposes to extend the range of their alliances and following, thereby helping to maintain the strength of the Congress organization.

It has been observed above that the triennial elections to the central and provincial legislatures under the 1919 Act provided a focus for organizational work at the provincial level. In this area of Congress activity there were several men who were relatively unimportant in the party's organizational wing. Many scions of well-to-do landed and commercial families joined non-cooperators like Motilal Nehru, Pant, Sri Prakasa and T A K Sherwani in the electoral contests of the 1920s. They included, for example, Thakur Sadho Singh, an influential *zamindar* of Shahjahanpur district; Lala Sangam Lal Agrawal, a substantial cloth merchant of Allahabad city; and Mukandi Lal, the son of a prosperous shopkeeper and contractor of Garhwal, an Oxford graduate and subsequently an advocate at the Allahabad High Court and the director of several companies.

The Independent Congress Party (ICP) set up by Malaviya to contest the 1926 elections in opposition to the 'official' Congress carried the representation of commercial and landed notables further. Among ICP candidates in UP were great landlords like Rai Rajeshwar Bali, Raja Durga Narain Singh of Tirwa, Raja Vishwanath Singh of Tiloi and Raja Raghuraj Singh of Mankapur, such men of commerce as Lalas Prag Narayan of Agra, Jwala Prasad Jigyasu of Aligarh and Chunnilal Garg of Kanpur, and the Calcutta magnate, mill-owner, merchant and *zamindar*, Ghanshyam Das Birla, who was also the chief financier of the party.[47]

When the Congress returned to the electoral arena after the years of Civil Disobedience there was again a need to find candidates who could largely pay their way and exercise a degree of traditional influence in their localities. Wealth was at a premium; Lady Wazir Hasan was considered for a Congress ticket in the 1936 elections to the provincial legislature since 'she can afford to spend a substantial amount'.[48]

Apprehensive of official sanction and displeasure, many of these leading Congress legislators withdrew from the limelight when periods of
civil disobedience began. Mukandi Lal, deputy leader of the UP Congress
Legislature Party from 1926 to 1929, his Oxford-educated colleague
Anandi Prasad Dube, a prominent member of the Allahabad Bar, and
the Dublin-educated Lucknow barrister and university lecturer in law,
Jaikaran Nath Misra, were among the Congress notables who held aloof
from the agitation of 1930–3.

Legislators like Motilal Nehru, Pant, Vidyarthi, Rafi Ahmad Kidwai
and Sri Prakasa, on the other hand, stayed on to lead the movement.
With them were other leaders from Non-Cooperation days, such as
Jawaharlal Nehru, Tandon and Shiva Prasad Gupta, who had chosen
to concentrate their organization and propaganda work outside the
constitutional sphere, though they were willing to use elections and
elected majorities in the districts and municipalities to further their
efforts. Below these groups, moreover, there was a second tier of
leadership, which throughout the 1920s had done more than most
Congress legislators to keep the organization going in the districts.

This middle leadership included activists like Baba Raghava Das,
Dr Vishwanath Mukherji and Vindhyavasini Prasad Varma, to take a
set of leaders from a single district – Gorakhpur. Better-known examples are the 'Shastris', Algu Rai, Harihar Nath and Lal Bahadur, each
of whom worked in a number of districts in UP. Less famous but not
necessarily less influential in the 1920s and 1930s were 'peasant leaders'
like Rae Bareli's Satyanarain Srivastava or Allahabad's Tikaram Tripathi
and Shivmurti Singh.

The Gorakhpur men mentioned above illustrate well the diversity of
social origins of this intermediate level of Congress leadership in UP.
Raghava Das was a Maharashtrian who came to UP as a young lad in
his teens after initial schooling in his home state. He became a disciple
of Anand Mahaprabhu, a renowned *sadhu* (hermit) of Deoria – then a
small town in Gorakhpur district, now the headquarters of an independent one – and soon became known as Baba Raghava Das. Gaoled
for Non-Cooperation, he worked after his release to strengthen the
Congress organization and spread the nationalist message in eastern
UP. Part of this work was concerned with elections; in 1926 he cam-
paigned vigorously for the protection of the Sanatan Dharrna and the
rights of Hindus, and therefore for Malaviya's ICP. More of his time
was spent in editing the religious and philosophical journal, *Kalyan*, in
promoting the *charkha* (spinning wheel) and *acchutoddhar*, and later

in flood relief work in eastern UP and Bihar. Living a life of extreme simplicity wearing a short loin-cloth and wooden sandals and subsisting chiefly on groundnuts and buttermilk, Raghava Das was soon acclaimed as 'the Gandhi of the eastern districts' – a reflection also of the following he had built up in the area.

Vishwanath Mukherji hailed from the other end of the country, the 24 Parganas in Bengal. A well-known homoeopath of Gorakhpur, he was drawn into politics through the influence of the renowned revolutionary terrorist, Rash Behari Bose. He too was gaoled for Non-Cooperation in 1920. Thereafter he worked chiefly among the Bengal and North Western Railway workers in Gorakhpur, organizing them into a union in 1926 and expanding the range of his political activities with the establishment of a Workers' and Peasants' Conference in 1929. Detained in the Meerut Conspiracy Case, he spent the next four years in gaol. But he returned in 1933 to resume work among the peasants and workers of his district, reorganizing the Bengal and North-Western Railway workers' union and the Kisan-Mazdoor Conference.

Vindhyavasini Prasad Varma was the only one of these men who was a native of Gorakhpur. The son of a successful lawyer, he himself practised at the Bar after graduating from Calcutta (BA, 1909) and Allahabad (LL B, 1913). As a student he had been a member and secretary of the Bihar Students' Conference. As a lawyer he established the Gorakhpur Home Rule League in 1916 with the help of two of his professional colleagues. In 1917 he accompanied Gandhi on his tour of Champaran. In 1918–9 he was president of the first Gorakhpur DCC and organized a *hartal* (general strike) to protest against the Rowlatt Acts. In 1920 he left his legal practice to become a non-cooperator, and throughout the 1920s and 1930s he worked to strengthen the nationalist movement in Gorakhpur, editing the weekly *Yugantar*, assisting in the organization of the railway workers and organizing numerous demonstrations and conferences. He lost his sight in 1939 and died in 1943, having donated most of his ancestral wealth to support the 1942 'Quit India' Movement.

Owing at least partly to the efforts of such workers, Gorakhpur came to be one of the strongest centres of Congress activity in UP during the Civil Disobedience Movement of 1930–3. None of these men was immediately concerned with obtaining seats in the provincial legislature or on local boards. But this was no bar to their devoting themselves to nationalist work or indeed to becoming the most important organizers of the Gorakhpur Congress.

The three 'Shastris' mentioned above gained greater prominence in the long run than any of our Gorakhpur examples, but in the period under study they did work of a very similar kind in other districts. All three were students at the time of the Non-Cooperation Movement. All took part in demonstrations and two of them, Harihar Nath and Lal Bahadur, were arrested. After the suspension of the movement all three went to the Kashi Vidyapith from where each received the degree of 'Shastri'. After that all of them joined the Lok Sevak Mandal (Servants of the People Society), Lahore, and devoted themselves to public work while living on the small allowance of about 60 rupees a month given by the Mandal to its members. Given the small number of men who were willing and able to devote themselves to full-time nationalist work when the Congress and all its associate bodies were considered 'subversive' organizations, the Shastris quickly gained a conspicuous and important place in the Congress organizations of the districts in which they happened to be working at different times.

Algu Rai went to Meerut, set up the Kumar Ashram as his headquarters and concentrated on *acchutoddhar*. He raised funds for this work, organized Sweepers' Unions and gave valuable publicity to the Congress and its activities, not only in Meerut but in neighbouring districts as well. Predictably he was among the chief organizers of the Congress campaigns in several of these districts in 1930–1 and afterwards.

Lal Bahadur also began his career in the Lok Sevak Mandal with *acchutoddhar* activity, beginning as Algu Rai's lieutenant in Meerut but then moving on to work among untouchables at Delhi, Banaras and finally Allahabad. Here Lal Bahadur's activities branched out into several areas. In 1928, at Tandon's suggestion, he successfully contested an election to membership of the Allahabad municipality. In the years following he was an active organization man in the district Congress. Later he was to be a Parliamentary Secretary, and then a minister in the Government of UP, before becoming a minister in the central cabinet in independent India. He served briefly as the Prime Minister of the country before his death in 1966.

Harihar Nath, like the other two, began his Lok Sevak Mandal work among the untouchables, in this case in Banaras. But soon afterwards he transferred to work among industrial labourers. After a period of training with trade union leaders in Bombay, he went to Kanpur, took up residence in the workers' quarter in Gwaltoli, and quickly established his influence in the area. By 1929 he was general secretary

Table 3.1
Occupational distribution of the members of the Council of the UP Provincial
Congress Committee, 1925–35

	1925–6	1929–30	1934–5
Lawyers*	5	8	8
Teachers	1	2	3
Journalists	2	4	3
Doctors	2	–	–
Ex-government service	1	–	–
Rais and **zamindars***	2	3	2
Men of religion	1	1	1
Public work**	2	2	4
Not known	(5)	(1)	–
Total	21	21	21

Source: For the membership, AICC Papers, Files 11/1926, P26/1929, P20/1934.

* All lawyers and advocates have been grouped together, as have all **zamindars** and **rais**. There were often wide variations in the wealth and social standing of men included in these groups, but by and large the less well-to-do lawyers and smaller **zamindars** predominated. In addition, certain men fall into more than one category. In such cases they have been classified according to their primary source of income, e.g. Sri Prakasa (a lawyer and **zamindar**) as a **zamindar** and Ganesh Shankar Vidyarthi (an ex-government servant and a journalist) as a journalist.
** 'Public workers' includes all those supported by nationalist social or political service institutions, such as the National Service, the Lok Sevak Mandal and the **Khaddar Bhandars**.

of the Kanpur Mazdur Sabha, by 1931 its president. He played an active part in the Civil Disobedience Movement of the early 1930s and took many of his local supporters into the campaign with him.[49]

The leadership of the Congress organization happened to be provided largely by men with some degree of economic independence from the Government and some amount of political education.[50] At the provincial level independent professionals were predominant in the leadership throughout the 1920s and 1930s (see table 3.1). In the second tier of the Congress leadership too the independent professionals were well represented. An overwhelming majority of the score or so of district Congress leaders whom Motilal Nehru referred to as 'thoroughly reliable' men in the course of preparations for local board elections in 1925 were lawyers.[51] But there was at the district level another kind of Congress leader who was important during this period. This was the man from an almost purely rural background, who was not directly involved in electoral contests for the provincial council or the local boards and who devoted his time primarily to work among peasant groups, helping thereby to keep the Congress organization alive in at least some rural areas. Naturally it was not from the bigger landowning families that such Congress workers came. Yet the leadership even at this level came from relatively privileged groups: men who had the economic independence, literacy, urban links and leisure to enable them to take up long-term national work.

Bayly suggests, on the basis of his study of the Allahabad region, that small *zamindars* and the 'upper tenantry' provided the most important organization men of the Congress in the districts and *tahsils* throughout the 1920s and 1930s. Brennan's work makes a similar finding about the new men who emerged as Congress leaders in the districts of Rohilkhand during the years of Civil Disobedience. Among them were an Agrawal paper merchant and moneylender, a Mahajan Vaishya *zamindar*, a young Chauhan *zamindar*, a Thakur with a BA, and two young graduates: 'young men from rural castes, or with Zamindari or money-lending connections with rural castes…[who had the] ability to influence the petty zamindars and tenants'.[52]

A sample survey conducted by the present writer of Congress leaders and organizers in Agra, Allahabad, Azamgarh and Rae Bareli districts in the 1920s and early 1930s also indicated a heavy representation of small *zamindars* and *pattidars*, and, especially in Agra with its important commercial and industrial position, petty and middling merchants and businessmen, apart from the independent professionals.

Rae Bareli's Satyanarain Srivastava provides one example of this type of Congress leader with a rural background. Born in a Kayastha family of strong Arya Samaji sympathies, Satyanarain developed nationalist views at an early age. After school he started work as a *peshkar* and honorary *munsif*[53] of Thakur Raghuraj Singh, the *taluqdar* of Semri, in whose domain his village, Bakuliha, and his small landholding lay. But in 1921 he gave up his *taluqdari* service to participate in the Non-Cooperation Movement. Afterwards he accepted a position as a clerk in the office of Kismat Rai Jagdhari, a noted lawyer of Rae Bareli and a Congressman until the time of Non-Cooperation, but only on the condition that he be allowed to continue Congress work. The front portion of the small house he rented on Station Road in Rae Bareli served as the district Congress office, and from there, for much of the 1920s, he ran the Congress organization and supervised what little Congress activity there was in the district. In 1930 he left his clerkship and returned to Bakuliha to organize locally for Civil Disobedience.

Allahabad had a greater abundance of such leaders. One was Shivmurti Singh, born in 1896 in a family of smallholding Thakurs of Kotwa in

Phulpur *tahsil*, some 15 miles across the Ganga from Allahabad city. The upper castes in the region did not touch the plough and Shivmurti's father occupied himself as a teacher in the village school. From there Shivmurti passed the Hindi Middle (Standard Eight) examination. He then went to Allahabad to continue his studies. Reading progressive and nationalist literature including such periodicals as *Karmayogi*, and attending political meetings at a time when the Swadeshi and the anti-partition agitations in Bengal were recent events, Shivmurti became a supporter of *swadeshi* (the movement for the boycott of foreign goods in favour of indigenous products) in his first year at Allahabad. In 1918 he left his studies and, at the suggestion of Purushottam Das Tandon, became a Hindi teacher at Gandhi's Sabarmati Ashram. Afterwards he taught in Allahabad and then at a school in Bikaner of which Sampurnanand, later an important Congress leader of Banaras, was principal.

When Non-Cooperation began in 1920, Shivmurti left teaching to take up Congress activities, working chiefly among the *kisans* in Allahabad and Pratapgarh districts. Following the decline of the movement he went to Lahore where he graduated from the Qaumi Vidyapith. He then returned to Congress work in Allahabad, working now under the guidance of Jawaharlal Nehru and still primarily among the *kisans*. Here he was largely responsible for the establishment of a more permanent Congress organization below the district level in the latter half of the 1920s. He recalled emphasizing that the *mandal*, which was the unit of district board administration, rather than the unwieldy *tahsil*, should be made the intermediate level of organization. At the end of the decade Shivmurti became an important organizer of the Civil Disobedience campaign in the district.[54]

Tikaram Tripathi's career was not dissimilar. From the village of Jamunipur, little more than a stone's throw away from Shivmurti's Kotwa, Tikaram was one of five Brahman brothers who inherited a small *Zamindari* that was divided among them. He went to the village school and then passed the Hindi Middle examination from Handia, a *tahsil* headquarters and important market town of the district. After that he taught in a district board school. Dismissed in 1910 for 'communicating his advanced views to the students', he was employed by Madan Mohan Malaviya at his Bharti Bhawan Library in Allahabad city. When the Non-Cooperation Movement began, he parted company with Malaviya, left the library and worked full-time for the nationalist organization, especially in the region of his native village. In 1923 he became secretary of the Allahabad DCC, and he played a prominent part in all subsequent Congress agitations against the British.

Tikaram's village provides an excellent example of organized and extended Congress propaganda and activity. Tikaram's son, Rup Narain Tripathi, followed him into active Congress work. Rup Narain in turn was followed by his wife and two sisters who took up the task of organizing the local women and courted arrest during the Civil Disobedience Movement. From about 1927 the Allahabad University Village Service League was active here, and in 1930 a Gram Seva Sangh 'consisting of the educated and energetic young men of the locality' also existed in the village.[55] In short, an active sympathy and support of the villagers was being generated for any future Congress campaign.

The presence of men like Shivmurti Singh, Tikaram Tripathi and Satyanarain Srivastava in leadership positions made a significant difference to the Congress movement. Their experience and education had made them articulate nationalists and enabled contact with senior Congress leaders. Their background equally fitted them to be spokesmen for the *kisan* and to interpret, for him, somewhat remote nationalist messages. Such men were unlikely to have found a place on Congress councils before 1920. After that date provincial and national leaders consistently worked through them to mobilize and retain popular support. As Satyanarain wrote, 'I was always [*sic*.] made a member of the PCC. I had been the Peshkar of a *taluqdari* estate and the clerk of a famous lawyer, and living amongst the peasants I knew the defects of the Awadh Rent Act very well. Hence I was able to make a useful contribution to PCC resolutions concerning the peasant.'[56]

V

If the presence of a core of committed leaders and workers was one reason for the continuing strength of the Congress organization in the years after Non-Cooperation, the availability of substantial financial support to the organization was another. It has been noted above that the success of the Tilak Memorial Swaraj Fund was never to be repeated. Indeed, there were occasions during the next decade and a half when the Congress faced major financial difficulties.[57] Yet for a number of reasons the post-War Congress was always in a stronger financial position than the party had been earlier.

In the first place, the open membership and four-anna fee introduced in 1920 proved, together with petty collections, sufficient for a great deal of local work. Secondly, the extensive sympathy for the Congress after the War, the strengthened organization and the increased propaganda produced promising results in many of the major and minor collections made for or by the Congress. Indeed, at moments of popular enthusiasm contributions to Congress funds came from some of the most unlikely sources. Old Congress leaders recall contributions during the Civil Disobedience period from the wife of Sir Jagdish Prasad, then chief secretary to the UP Government; through a secret collection made at the Allahabad police lines; and from a police inspector sent to arrest an organizer of the 'no-tax' campaign in that district.[58] Later the wife of Sir Jwala Prasad Srivastava, a Kanpur *rais* and businessman and minister for education in the UP Government from 1931 to 1937, signed an appeal for subscriptions to Gandhi's Harijan Fund; and Srivastava had to make a hasty apology disclaiming prior knowledge of the act.[59]

Above all it was during the years after the First World War that the Congress began increasingly to ally itself with elements of the Indian commercial and industrial bourgeoisie. The Swadeshi agitation in Bengal and the strong campaigns for the boycott of foreign cloth during the Non-Cooperation and Civil Disobedience Movements indicated the direct aid that a powerful nationalist movement could give to Indian industrialists.[60] The changes introduced by the 1919 constitution made it possible for the Congress to promote the interests of this class through the legislatures as well.

The public pronouncements made by the Congress were marked by a certain ambivalence regarding the importance of industrialization in India, as opposed to the encouragement of Indian handicrafts.[61] But no one at the highest level of the Congress leadership had any doubts about the need for a long-term link between the Congress and the capitalist class. Gandhi put it succinctly in an article published in *Young India* in July 1929:

> The exclusive preaching of khadi does not mean hostility to indigenous mill-cloth... It is the popular indifference that has given the foreign cloth dealer his vantage ground. The moment the people are induced to think for themselves and make their choice, the boycott is a certainty. The indigenous mills are therefore playing their part in the movement and profiting by it without the assistance from Congressmen.[62]

The concessions sought from the British at this time also made the Congress position in this matter abundantly clear. The 'substance of independence', contained in Gandhi's 'Eleven Points' of 1929, included a wholesale acceptance of the demands of the Federation of Indian Chambers of Commerce and Industry. In the 1930s the demand for industrial protection and financial independence was articulated more clearly than ever before.[63]

During the Civil Disobedience period the Congress concluded a far-reaching agreement with a number of Indian textile mills. On the acceptance of various conditions, including a pledge to deal only with Indian banks, the mills were placed on an 'approved' list and the sale of their products was to be permitted by Congress picketers.[64] The favored mill-owners reaped some immediate rewards. In UP at least Gandhi's prediction was borne out. The supply of *khadi* was far outstripped by its demand in 1930 and had to be supplemented by Indian mill cloth.[65]

There were of course other grounds, too, for the support that businessmen and industrialists gave to the Congress. They often shared the nationalist sympathies and anti-British feelings that were spreading among the urban population generally. 'If it is absolutely certain that we are going to stamp out boycott,' Hailey wrote about the UP business community, 'it will cooperate, though not very openly, for the Marwari tradesman is not only very timid, but at heart has all the Hindu feeling in favour of Congress. The Marwaris as a body tend to place Hinduism before almost any other consideration.'[66] N.B.

Whatever the reason, it is beyond doubt that men of commerce and industry were the chief source of Congress funds in the 1920s and 1930s. Calcutta's Ghanshyamdas Birla made handsome donations for *acchutoddhar* work in the mid-1920s, towards the costs of the election campaign of the ICP in 1926, for the propagation of the Nehru Report in 1928–9, and indeed for almost any other cause that Gandhi deemed it fit to recommend to him.[67] Congress leaders everywhere turned to Bombay and Calcutta whenever there was a need for substantial funds.[68]

In UP local industrialists and businessmen also made large contributions to the Congress coffers.[69] This was probably an important reason for the vigour of the Civil Disobedience Movement in major centres of commerce and industry like Kanpur and Agra. By the mid-1930s, secret support was giving way to more open association between the Congress and industrial and commercial men in UP: one indication of this was the appointment of several important Congressmen as directors or agents of the new insurance agencies being established to fill a gap created by the disruptive effects of the Depression.[70] Very large contributions to the UP Congress funds were also made by prosperous advocates and other professionals, several substantial landlords and the ruler of a princely state.[71]

In return for such support, the Congress sometimes felt obliged to make important concessions. The Kanpur TCC, for example, acquiesced in the continued sale of foreign cloth during the Civil Disobedience Movement when other strong Congress centres were clamping down on the trade. The result was a weakening of boycott not only in Kanpur but also at other places in UP. The secretary of the TCC explained the position regarding one of the 'culprits'. Lala Lallu Mal Dalai, a member of the TCC Executive, was a working partner in the firm 'Babu Ram & Co.', which had sold some foreign goods in 1930–1. Besides, Lallu Mal was the Kanpur broker for the firm Messrs Jugal Kishore Baldeo Sahai of Gonda district. In this capacity he still sold some foreign piece goods, though, the TCC secretary suggested, most of his sales were of *swadeshi* cloth:

> All the same he is very useful to us in more than one way. He has been the mainstay of our financial resources, since the last 11 years. He has helped us in the establishment of the Congress Khaddar Bhandar and he is a director thereof. He has been contributing handsomely towards the political sufferers' fund. In short there is no national scheme in which we do not avail of his generous help.[72]

In a word the Congress, depending heavily on the donations of the Birlas and Bajajes and sympathetic Rajas and notables, recognized in them exceptional cases, not subject to the normal demands of personal sacrifice made by a nationalist movement, and made major concessions to them, not only in Bombay and Calcutta, but in Kanpur and Agra and Almora too.[73]

VI

There was one other factor that sustained the Congress organization through periods of slackness in the nationalist camp after 1920. This was the presence of 'feeders' in the form of 'national' institutions and 'constructive' work organizations. The establishment or, in some cases, further development of select national institutions, opposed to British and British-aided institutions in India, was one of the features of Non-Cooperation. Of these, educational institutions were among the most important, on account of the groups they affected and the ideological guidelines they provided.

National education had been advocated by the Arya Samaj since the late nineteenth century. At many places in UP the Samaj had established Dayanand Anglo-Vedic schools and colleges, as well as more traditional Gurukuls. The Gurukuls were particularly influential with their pronounced Indian-ness, their denunciation of distinctions based on caste and their provision of free education, which attracted many poor students. 'The cultural nationalism emerging from the Gurukul', writes a historian of the Arya Samaj, 'became the mother of political nationalism in India.'[74] While the Hindu bias of the 'national' education provided here added to the unfortunate Hindu appearance of Indian nationalism, the presence of these institutions did strengthen the Congress movement. For example, the Gurukul Kangri at Hardwar in Saharanpur district was particularly noted for its prominence in the early stages of the Civil Disobedience campaign in 1930.[75]

Individuals had also supported national education. Raja Mahendra Pratap of Mursan founded and sustained a number of national institutions in Mathura and other districts of western UP, the Prem Mahavidyalaya of Brindaban (Mathura) being the most notable among them. Men who were later well-known Congress figures, such as Acharyas Jugal Kishore, Gidwani and Sampurnanand, were associated with the Prem Mahavidyalaya. In 1929 the institution provided for lectures on citizenship, economics, spinning and carding work, cleanliness and medicine, and organized a tour of villages at least once a week to collect statistics regarding village conditions. Before admission students had to pledge themselves to at least ten years of village work. Needy students received a stipend of Rs 15 to Rs 20 per month, and, after completion of their course, from Rs 35 to Rs 75 per month for continued public work. There was a branch of the Hindustani Seva Dal in the college, and there was an effort to establish one or two small centres in the villages to increase rural contacts. Understandably, the Prem Mahavidyalaya earned the Government's displeasure during periods of nationalist agitation. It was closed down for some time by a special government order in 1932.[76]

The Non-Cooperation Movement produced a tremendous spurt in the establishment of national educational institutions. By the end of July 1921 UP had 37 such institutions with as many as 8,476 scholars.[77] Probably the most famous of these was Kashi Vidyapith, established through the munificence of Shiva Prasad Gupta, the Banaras *rais* and

Congressman, modelled on the Gujarat Vidyapith, and inaugurated in February 1921. From the start the institution was organized and run by well-known nationalist leaders. Dr Bhagavan Das, a leading Congressman in the early 1920s, was its chancellor from 1921 to 1940. J B Kripalani, Narendra Deo, Sampurnanand, Birbal Singh and Yajna Narain Upadhyaya, all of whom attained prominence in the Congress, were among its earliest teachers.[78]

In 1925 Kashi Vidyapith was extended to include a college. Forty-two students passed through this college in the first four years of its existence. The work they then took up was as follows:

Table 3.2

National education	10
Newspaper editing	5
Acchutoddhar	5
Khadi work	2
Unpaid Congress work	7
Other public work (unpaid)	7
Total	36

Of the remaining six, at least three combined some public work with their personal vocation. Five of those involved in 'national' education were teachers at the Vidyapith itself. Others taught elsewhere in UP, Bihar and Rajputana, and trained numerous young men for national work. The journalists were working with *Aj, Pratap, Sainik, Vishal Bharat* and *The Hindustan Times*, again in positions of some public influence.[79]

In general, institutions like Kashi Vidyapith inculcated a public spirit rarely found among the products of government schools and colleges. It was claimed that almost all the students and teachers of the Gujarat and Kashi Vidyapiths participated in the Civil Disobedience Movement of 1930–1.[80] 'The Kashi Vidyapith, as its prototype in Ahmedabad, has really always been the seminary where students are trained in extremists' methods of thinking', the UP Government observed.[81] But perhaps the Deputy Commissioner of Rae Bareli made the most revealing comment when the provincial Government was considering the issuing of a communique declaring students participating in 'subversive' movements disqualified from future government employment. The nine students then in the Rae Bareli gaol were all from Kashi Vidyapith and the Deputy Commissioner pithily observed: 'The students of Kashi Vidyapith are not likely to seek Government employment.'[82]

Certain government-aided educational institutions also stood out from the general run of such bodies by virtue of the education they provided and the results they produced. One was Madan Mohan Malaviya's Banaras Hindu University, which began functioning in 1917 with all of Malaviya's emphasis on 'Hindi, Hindu, Hindustan'. It was observed in September 1930 that, while the students of Allahabad, Lucknow and Agra Universities had shown sympathy for the Civil Disobedience Movement, none of these institutions was as enthusiastic as Banaras. Over a hundred students had left the University to take part in the movement, extending their activities beyond UP to Bihar and Orissa, Bombay and Madras. It was chiefly because of the activities of members of the University that two years later Banaras was considered to be the principal centre of the movement in the province. Again when Gandhi's Harijan campaign took over the political stage some 500 Banaras Hindu University students pledged to work for it during their vacations.[83] At the start of the Quit India Movement in 1942, students of the university even declared the establishment of a state of Free India on their campus, which the colonial armed police was forced to come and re-occupy.

Non-educational public (or social) service organizations that emerged in the Non-Cooperation years also provided valuable support for the nationalist movement. One that was of special importance in UP was Lajpat Rai's Lok Sevak Mandal. Modelled on Gokhale's Servants of India Society but more openly political, the Mandal was officially inaugurated by Gandhi at Lahore on 9 November 1921. Lajpat Rai was president of the Society from then until his death in 1928. He was succeeded by Purushottam Das Tandon, the Allahabad and UP Congress leader. Partly owing to a shortage of funds, and partly on account of great selectivity, the Society remained a small band of trained public workers, maintained by the Society and working full-time in an allotted sphere. In 1934 it had only 14 members, with three assistants.

The area of work was mainly Punjab and UP though a few members worked in Gujarat and Orissa. In UP, Meerut, Allahabad and, later, Kanpur were the chief centres of Lok Sevak Mandal activity. In the 1920s the members concentrated on *acchutoddhar* and ran *ashramas*, libraries and other social services.[84] Nevertheless the Government was of the opinion that, by 1927:

> …members of the Society were engaged in endeavouring to meddle with the administration in the villages. Though some of their activities, such as an endeavour to improve sanitation and

education, were apparently not open to reproach, yet the fact that they persuaded villagers not to call upon the police or courts to help them settle their disputes, and that they opened registers of births and deaths, showed that the Society was beginning to put into force what Congress had been advocating – the gradual establishment of parallel government.[85]

The fact was that in the political conditions of the 1920s the dividing line between social and political work was a thin one. Besides, there was a frankly political aspect to the Lok Sevak Mandal's work. During the Civil Disobedience campaign of 1930, officials reported that all the members of the Mandal had been 'lent' to the Congress.[86] The truth was rather that these men, many of whom were members of the Congress before they became members of the Mandal, turned at this stage from quiet and unostentatious national work to open anti-imperialist agitation because the times and the leaders so dictated. One might describe it as a change of tactics, not however of the battlefield.

Less centralized and perhaps less well organized institutions, like the Khaddar Bhandars and the whole range of *ashramas* run by nationalists all over the country, performed similar functions. They were the chief agencies for Gandhi's programme of 'constructive' work and did much to propagate the fame of the Congress in remote towns and villages. In a period of two or three months in early 1929 Congress committees in UP alone, working in concert with the Khaddar Bhandars, sold *khadi* worth Rs 7,650.[87] Over the next decade, these 'non-political' institutions for 'constructive' work did far more than simply to make financial or moral contributions to the regular Congress organization. Of the Allahabad Khaddar Bhandar an intelligence report said in 1933, 'This...is in fact a branch Congress Office. The employees receive and carry about from place to place objectionable literature, etc. Since the closing of the Congress office in Allahabad, the local khaddar bhandar has been the focus of all illegal activities of the Congress.'[88]

An important function performed by national educational and social service institutions was that of grooming and supporting nationalist workers and leaders at many different levels. The Lok Sevak Mandal, in spite of its limited membership, gave to the UP Congress such leaders as Algu Rai Shastri, Harihar Nath Shastri, Mohanlal Gautam, Lal Bahadur Shastri and Raja Ram Shastri. Kashi Vidyapith trained an even larger number of influential Congressmen. In addition to the four Shastris just mentioned, Kamlapati Tripathi, Tribhuvan Narain Singh,

Balkrishna Keskar and Paripurnanand Varma studied there. Several teachers of the Vidyapith also became important Congress leaders, as noted earlier. In a similar way, the Khaddar Bhandars, the Gandhi *ashramas* and so on provided training and livelihood for numerous Congress workers.[89]

As the value of full-time national workers became obvious, other institutions were set up to provide for them. In 1929 a National Service was established in UP, the delayed fulfilment of an idea first mooted in Non-Cooperation days. Gandhi's tour of the province, from September to November 1929, was utilized for the collection of funds for the service. By the time Gandhi left, over Rs 12,000 had been collected, without doubt a good start. Gandhi commented:

> The idea of such a service has been before the country since 1920…Pandit Jawaharlal [Nehru] has given it a shape and a habitation. National work must suffer so long as we have to depend upon volunteers who give only a part of their time and that too in fits and starts. Permanent work requires permanent whole-time workers.[90]

In 1931 the Ganesh Shankar Vidyarthi Memorial Committee, appealing for donations of Rs 1 lakh, declared that any money left after the erection of a suitable memorial to the Kanpur Congress leader, who lost his life in a communal riot in that city earlier that year, would be used to set up a Ganesh Shankar National Service.[91] About the same time Jawaharlal Nehru proposed, and Gandhi supported, the establishment of a National Workers' Association with full-time, paid workers.[92]

In 1934, in the big Congress reorganization before the elections, the National Service Board, which had ceased to function during the Civil Disobedience Movement, was reconstituted. The National Service was now divided into a provincial and a district branch. Members of the former were given a monthly allowance of up to Rs 40 and of the latter up to Rs 25. Provincial members were placed in charge of whole districts. Paucity of funds was still a problem and the number of members remained small. In June 1934 there were 12 members in the provincial and 14 in the district branch.[93]

The major weakness in all this organizational activity was, of course, the absence of any specific appeal to the mass of the rural and urban poor. The *khaddar* and *swadeshi* campaigns may have gone beyond the 'Indian gentlemen of the middle class…clerks, pleaders, etc.' who alone were substantially affected by the Swadeshi Movement in Bengal early in this century.[94] But, except in those villages where a Khaddar Bhandar or a nationalist *ashrama* existed, these campaigns do not seem to have made much of an impact on the poorer classes in the rural areas.[95] National educational institutions, too, even with their stipends for poor students, recruited mainly from rich peasant groups and the lower middle classes in the towns; it is indeed significant that not a single Dalit name is found among the Congress workers who emerged from these institutions. Not until the end of the period under study was any attempt made to redress the balance in this regard.

The view that the Congress organization took a radical turn in 1928[96] is not borne out by the evidence from UP, supposedly one of the more radical Congress provinces. About that date a restless Jawaharlal Nehru, strongly influenced by his visit to Europe and particularly to Soviet Russia in 1926–7 and increasingly frustrated by the conciliatory character of Congress policies in the mid-1920s, sought to extend the scope of Congress concern. His was a personal, emotional commitment, backed by other individual commitments and a growing, though vague, sympathy for socialism or egalitarianism among young people all over India. There was, however, little in the way of detailed study or solid organizational work.

The linking of the provincial Trade Union Congress with the PCC in 1929, when Nehru was president of the All-India Trade Union Congress, remained a token gesture. The Workers' and Peasants' Party, branches of which were being established in many parts of the country in 1928, appears to have been inactive at the provincial level in UP.[97]

More important in this province was the Independence for India League and the youth movements, which were again gathering momentum about this time. The Independence League, founded in 1928 by the 'radical' wing of the Congress led by Nehru and Subhas Bose, set up a new ideal of considerable emotive power that had an obvious impact on the youth, especially students. Some of the most active and influential of the younger leaders in the UP Congress joined the new organization. But the League made little tangible progress[98] and became superfluous once the Congress itself had adopted the goal of 'complete independence'. Thus the Independence League helped to give a new vigour to Congress activities and propaganda. It did not, however, perceptibly radicalize the organization or broaden its social base.

The same is true of student and youth organizations, which generated considerable enthusiasm at the end of the 1920s and in the 1930s. In UP a large number of youth leagues and student associations sprang up. The big educational centres – Allahabad, Lucknow, Banaras, Gorakhpur and so on – were prominent in this regard. But smaller towns – Mathura, Mainpuri and Moradabad, Jhansi, Jalaun, and Jaunpur – also came to have youth organizations that were vociferous and active.[99] The declared objects of these associations generally included the abolition of outmoded social and religious customs, the combating of communalism, the boycott of British goods and the independence of India. They called for physical training, the study of international questions, an understanding of the causes of growing unemployment among the youth and practical welfare work among workers and peasants.[100]

Since youth leagues and their branches were established in areas where other nationalist associations were not very active or well organized, and several of the young men and women who participated in their activities came from rural or semi-rural backgrounds, these organizations proved to be of value. They helped to extend the links between 'advanced' centres of nationalist activity and the politically 'backward' areas. Nationalist public meetings, processions and demonstrations also owed much of their success to the student and youth associations and their junior partners – the Bal Bharat Sabhas and Vanar Senas. Besides, a fair number of Congress leaders who emerged during the late 1920s and 1930s had their initial training in public work in the incompletely organized and sporadically functioning youth movement.[101]

Yet the fact remains that the organization of students and youth did not extend very far. Little came of a number of attempts to set up a provincial organization to coordinate the work of the various youth bodies; even Jawaharlal Nehru grew dejected on this score.[102] Perhaps more important, these organizations, like the Independence League and others discussed above, failed to reach the poorer sections of the society. This was so partly because their leaders were not from those sections and more especially because they were not given to sustained propaganda work, nor was their language – 'India First', 'We are helots in our own country' – easy for the poor and the illiterate to understand. Militancy these educated young men may have re-introduced into the nationalist movement; a radical departure they did not bring.

It was indeed not until 1933 that Nehru publicly posed the question, 'Whose freedom are we particularly striving for, for nationalism covers many sins and includes many conflicting elements?'[103] In the following year a number of developments suggested a definite Congress shift to the left. The 1934 Congress constitution, the emergence of the CSP and even the Harijan movement were indications of this. These new factors certainly made some difference to the Congress's organization and approach. Yet one must be wary of taking the developments at their face value and of suggesting a major change in the orientation of the Congress at this time.

Some of the changes made in the organization are likely to have been guided by expectations about the forthcoming revisions in the Indian constitution and the needs of the coming elections. Moreover, many of the new provisions in the Congress constitution were scrapped within a short time. The condition of six months of labour to qualify for membership of Congress committees and their executive arms very quickly became a farce. After prolonged discussion about how much spinning constituted how much manual labour, the CWC declared that 'it shall be open to members to offer their work consolidated for a period of six months.' Even this condition was dropped by the Lucknow session of the national Congress in April 1936. In addition, that Congress reduced the minimum length of membership before a member was qualified to vote in Congress elections from six to three months, and reduced the ratio of members to delegates, laid down by the 1934 constitution as 500:1, to 250:1.

To a certain extent these amendments regularized the position created by the breach of the labour qualification and the backdating of people's membership forms in order to enable them to vote in Congress elections, practices that had become a feature of Congress politics in UP in the mid-1930s.[104] At the same time they made it easier for Congress leaders to recruit new members in order to further personal or factional ambitions and also facilitated the entry of less committed men and women into the organization, especially after Congress became the party of Government in 1937. It is not at all surprising that the claimed membership of the provincial Congress shot up from a little over 62,000 in mid-1935 to nearly 1.5 million towards the end of 1938. New organizations for 'constructive' work launched by Gandhi in the early 1930s, such as the All-India Village Industries Association and the Harijan Sevak Sangh, also need to be analysed critically. Consider the latter. The Harijan movement was in one sense a culmination of the anti-untouchability work undertaken by Congressmen and Arya Samajis in the 1920s and even earlier. Its immediate cause, however, was the British Premier's Communal Award made in September 1932, which gave separate electorates to the 'depressed classes'. Gandhi's fast to prevent such an electorate was the first step in the new movement. The 'untouchables' now became 'Harijans' or children of God; and in October 1932 the Harijan Sevak Sangh was established, with Malaviya as president, to work for Harijan uplift.

The Sangh's activities covered a fairly broad social and economic field. It aimed to secure for Harijans the civic rights enjoyed by other Hindus. It worked for their educational advancement, instituting scholarships and helping to open new preparatory schools, hostels and homes for Harijan children. Attempts were also made to employ Harijans in the offices and welfare centres of the Sangh and in newly established industrial homes.[105]

This work received a considerable fillip when Gandhi undertook an all-India Harijan tour from November 1933 to July 1934. When the tour finished at Banaras, Gandhi had collected nearly 821,180 rupees for Harijan uplift. The largest provincial contribution of Rs 116,458 came from Tamilnadu and the largest contribution by any one city from Calcutta, over Rs 70,263. But even the poorer provinces and districts made a substantial contribution. The total from UP was 60,337 rupees, 8 annas and 3 paise. Kanpur gave more than a third of this amount, over Rs 20,320, Banaras over Rs 9000, Allahabad over Rs 8000, Lucknow over Rs 5000 and Gorakhpur, Meerut, Agra, Mathura and Jhansi over Rs 1000 each. As in several other provinces, the entire UP collection was given to the provincial Harijan Sevak Sangh on the grounds of the general poverty of the region. With this sum at its disposal the provincial board expanded its activities. By the middle of January 1934 there were affiliated branches in 31 districts. In the year that followed UP was divided into an eastern, a central and a western part to facilitate Harijan work; branches of the Sangh were opened throughout the province; and Harijan welfare became one of the major areas of Congress concern.[106]

This extension of Congress activities among the section of society that provided the largest number of cultivators in UP was obviously important. It enabled the first organized contact between the Congress and some of the poorest in Indian society. Gandhi's movement was able to gather substantial support even in the teeth of much orthodox Hindu opposition.[107] In many parts of the country, temples and public wells were now thrown open to the untouchables. The movement created a heightened awareness of the Harijan problem, not least among the Harijans themselves. For all these reasons it brought rich dividends to the Congress, especially in elections.

Nonetheless this should not obscure the very great limitations of the Harijan campaign. A few scholarships and industrial homes were scarcely an adequate answer to the problem of untouchability. Nor was the separation of economic oppression from social depression conducive either to a real improvement in Dalit conditions or to the winning of long-term support for the Congress.[108]

A more promising development in the Congress in the 1930s was the formation of the CSP. Like the Swaraj Party organized a decade earlier, the CSP began as a minority movement in the Congress. Like the Swarajists, the Congress Socialists remained in the parent organization and hoped, 'while concentrating on the organization of Labour and the Peasantry,' to capture the Congress organization from the inside.[109]

UP very quickly became one of the strongholds of the Socialist Party. A large number of prominent Congressmen joined the new body. After the PCC elections in September 1934 the Government reported that the president and 4 vice-presidents, 4 of the 6 secretaries and 7 of the 11 members of the executive council belonged to the socialist camp, as did 26 of the 46 provincial representatives to the AICC. In Banaras district the CSP had evidently gained 'complete control of all local committees'. There were reports of strong CSP branches from a number of other districts as well.[110]

The CSP did some valuable organization and propaganda work among groups of workers and peasants in UP. Its role as defence counsel for the 'exploited' against right-wing elements in the Congress was of special importance. The UP Socialists attacked the right wing Congress position, represented strongly in its provincial Parliamentary Board, that the Congress must preserve and strengthen the position of zamindars even as it sought to ameliorate the conditions of the peasantry. They called, instead, for the elimination of middlemen, the abolition of illegal cesses, a graded land tax, the wiping out of arrears of rent and debts owed by tenants and petty *zamindars*, and so on.[111] One of their most creditable battles was fought in connection with the UP Tenancy Act, 1939, passed by the first Congress ministry in the province. This measure, in any case a compromise, might easily have emerged from the Congress councils indistinguishable from British reforms that preceded it but for the resistance of the Socialists.[112]

The weakness of the Socialist position lay in the fact that, as a focus for opposition to the 'official' Congress leadership, the CSP attracted a bundle of disgruntled elements not necessarily bound by a common ideology. The party's anomalous situation was highlighted by Nehru's refusal to join it, in spite of his well-advertised socialist sympathies. It was also revealed by the numerous entrances and exits of Congressmen at all levels through doors that the CSP had opened to all Congressmen who were not members of communal organizations.

Many members accepted the general drift of the socialist programme but opposed some of its most important immediate applications. The question of whether socialists should participate in parliamentary activity proved particularly controversial. The UP branch disagreed with the all-India CSP, and ultimately itself split, on the issues of participation in the Legislative Assembly elections of 1934 and acceptance of offices in Congress committees.[113]

Even in a senior and sophisticated Congress leader like Sri Prakasa there was evidently no more than a sentimental attachment to the concept of socialism, brought about by the experience of *kisan* conditions and agitation during the Depression and the rhetoric of Jawaharlal Nehru. In 1934 Sri Prakasa was an active member of the CSP. But he was also president of the PCC and a member of the UP Congress Parliamentary Board that the Socialists so vehemently attacked. Later he accepted a Congress ticket for the Legislative Assembly elections and, before his election by a thumping majority, resigned from the CSP when the split in the party occurred.

Others who joined the CSP could not be credited even with a sentimental attachment to socialism. 'Socialist' and 'non-Socialist' very quickly became catchphrases and slogans in a whole range of intra-Congress factional disputes.[114] All but a select group of committed Socialists turned their attention inwards on the Congress. The 'outside' work of mobilizing and organizing the masses for a wider social transformation waited for another day.

In summary, even the 'radical' developments of the mid-1930s did little to bridge the gap between the leadership of the major nationalist party and the majority of the 'nation' it fought for. On an organizational level there was still no substantial representation of the poorest classes in the Congress. What had happened in the period since the First World War was, first, the creation of an extensive organization with much popular support and, then, a consolidation and strengthening of this organization among certain limited sections of the society and a toning up of central control and general efficiency. A primary reason for this was the very general nationalist approach of the Congress, which made only belated and rather feeble efforts at providing specifically for the 'masses'. The language of the propaganda and appeals emanating from the nationalist leadership in the 1920s and 1930s indicates this even more clearly than does the nature of the nationalist organization.

4

Spreading the Nationalist Message

The British rulers of India apparently never ceased to be amazed by the proportions assumed by the nationalist movement. They were shocked by the fury of Non-Cooperation, surprised by the successful launching of the Civil Disobedience Movement eight years later and still unprepared for the sweeping Congress victories in the elections of 1937. The vigour of the Congress organization was only one factor that officials picked out in trying to explain these repeated successes. More fervently they argued that economic pressures and an absence of political sophistication led to the strength of the opposition movement. 'Failed BAs and students', 'paid volunteers' and 'bazaar riff-raff, allegedly accounted for the success of nationalist demonstrations and agitations.[1]

The people of India were of course overwhelmingly illiterate,[2] and it is not uncommon to mistake an absence of public school manners and book-learning for a lack of political sophistication or even basic intelligence. In addition it is undeniable that very large numbers of people in the country lived in appalling conditions at the best of times, let alone in situations of economic crisis. We have already noted above what these conditions were like in UP during the early decades of the twentieth century[3] – conditions made even worse by the growing problem of unemployment among the educated in the province in the 1920s and by the Depression at the end of that decade. All of this might appear to support the government interpretation of why the nationalist movement prospered.

Yet neither extreme poverty nor political naivete has ever been a sufficient condition for the rise of large-scale political movements. It has taken stirring ideas and persistent propaganda to draw discontented men into open and extended political action. In UP itself, as Peter Reeves has observed, the economic crises that precipitated the Awadh peasant agitation of 1920–1 were not unprecedented in their gravity. In the early 1920s 'they were associated with new forces at work in the villages: nearly half a million returned soldiers who brought with them a new awareness of their plight and grumbles of their own about unfulfilled recruiting promises and hasty demobilization; and new peasant leaders who spoke of direct action against the British to end their problems.'[4]

The Congress was by no means the only or the obvious choice as a channel for the expression of popular grievances. Other bodies, such as chambers of commerce, landlord leagues, reform societies and caste associations, and forms other than mass agitation, for instance independent deputations and petitions to the local notable, the district official and the provincial governor – all these could have served as well. Even among the intelligentsia, not all who suffered economic hardship necessarily, or automatically, jumped onto the Congress 'bandwagon'. 'The main class of people here sympathetic with the civil disobedience movement are the lawyers', wrote the District Magistrate of Mathura in 1932. 'The few lawyers who assist me in my publicity campaign belong to the rural area and are zamindars, with one exception; this exception is a lawyer with little practice, who aspires to employment in an Indian State.'[5] Economic grievance could cut either way.

Congress propaganda and initiative played an important part in channelling disparate economic grievances, and perhaps a more general feeling of national discontent, into a non-violent anti-imperialist agitation. A Liberal leader noted in 1930, for instance, that as a result of this propaganda racial feelings had been fanned and an intense distrust of the British had arisen.[6] In creating such a condition the Congress was, of course, aided by other forces. The racial arrogance and self-interested policies of the colonial regime provided the ground for anti-British feelings. The economic situation of the late 1920s and early 1930s and the growing impatience of numerous young men with the staid nationalist politics of the mid-1920s had a major impact. Revolutionary terrorists caused excitement with their philosophy of the bomb. We shall see also that local leaders in the rural areas, not directly connected with the Congress, mobilized large numbers of peasants for political action. Moreover, popular agitation, once begun, tended to generate its own momentum. But the Congress's propaganda and mobilization efforts were important as starting points.

II

With fairly substantial funds available, and a larger number of organized cadres than before, the Congress used a whole gamut of techniques to reach different sections of society: from women picketers blackmailing a rich family by placing a curse upon a wedding in the house should foreign cloth be used in it, to Congress workers cycling from village to village distributing leaflets among literate and locally influential men and speaking to small meetings called by the latter, to practised orators addressing meetings of thousands in the cities, small towns and even large villages.[7] In the initial stages certain kinds of loud and sometimes aggressive public activity proved especially effective. One was the relentless propaganda of the nationalist press. Then there were public tours by renowned leaders who had come to symbolize the nationalist spirit and people's hopes – often very diverse and even conflicting hopes – for the future. Perhaps as important were public demonstrations of fearlessness in the face of the Raj, what might be called 'propaganda by deed'.

In the build-up to Civil Disobedience, and at various turning points in the campaign, the press, not only periodicals, but also pamphlets, leaflets and posters and, indeed, cyclostyled and handwritten notices played a crucial part:

> Never before [1930] had the press played so important a part in the national campaign [wrote one commentator],...enthusiasm was kindled and maintained by the vigorous action of the Nationalist newspapers. The facts of daily arrests of leaders, vast processions, injuries to Congress volunteers who had come into conflict with the police, were all displayed in bold type. Indeed, all the methods which a nationalist press might be expected to use in a country at war were employed by the journals supporting the movement.[8]

In UP the number of periodicals directly supporting the Congress programme or openly sympathetic with it had increased since the early 1920s. By 1930 they had, in the case of those of longer standing, generally regained their circulation of the Non-Cooperation period and in a few important cases even surpassed it (table 4.1). This showed a return to something like the enthusiasm of Non-Cooperation times, at least among groups that could afford to buy newspapers and journals. On the other hand it is significant that both the Urdu periodicals listed in table 4.1 declined in circulation in the 1920s, perhaps an indication of the growing Muslim disaffection with the Congress programme, as well as of a growing Hindi-reading public.[9]

Table 4.1
Statement of Important Nationalist Periodicals in UP, 1922–30

Name	Language	Place	Period	Circulation 1922	1927	1930
Abhyudaya	Hindi	Allahabad	Weekly	3000	2500	3000
Aj	Hindi	Banaras	Daily	4000	4000	5000
Bharat	Hindi	Allahabad	Bi-weekly	N/A	3800[a]	9000
Bhavishya	Hindi	Allahabad	Weekly	N/A	N/A	11,000
Chand	Hindi	Allahabad	Monthly	N/A	8000	15,000
Hind Kesari	Hindi	Banaras	Weekly	4000	3000	3000
Indian Daily Telegraph	English	Lucknow	Daily	2000	2500	3000
The Leader	English	Allahabad	Daily	5000	8000	9000
Mazdoor	Hindi	Kanpur	Weekly	500	1000[a]	1500[b]
Medina	Urdu	Bijnor	Bi-weekly	12,500	6500	6000[b]
Mustaqil	Urdu	Kanpur	Daily	N/A	700[a]	500
Pratap	Hindi	Kanpur	Weekly	10,000	7800	16,000
Sainik	Hindi	Agra	Weekly	N/A	3000	4500
Samaya	Hindi	Jaunpur	Weekly	N/A	550	750
Shakti	Hindi	Almora	Weekly	1000	1100	1000
Swadesh	Hindi	Gorakhpur	Weekly	N/A	1300	3700[c]
Tar	Hindi	Gorakhpur	Daily	N/A	N/A	1200
Vartman	Hindi	Kanpur	Daily	8000	3000	4000

[a]Figure for 1928   [b]Figure for 1931   [c]Figure for 1929
The large number of N/As in the column for 1922 occurs because many of these periodicals had not started then.
The importance of periodicals has been judged from their circulation and ascribed political standing. A majority of those listed here were included in the list of important periodicals given in: *Indian Statutory Commission, Vol. IX. Memorandum submitted by the Government of the United Provinces to the Indian Statutory Commission* (London 1930), 209.
Source: *Statement of Newspapers and Periodicals published in the UP* (Government Press, Allahabad) for the relevant years.

Circulation figures are of course deceptive. Periodicals were very cheap in the 1930s – the daily *Aj* cost only 2 *paise*. Even so the number of buyers gives no indication of the actual readership. Even today the *Aj* newspaper, posted up on a wall outside the paper's office in Banaras, attracts scores of readers throughout the day. In the 1920s and 1930s many vernacular newspapers and journals in India bore such slogans as: 'Read this yourself, read it to others, and give it to a peasant'. The Indian Statutory Commission noted in 1928 that vernacular papers 'can be, and are, read to illiterate hearers by their literate fellows in town, villages, railway carriages, public meetings and so on'.[10] Only some kind of geometric progression, then, would give us an idea of the number of buyers, readers and listeners reached by the press.

I have argued elsewhere that this was probably truer still of the non-periodical literature put out by nationalists in the late 1920s and early 1930s.[11] 'Following the publication of resolution number 6 of the Congress Working Committee', said an Intelligence report in July 1930, 'numerous copies of this resolution and of pamphlets based on it have come to notice.'[12] Further leaflets and pamphlets based on the resolution were noticed in the following weeks. Resolution 6 was an appeal to the army and the police to support the national struggle for independence. Therefore the Government took special note of it. But the same method of dissemination was used for other important nationalist resolutions and messages. Congress committees at different levels published notices of meetings, circular letters, resolutions and general information for workers in the columns of newspapers. Apparently much of this was passed on through the medium of the non-periodical press.

This is why Madan Mohan Malaviya's indictment of 'Repression in India', written in English, is found in Hindi among the publications confiscated by the UP Government. Thus the whole history of the freedom struggle since 1857 was printed in verse for wide distribution. Thus, too, there were songs detailing Gandhi's 'Eleven Points', or Vallabhbhai Patel's speech to 5,000 school and college students in Bombay, or the heads of income and expenditure under the British Raj and the fact that the amount of money spent annually on every single Indian convict was greater than the *per capita* income of the rest of the population.[13] This again is what inspired a lieutenant of Jawaharlal Nehru to write to him in 1934 about an article in which Nehru had propounded his socialist views; 'You have only introduced the [socialist] idea to the uppermost crust of the population... Your message must be carried to the millions through a flood of easy straightforward and cleverly worded literature.'[14]

Let me cite one more example to illustrate the place of the press in nationalist propaganda. One of the many thousands of pamphlets proscribed by the UP Government in the course of Civil Disobedience was entitled *Jwalamukhi arthat dabi hui aag* ('Volcano, that is, Suppressed Fire'). It was written by Gopinath Vaidya, secretary of the

Haldaur Congress Committee, Bijnor, and published by that committee in 1930. The preface to the 14-page pamphlet said that it was written for Congress propaganda in the villages. The author claimed to have written it in such a language that even a schoolboy reading in class II would be able to read it out and illiterate villagers could comprehend it easily. It was hoped that Congress committees would use it fully in village propaganda. They could have the pamphlet at cost price (two paise) and were at liberty to print further copies themselves.[15] In a very real sense it seemed that if 'the movement made speakers of us all',[16] the press provided the texts.

The tone of these texts is often dramatic. 'Foreigner! You have tasted the blood and the flesh of Pathans, Gujaratis, Bengalis, Punjabis, Sindhis, Biharis, Madrasis, all... Speak! Did you find the flesh of our little children delicious?' This is an extract from a bulletin issued by the non-violent TCC of Allahabad. The bulletin went on: 'Foreigner. Do not get tired... Do not let your *lathis* and guns rest. Do not talk of compromise and truce. Today, on the day of Holi, we issue you a new invitation to war:

> *Khoon ka keechad faag machao, laashon ki rangroli hai.*
> *Khel phirangi khoob khel le, lahu loth ki holi hai.*
> (Blood mingling with mud, lusty songs, corpses merry-making.
> Play, foreigner, play all you can, this is a Holi of flesh and blood.)[17]

Such propaganda was of course bound to create a certain amount of xenophobia against the British. The Hindu slant of much of the propaganda – noticeable, for example, in the reference to Holi in the bulletin quoted above – also created special problems of identification with the nationalist movement for non-Hindu groups. Many nationalist leaflets and pamphlets depicted the British imperialist as 'Kumbhkaran' or 'Ravana'; 'Ramrajya' was a convenient and appealing description of *swaraj*; and to many there seemed to be no anomaly in prefacing an exhortation for Hindu-Muslim unity with a quotation from the *Bhagavad Gita*.

After the experience of communal friction in the mid-1920s even a simple call for organization (in Hindi, *sangathan*) appeared to carry suggestions of communal hostility. Sangathan now had the connotation – and one that was sometimes made explicit with the call for organization[18] – of Hindu unity against all non-Hindus and not only the British. Moreover, direct religious appeals, though less in evidence now than during the Non-Cooperation movement, still remained an important element in the Congress campaign. No longer did Gandhi say: 'I look upon the Khilafat problem for the Mussulmans in the same light as the cow problem for the Hindus. It is my firm belief that the solution of one will automatically lead to the solution of the other.'[19] But Allahabad villagers were still told that Indians using foreign cloth were indirectly responsible for the slaughter of more than 40 lakhs of cows every year. Together with the alleged increase in the consumption of liquor and in prostitution, the alleged growth in the number of cows killed remained a symbol of the injustice of imperialism. 'Is not this question of cow-protection sufficient in itself to inspire us to strive for the attainment of *Swaraj*?' asked the Liberal daily, *Bharat*, in 1929.[20] Inevitably such propaganda contributed to the increasing fears of large numbers of Muslims regarding the 'Hindu' movement for freedom, even as it helped to mobilize support for the Congress campaigns of civil disobedience.

III

The press was of course only one of several means of nationalist mobilization. The years 1928–9 saw a renewed organization of nationalist meetings and demonstrations on a fairly large scale. Table 4.2 shows the expenditure incurred by the Agra DCC and the Kanpur TCC for propaganda during the first phase of Civil Disobedience in 1930–1. While the expenditure on publications was fairly substantial in both cases the main charges were for 'travel' and 'district propaganda'. Much of the latter is likely to have been concerned with the organization of public meetings in villages and small market towns.

Altogether the late 1920s and the 1930s more generally saw a gigantic propaganda campaign through nationalist meetings and conferences from the annual provincial political conference down to the gatherings at the weekly or bi-weekly markets (*hat, painth* or *bazaar*) that served groups of villages throughout UP. In addition there were specially celebrated 'days' and 'weeks' with a particularly strong emotional appeal to memories of national suffering or national achievement: National Week, Jallianwala Bagh Day, Independence Day, Gandhi Day, Lajpat Rai Day and so on. 'Traditional' elements associated with nationalist meetings served to add to the enthusiasm. *Prabhat pheris* (nationalist groups which went out in procession every morning singing and raising slogans) became a part of the Congress's Sunday programme of flag salutation. Bugles, in earlier times signals of war, were sounded in the Shult *pattis* of Ranikhet *tahsil* (Almora) to indicate the place of a meeting. Drums were used more widely for publicizing nationalist news of all kinds.

Table 4.2
Congress Expenditure on Propaganda

	Agra DCC I April 1930 – 24 June 1931 Rs.	Kanpur TCC 24 March 1930 – 24 April 1931 Rs.
Travel	8,659	–
Wages and fares of volunteers	3,372	2,746 (fares alone)
District propaganda	–	4,997
Tahsil account	3,131	–
Muslim propaganda	–	1,070
Khadi propaganda	1826 (includes uniforms)	910
Aid to political sufferers	2,226	475
Publications	3,926	3,378
Total Expenditure	39,187	34,310

Source: **Agra Satyagraha Sangram** (DCC, Agra, 1931), P.P. Hin. B. 33 (IOL), 116–7: AICC P21/1931, Statement of Kanpur TCC Income and Expenditure for 1930–1 (in Hindi). The nearest rupee figure has been used.

Alas and *dolas*, *bhajans* and *ghazals*, all traditional forms of vocal music, became an integral part of public meetings and processions. The *nautanki* or travelling theatre was put to a new political purpose in the rural areas of Allahabad. The great Bageshwar Mela, when thousands of Kumaunis camped at the confluence of the Sarju and the Gomti, was made the occasion for an organized protest against the system of forced coolie labour that government officials in the hills now used as of right.[21] Such activities were intensified at the time when the Congress began mobilizing for campaigns of civil disobedience, and they had a considerable impact.

Jawaharlal Nehru noted the special significance of the mass meeting as an instrument of mobilization. Referring to a *kisan* conference held at Allahabad for the launching of the 'no-tax' campaign in October 1930, he wrote:

Delegates had come to it from practically every important village in the district and, when they dispersed, they carried the news of the fresh decisions affecting the peasantry, and of my arrest in connection with them, to every part of the district. They became, 1,600 of them, effective and enthusiastic propagandists for the no-tax campaign.[22]

Table 4.3

Meetings and Collections during Gandhi's Tour of Various UP Districts, 1929

Place of meeting	Audience	Purse presented	On-the-spot contributions
AGRA (11–18 September 1929)			
Hewett Park	10,000	Rs 4,000	Rs 110 + gold buttons
Bagh Muzaffar Khan	2,000 women	Rs 300	
Meston Hall	100 students	Rs 1,031	
Village Fatehabad	4,000	Rs 501	
Village Achnera	2,000	–	
Fatehpur-Sikri	2,000	–	
Village Kiraoli	3,000	–	
Village Etmadpur	4,000	Rs 501	Rs 25
Firozabad	10,000	Rs 1,000	
Dayal Bagh	1,000		
AZAMGARH (3-4 October 1929)			
Kshatriya School	several thousands	Rs 2,500	Rs 182 + sale of 1500 tickets at rates of 4 annas to Rs 100
Village Azmatgarh	–	Rs 1,000	
Village Dohri Ghat	3,000	Rs 320	
RAE BARELI (13-14 October 1929)			
Village Bachrawan	400	Rs 160	
Headquarters town	3,000	Rs 3,760	Rs 157
Hindu High School	300 women	Rs 82	
Lalganj	8,000	Rs 1,857	
Village Salon	–	Rs 385	
ALLAHABAD (16-17 November 1929)			
Ewing Christian College	1,500	Rs 732	
The University	4,000	Rs 3,000	Rs 352
Municipal Board Office	2,000	Rs 2,094	Rs 1,125
Purushottam Das Park	8–9,000	Rs 31,000	Rs 150

Source: PAI (21 September, 19 October, 23 November 1929). The figures given may not be entirely correct, and are besides incomplete, but they do give a fair idea of the enthusiasm generated by Gandhi's visit.

Gandhi's tour of the province in the latter half of 1929 showed the effectiveness of this kind of propaganda. Table 4.3 indicates the enthusiasm it generated not only in districts with large cities and major educational centres (Agra and Allahabad) but in 'backward' areas where the headquarters town was distinguished from the rest of the district chiefly by the presence of the civil courts and the gravelled drive that led up to the district officer's residence (Azamgarh and Rae Bareli).

Nehru's whirlwind tour in the same year, when he was president of the Congress and widely looked upon as the rising star in the Indian political firmament was almost as important.[23] He repeated the exercise as the Congress's star campaigner in the election campaign of 1936–7; and Government sources listed his tour as one of the major causes of the party's remarkable victory in that election.[24] Indeed, this was a pattern of mobilization that was clearly cemented for the future by the successes of this period.

I V

The public burning of foreign cloth had been a feature of Gandhi's meetings throughout UP in 1929. Like the wearing and sale of *khadi* – as a means of support for the boycott of foreign cloth, as well as symbolic acts of national pride – this, too, was an instance of 'propaganda by deed' used effectively by the Congress in the 1920s and 1930s. The Bardoli *satyagraha* of 1928 and Gandhi's salt *satyagraha*, beginning with his march to Dandi in March-April 1930, were even more spectacular examples of demonstrations against the 'evils' of British rule. The former, occurring as it did when politically conscious groups in India were already exercised on the question of the Simon Commission, aroused considerable enthusiasm and revived popular interest in the efficacy of *satyagraha*. 'Bardoli became a sign and a symbol of hope and strength and victory to the Indian peasant', wrote Nehru in typical hyperbole.[25] Yet it is clear that the capitulation of the Bombay administration in Bardoli became an ideal that nationalist cadres exulted over in their speeches and writings[26] – just as earlier generations of nationalists had enthused over the victory of Japan over Russia and later over the Bolshevik Revolution in Russia itself. Gandhi's salt march similarly captured the imagination of the educated and other politically 'advanced' groups, though the Government substantially weakened its impact by deliberately delaying Gandhi's arrest.[27]

Equally important for nationalist mobilization in UP, though less noticed in the historical literature, were the demonstrations against the Simon Commission when it visited the province in 1928, and – an initiative that was not controlled by the Congress – the deeds of the revolutionary terrorists. These activities and their effects bear examination in some detail. The appointment of an 'all-white' commission to review the progress of the reforms in India brought forth loud protest from virtually every major political grouping in the country. The Congress and Liberals, the All-India Muslim League (or, at least, one section of it), the national Trade Union Congress, the Sanatan Dharm Pandit Sabha of Banaras and even some UP landlords joined in the chorus. But the Simon Commission and its boycott were not issues that fired the popular imagination from the start. The *hartal* of 3 February 1928, the day on which the Commission landed in Bombay, was incomplete. The UP Government cynically reported: 'The Muslims held aloof, the Hindus were half-hearted, and the rain spoilt the public meetings.' Even in Allahabad, the hometown of the Nehrus, Muslim shops and many of the smaller Hindu shops remained open.[28]

Throughout the country students were the main supporters of the boycott programme. In the second half of February the Simon Commission paid a private visit to Banaras. Students of Banaras Hindu University led by Govind Malaviya, the son of the vice-chancellor Madan Mohan Malaviya, staged a noisy and to that extent successful demonstration on the occasion, in spite of the opposition of the university authorities and the precautions of the police.[29] It was a foretaste of the reception accorded to the Commission when it returned to the province on business at the end of the year. Then students and youths were still the leaders in the demonstrations but enthusiasm was greater than before and support far more general. The Government observed that the Congress would have achieved little or nothing in Lucknow without the university students and schoolboys. But it noted also that 'the Hindu community as a whole is in favour of the political boycott of the Simon Commission.'[30]

An event of major importance in bringing about the changed atmosphere was the death of the Punjab Congress leader, Lajpat Rai, shortly after the visit of the Simon Commission to Lahore, the capital of the Punjab. In the course of that visit Lajpat Rai had received a lathi-blow during demonstrations against the Commission and his death was freely attributed to that blow. Martyrdom has a unique and compelling force. Condolence meetings, which served at the same time as meetings agitating for a more complete boycott of the Simon Commission, were held all over northern India. Even such UP districts as had hitherto shown few signs of Congress activity were affected.[31] Nationalist Muslims like Mukhtar Ahmad Ansari and Abul Kalam Azad now expressed their grief for one who had come to be feared as a communal Hindu leader. Motilal Nehru, who had suffered at the hands of Lajpat Rai when the latter teamed up with Malaviya to oppose the Swarajists in the 1926 elections, joined in the call for the observance of Lajpat Rai Day on 29 November 1928.[32]

In Agra and Meerut strongly worded leaflets were distributed in the name of Mrs C R Das, widow of the respected Swarajist leader who had died in 1925. 'I am ashamed...to think', the leaflets read, 'that those base...hands had the audacity to attack this aged man who was beloved by 30 crores of Indians. Are there still men and youths living in this country?'[33]

Despite a reasonably good response from students, however, there was but a small and quiet black-flag demonstration when the Commission reached Agra on 28 November 1928. The local Congress leadership restrained the demonstrators, partly because of a pro-Commission demonstration by a group of Agra Muslims.[34] In Lucknow and Kanpur, which the Commission visited next, there were no such constraints. Muslim leaders were prominent in the organization of the boycott and they had the support of one of the leading Muslim *taluqdars* of Awadh. Congress leaders also concentrated their efforts on the boycott demonstrations in Lucknow. Events therefore turned out differently.

The Simon Commission Boycott Committee in Lucknow included not only Congressmen – Mohanlal Saxena, Khaliquzzaman, Mrs Suniti Mitter and K Pestonji, a happy 'national' combination of a UP Kayastha, a UP Muslim, a Bengali Hindu and a Parsee – but also Liberals such as Rahas Behari Tewari and Krishna Prasad Kaul.[35] Shortly before the coming of the Simon Commission Jawaharlal Nehru and Govind Ballabh Pant, the most respected Congressmen of the province after Motilal Nehru and Madan Mohan Malaviya, and with them Gauri Shankar Misra, arrived to strengthen the hands of the local boycott committee.

The Liberals reportedly concentrated on the *hartal* of 29 November 1928, Lajpat Rai Day, which proved a great success. Others, led by Khaliquzzaman, acted on the impulse of the moment on the day the Commission arrived, flew black kites over the grounds where the *taluqdars* were holding a garden party for the Commission and cut them ingeniously so that they dropped into those grounds. At least a little commotion resulted. But the most important part of the Lucknow boycott programme was the black-flag demonstration organized to welcome the Commission outside the Lucknow railway station.

In preparation the Boycott Committee started organizing processions and public meetings several days before the Commission's arrival.[36] With these activities there began a regular jousting match between the Congress leadership and the local administration. The administration insisted that licenses were needed before processions could be taken out and emphasized that licenses would be issued only if processions remained orderly and kept to specified routes. The Congress leaders questioned the rules regarding licenses and declared that Congress processions could never be disorderly. After the first few days the jousting took a serious turn – and the use of force followed. On the last three days of November the police forcibly dispersed what the Government called 'aggressive demonstrators'.[37] On the last of those days Jawaharlal Nehru and Pant were among the injured.

It was the Government's view that Nehru's intervention was responsible for the ugly turn of events in Lucknow. Certainly Nehru's hectic activity and emotional appeal played a part in what happened. His addresses to students were especially important. A characteristic circular read:

> It is announced in the public press that the Lucknow University authorities have invited Sir John Simon and his undistinguished crew to the University Convocation... Every schoolboy knows that India has resented the appointment and the coming of the Simon Commission and has boycotted it. Has no whisper of this reached the academic ears of the Lucknow University authorities? Have they not heard or felt in their boudoirs the deep rumble of a nation in anger? Do they not know how one of the greatest of India's sons was treated in Lahore city less than a month ago because he would not bow his head to this Commission...?
>
> ... Will you not make it clear to your University authorities, to the Simon Commission, and to all whom it may concern, that the young men and young women of Lucknow cherish the memory of their departed leader and stand for the boycott of the Simon Commission and will not permit anyone to exploit them on behalf of the enemies of Indian freedom. Will you not take full part in the boycott demonstrations in Lucknow, and above all, boycott the Convocation to which your University authorities have invited the Simon Commission? They have dared. Do you also dare?[38]

Others followed Nehru's lead, in speech[39] and in action. On Lajpat Rai Day, the Municipal Board, significantly not in Congress control, closed all its schools and offices. University students went on strike and, with schoolboys, spent the day 'working for the boycott demonstration of the 30th'. In one sense the Congress had already achieved success in its campaign.

It would appear that the successive processions and demonstrations were themselves the main cause of the rising militancy. The Government's charge that the Congress–Government clash occurred because Nehru had on his arrival in Lucknow asked local Congress leaders to disregard orders seeking to regulate the path and timing of processions was incorrect. The first open clash occurred on 28 November, while Nehru returned to Lucknow only on the following day. Lucknow's Congress leaders were themselves reluctant to accept the Government's suggestion that the Congress must obtain a license each time it wished to take out a procession, and apparently the growing support for the boycott and the rising militancy all around them gave them the confidence to oppose the Government's stand. Nehru's presence on the scene made the question more clearly one of prestige; he was firm in his refusal to kowtow to the British authorities, as the events of 29 November were to show.

On that day Nehru and other Congress leaders started a procession from Narhai, near the European shopping centre, which was to go to Aminuddaulah Park on the outskirts of the city's Indian quarter. They had no license and were stopped a few hundred yards from Narhai by mounted police armed with *lathis*. The Deputy Commissioner, who arrived on the scene soon afterwards, reported that 'The processionists maintained...that they were not taking out a procession, but were merely proceeding in three companies of 12 men each, carrying black flags, and singing songs, to Aminuddaulah Park.' The growing crowd and the arrival of more Congress volunteers heightened the tension. The Deputy Commissioner then agreed to allow the procession in the manner mentioned above – 'if the leaders would merely make a verbal request for permission. Pandit Jawahar Lal Nehru declined to do this, but Pandit Govind Ballabh Pant said they would not proceed without permission, and they wanted to go. This was so little different from a request for permission that I agreed.'[40]

These verbal niceties and legal technicalities did not end the matter, however. The 3 groups of 12 each that started out from Narhai rapidly grew in size. The procession stopped and shouted slogans outside the Deputy Commissioner's house. By the time it reached its destination it had assumed 'considerable dimensions'. With every act of protest and every inconclusive clash between 'the people' and the police, militancy grew.

On the day the Simon Commission finally arrived in Lucknow (30 November) a very large number of demonstrators gathered at the railway station with black flags and armbands. The Congress leaders refused to take up the position allotted to them for the demonstration, claiming that it was too far from the route the Commission would take.[41] Moreover the demonstrators were apparently in such a state of excitement that the leaders could not have stopped them from approaching the station, even had they so desired. The occasion was marked then not only by shouts of 'Simon, go back', black flags and later that day black kites, but also by action from the mounted police, the beating back of demonstrators, the throwing of stones and bricks, and injuries on both sides. Pant suffered rather serious injuries; and the Government was already beginning to appear guilty of the repression that drew hundreds of conscientious objectors into Civil Disobedience when that movement began a year and a bit later.

The Lucknow events, connected with the visit of the Simon Commission, had important repercussions in Kanpur city, 45 miles away. College students went on strike and joined the anti-Simon demonstrations in large numbers when the Commission reached Kanpur on 3 December. They were so militant that the Kanpur Congress leaders, Vidyarthi and Jawaharlal Rohatgi, were evidently in no position to control them. The cars carrying Simon and his colleagues were at one point surrounded by slogan-shouting demonstrators. One or two were hit by stones. 'Altogether the visit was an unpleasant one for them [the Commission]', wrote Hailey in a characteristic British understatement.[42]

The nationalists took a rather different view of the matter. 'Lucknow', wrote Nehru with reference to the events of 30 November, 'has reason to be proud of the events of this morning and the officials, who were responsible for this morning's events, have helped greatly in producing an atmosphere in India which will put an end to British rule.'[43] *The Leader*, the influential Liberal daily, echoed him in more explicitly jubilant tone: 'The purpose of the boycott demonstrations has been more than achieved and the victors are those who carry the marks of police batons on their bodies.'[44]

Several developments proved the force of these assessments. In the press and on the platform there was a round of condemnation of police brutality and the insult to so 'respectable' a person as the Maharaja of Mahmudabad,[45] a leading *taluqdar* and an ex-minister of the UP Government whose house was surrounded along with others in the official effort to keep out demonstrators during the *taluqdars'* garden party. Motilal Nehru, the Liberal leader Sapru and Annie Besant issued a call for a complete ban in the columns of the nationalist press on all news concerning the Simon Commission and for the social boycott of the Commission and all who cooperated with it.[46] The Liberals had never been so angry before. In the UP Legislative Council (UPLC) a resolution condemning the action of the Lucknow authorities was moved by the Liberal leader C Y Chintamani and was carried unopposed. The Government wisely refrained from asking for a division.

Apart from Jawaharlal Nehru, Pant, the leader of the Swaraj Party in the Council, Rahas Behari Tewari, a Nationalist Party member of the Council, and also Andrews Dube and Krishna Prasad Kaul, members of the Servants of India Society, were involved in the clashes. Besides, the Chief Secretary noted, 'Many non-officials, who often supported Government, felt that if they opposed the adjournment motion, they would be pilloried in the press and in their constituencies as approving of police assaults on prominent and patriotic Indians. The racial issue was prominent throughout.'[47] In the elections to local bodies and the Congress's own organizational elections held at the end of 1928, this widespread expression of sympathy assumed a more tangible form. In both there were notable successes for the boycotters, particularly for Jawaharlal and his 'independence' men.[48]

Clearly, the mobilization process, once begun, tended to generate its own momentum. Processions and demonstrations acquired a significantly spontaneous element. The refusal to follow government orders regarding processions was not only yet another symbolic act of protest against alien rule. It also gave to nationalist demonstrations the flexibility and the time they needed for maximum public impact. Its importance lay, above all, in bringing about a direct confrontation with the Raj in a manner that was likely to influence many more people than a quiet, orderly march. In the course of the Non-Cooperation and Civil Disobedience Movements of the 1920s, 1930s and 1940s, such confrontations, the beating or trial of venerated Indians at the hands of British officials and their native henchmen, and the apparent fearlessness of Congress volunteers in the face of brute force contributed to the rapid spread of strong anti-imperialist feelings. When unknown, poorly clad villagers, quite apart from the

Congress's well-known leaders, stood up to the 'awesome' foreigner on the streets or in the court, something snapped inside the men who watched. The special merit of propaganda by deed lay precisely in this, in ridding men of the mentality of dependence, of the inferiority complex that long subjection brings and of fear.

The most dramatic actions in this regard came of course from the revolutionary-terrorists. Through them men like Bhagat Singh and Chandrashekhar Azad became legendary in the 1920s and 1930s. 'The popularity that the man achieved was something amazing', Jawaharlal wrote about Bhagat Singh.[49] The political activities of students and other youths in 1928–9 indicated the extent of the revolutionary-terrorists' impact. At the Karachi session of the Congress in March 1931 even Gandhi had to face black-flag demonstrations for his refusal to appeal to Irwin for the commutation of Bhagat Singh's death sentence.

Earlier the Kakori Conspiracy Case had aroused sympathy for terrorists, and condemnation of the treatment the Government had meted out to them, throughout UP. The Kakori 'dacoits' followed up their daring train robbery at Kakori, near Lucknow, in 1925 with a protest by fasting against the inhuman conditions of their treatment in gaol. For several months the entire nationalist press expressed concern for the Kakori men. Wild rumours circulated especially about the 'worsening condition', 'impending (or actual) death' and constant transfers of Damodar Swarup Seth, later an important Bareilly and UP Congress leader.[50]

The political implications of Kakori became clearer after the trial. The sentence of death passed on four of the accused brought pleas for commutation not only from the pro-Congress *Aj* and *Abhyudaya* but also from the Liberal papers, *The Leader* and *Awadh Akhbar*, and what Congressmen called the 'half-English paper', *The Pioneer*. An appeal for mercy was made by legislators belonging to a wide range of parties: Congressmen like Pant and Vidyarthi, Liberals such as Chintamani, independent notables such as Khan Bahadur Fazlur Rahman Khan and Rai Bahadur Pandit Sankatha Prasad Bajpai, and the industrialist and future minister in the British-dominated provincial government, Jwala Prasad Srivastava, among others.[51]

Congress support was especially strong. Congress papers commended the spirit of patriotism that had swayed the Kakori men. Ganesh Shankar Vidyarthi, Shiva Prasad Gupta, Manjit Singh Rathore and other Congress leaders visited those under trial in gaol and provided them – as also their revolutionary-terrorist colleagues outside – with financial and other support.[52] Pant, the Congress leader in the UPLC, became the chief defence counsel for the accused. His assistants included Mohanlal Saxena and Chandrabhanu Gupta, Lucknow men who were to be prominent later on in nationalist protests, both constitutional and unconstitutional. Thus the Kakori men sparked off, however briefly, a nobler struggle at a time when large numbers of nationalists were either getting bogged down in factional conflicts over electoral and legislative politics or even helping to spread the virus of communalism.

The fact that the Lahore Conspiracy Case followed not long after Kakori and that 13 of the 24 accused in this case were residents of UP strengthened their plea. The staging of the Meerut Conspiracy Case of 1929 in UP, because it was easier to obtain conviction here,[53] added further to the force of their appeal.

The Government noted that the arrests in the Meerut Case in March 1929, especially that of the Allahabad student, P C Joshi, became the focal point for much student activity and protest in the province.[54] Understandably, Allahabad and Meerut led in this agitation. The months that followed saw a certain slackening of tempo but rapid revival came in September 1929. The death of Jatindranath Das in the course of a hungerstrike in Lahore gaol brought emotion among young men and women in UP to a high pitch. Protest meetings and demonstrations were held, especially at the more important student centres, and at the Provincial Youth Conference held in Lucknow that month Congress leaders were constrained to water down some of the resolutions proposed.[55] 'The emotional character of India came out at its very worst over the death of Jatin Das',[56] Hailey wrote in a letter to a man who himself had experienced that 'emotional character' a decade earlier. There can be little doubt that the nationalist fervour thus generated did much to strengthen the hands of the younger Nehru and the Congress 'Left' at this time and helped them carry the party into a more militant stance.

V

There were two features of these early propaganda and mobilization efforts that could place serious limitations on the movement as a whole. One was the concentration of nationalist propaganda in the towns, partly by force of circumstance – most obviously in the case of the press – and partly because of the need to create maximum impact. The other was the making of a very broad, nationalist appeal in order to draw into the movement several diverse groups. The former limitation was overcome by the chain reaction created in the politicizing and mobilizing process itself and by the UP Congress's heavy concentration on the rural areas from the last quarter of 1930 onwards. The limitations of the broad, nationalist appeal proved more difficult to circumvent, for this was at once a point of strength and one of weakness for the Congress movement. Ultimately it meant the failure of the Congress to mobilize the long-term support of the mass of the poor, especially in the villages.[57] At the same time it enabled the mobilization of a wide array of social groups on behalf of the nationalist cause in successive campaigns.

'The next anti-Government movement…may be supported by fewer people than in Non-Cooperation times', the New Delhi Intelligence Department observed in mid-1929, 'but the agitation will be more intensive and more dangerous, because of the class and character of the people conducting it.'[58] The groups referred to here, students and youth generally, teachers and members of other middle class professions such as law and journalism, in fact provided a smaller proportion of volunteers for Civil Disobedience in 1930–2 than they had done for Non-Cooperation in 1921–2. There were fewer resignations too from schools and courts this time.[59] However, as influential 'educated' men, such groups proved invaluable in the process of general mobilization for the inflammatory movement. Teachers in 'national' institutions, and in municipal and district board schools, which were only indirectly tied to the Government, became a major headache for the UP Government during this period. In April 1930, when the Civil Disobedience Movement had just begun, the Government drew the attention of the Education Department to paragraph 169A of the Educational Code, 1927, whereby 'no teacher in a recognized vernacular school shall take part' in any anti-Government political agitation or inculcate opinion that tends to support such agitation. Later in that month, and sporadically during the year 1930, action was urged and taken against teachers involved in or encouraging the movement.[60] Yet in September 1930 Hailey complained: 'Until we can have summary powers for suspending the district boards or their education committees, we shall never be able to tackle the rural areas effectively'.[61] In mid-1932 when, according to numerous government reports, Civil Disobedience had virtually run its course, district officials were still concerned on this score.[62]

Students too exercised an influence out of all proportion to their numbers among the *satyagrahis* in the 1930s and 1940s, as in the 1920s. Gopal Narain Shiromani and Niranjan Singh of Agra are typical examples of those who gave up their studies in 1930–1, joined the Civil

Disobedience Movement and rapidly rose to Congress leadership in their districts. Many more were carried into the anti-imperialist campaigns for a short while before parental or other pressures took them back to their homes or colleges. They too performed a critical function as 'shock-troops' and 'leaders of opinion'.[63] In 1932–3, when enthusiasm for civil disobedience had begun to flag, it was the student volunteers who made a valiant bid to revive agitation through attacks on government property in town and country, which they planned and executed on their own initiative; and this was one element of the population that was to the fore again in 1940 and 1942.[64]

These groups helped substantially to extend the nationalist appeal in rural areas. It was in the early 1930s that the Congress actively began this task. On the broad, anti-imperialist platform adopted by the Congress there was room for direct address to discrete sections of the population. Pamphlets and leaflets surviving from these years provide examples of calls to students, to shopkeepers, launderers and barbers, to factory workers and above all to the general category of *kisans* – who were urged to set up their own law courts in every village and fight for food and independence, and were asked: 'Kisan brothers, how long will you let these leeches suck your blood?'[65] After October 1930, when the decision to start a no-tax campaign was taken, much of the UP Congress's propaganda effort was concentrated on the *kisan*. Propaganda among the peasants was especially strong in a number of districts towards the end of 1931, just before the renewal of the Civil Disobedience Movement, when the extent of peasant distress and agitation was manifest. The Intelligence Department reported the distribution of a 'considerable amount' of literature in rural areas at this time. In Kanpur, Unnao, Rae Bareli and elsewhere, there was an effort to broadcast thousands of leaflets and notices regarding rent and revenue questions.[66]

The message was simple: that the Congress was the *kisan's* protector against an oppressive, alien regime and the *kisan* must support the Congress. One leaflet asked all Allahabad tenants who had been ejected, whether subsequently restored to their land or not, to file details of their lands and ejectments at a Congress office in any one of a number of specified places. It listed the names of some twenty places in the district and promised that 'The District Congress Committee will do all it can to help the kisans once it has all the information necessary.'[67] In November 1931 another leaflet was distributed along with copies of *Abhyudaya's* 'Kisan' number. It outlined the Congress's efforts to obtain concessions for the peasants, emphasized the Government's un-responsiveness, and called for the withholding of rent and revenue until the Congress issued further orders.[68]

Other messages to 'Our Brother Cultivators' made the appeal even more pointed:

> Just as on behalf of Congress notices are being sent to 'you', Government is also sending you notices to frighten and threaten you through the police, etc... You know that Government has not granted remissions with any graceful clemency. Government has been governing 150 years, there have been many droughts and famines, why did not Government give remission then. For the last two years why has Government begun to give in succession remissions; why was Allahabad given the most remission? There is only one reason: your obstinate defiance and your *satyagrah*...if you remain firm...and don't pay a single paisa, you will not only get back the fields from which you were ejected and get four times as much remission, but cultivators will get the Raj later.[69]

The Congress had a point, of course. Whereas during the partial famine of 1907–8, the UP Government had remitted Rs 76 lakhs of revenue and during the scarcities of 1913–14 and 1918–19, Rs 46 lakhs and Rs 61 lakhs respectively, in the difficult but much less severe year 1928–9 it felt constrained to remit Rs 60 lakhs. The amount remitted in Meerut for that year substantially exceeded the total amount remitted in that district in the preceding 30 years. The remissions granted in the following years, which were marked by uncertain seasons and exceptionally low prices, were on an even more liberal scale.[70] In addition the administration suspended operations for the revision of settlements in five districts and postponed the beginning of operations for such revision in a number of others.[71] A certain amount of relief was also granted on canal dues and debts from *taqavi* loans, mainly in the province's western districts which were better provided with canals and where relative prosperity had enabled some use of the provisions for these official loans for development purposes.[72]

The Government's niggardliness in this respect is now well established.[73] Remissions were made very reluctantly indeed at the time of the Depression. As a senior official explained the position:

Land revenue is easily the main source of provincial revenue. Normally, and even as now reduced, it exceeds 50 per cent of the whole revenue, and more than equals the combined receipts from irrigation, stamps and excise. No reserve had been set aside year by year from which Government could meet remissions of revenue made necessary by any cause. The result was that when the fall in prices came Government were in no position, *and in no hurry*, to deal with it, and hoped that the slump might prove to be of temporary duration.[74]

Consequently though a sharp decline in prices was evident by the end of 1930, the UP Government took little account of it until Hailey's return from the Round Table Conference at the end of April 1931. Then Hailey wrote of how revenue remissions had reached 'a horrible total of nearly 70 lakhs'.[75] A little less than two years later he observed that the price of wheat had improved considerably but other crops lagged behind and *gur* was at least 50 per cent cheaper than it was three years earlier. 'If we could only get an improvement of price there,' he said, 'I really think that we would begin to move rents up again a little.'[76] The human approach was no more in evidence at the district level. Andrew Park Hume, an ICS man stationed in Rae Bareli in 1931, found that tenants were not paying their rents partly because of their financial straits, but, he wrote to his parents, 'they are going to be made to all right.'[77]

With officials in this frame of mind, the Congress's representation of the interests of *zamindars* and tenants was important. There was endless controversy as to whether prices had fallen to the level of 1915 or 1901 or an even earlier date. The authorities talked of the need for all the concerned parties – Government, landlords and tenants – to share the burdens of the crisis. They argued correctly[78] that occupancy tenants had done well out of the era of high prices and that landlords had also received some benefits through higher rents, while the Government's share of the landlord's assets had actually decreased. In 1929 the land revenue was reduced by law from 50 to 40 per cent of the assets. What no one took notice of were the variations within the categories of 'landlords' and 'tenants' and the differential degrees of loss they suffered at this time. In the circumstances the Congress's part as counsel for various groups in rural society proved to be a crucial one. Ultimately peasant discontent and unrest were suppressed by large-scale rent and revenue remissions and a fairly liberal use of force. Without the presence of the Congress the task might have been accomplished through smaller remissions and a freer use of force.

In 1928–9 when settlement operations resulting in an enhancement of revenue, and consequently rent, had combined with a series of poor harvests to cause severe hardship in parts of UP, the Congress was quick to take up the question of relief. 'The tenants are shrieking, but the Government is indifferent', declared *Sainik*, Sri Krishna Dutt Paliwal, the Agra Congress leader's Hindi weekly, in August 1928.[79] A month later it commented on the Government's grant of Rs 20 lakhs for *taqavi* loans to peasants, announced at an interim measure while the administration awaited future developments:

> How long will the Government watch the situation?... We would tell the Government that it has watched long enough, now it should act. Your machinery is notorious for its dilatoriness. The system of your administration is vicious. Not to say of crops there is not even a blade of green grass in villages. Yet the *patwaris* report that the crops are eight annas and even more... They think that such reports please the officers and that there would be a danger of incurring their displeasure if true reports were submitted.[80]

Jawaharlal Nehru and other Congress leaders made this into an issue of some agitation. Baba Ramchandra, the renowned leader of the Awadh *kisans* in the early 1920s, followed suit. At numerous village meetings they urged the need for rural organization, pointing for inspiration to the achievements of workers and peasants in the Soviet Union, and from the beginning of 1930 many nationalist leaders also called for the nonpayment of any increase in rents and revenue.[81]

Many groups of peasants felt encouraged by Congress support to resist illegal exactions and rentals higher than those recorded in their *parchas* (slips laying down rental agreements). It is also likely that the use of force to collect dues and to discipline tenants declined somewhat when Congress leaders began their widespread investigations of police and landlord repression in the latter half of 1931.[82]

By detailed investigation of agrarian conditions, then, and by prolonged negotiations with the Government on the subject of remissions and the treatment of defaulting peasants, as well as by rural meetings and organization and the partial encouragement of the policy of withholding rents and revenue even during the 'truce' of March to December 1931, the Congress made a major contribution to the obtaining of relief. A striking illustration of this comes from Allahabad district. Here the total rent due in the agricultural year amounted to Rs 57 lakhs. For 1338 *Fasli* (1 October 1930–September 1931) the District Magistrate, R F Mudie, remitted Rs 11 lakhs of this amount out of a possible Rs 12.3 lakhs sanctioned by the provincial Government. For the subsequent agricultural year when conditions were no better he wished to remit Rs 9.5 lakhs. Congress leaders, however, latched on to a 'technical' flaw in his calculations, and at the end of October 1931, when the scale of remissions for the entire province had already been announced and indeed all remission slips distributed, the Government had to announce the remission of an additional lakh of rupees in the rental due from Allahabad.[83]

V I

Thus nationalist mobilizers made significant inroads into the rural areas and their presence made a difference to the political situation that existed in the villages. It must not be forgotten, however, that from beginning to end there remained an ambivalence in the Congress position vis-à-vis agrarian problems and indeed any question concerning the interests of the 'masses'. The leaders laboured under ideological restrictions derived from a particular understanding of nationalism that was well reflected in Gandhi's doctrines. Conceived in these terms, the nationalist movement under the aegis of the Indian National Congress was to be an anti-imperialist war on the widest possible front. Landlords and princes were the trustees of the people. Class war was unethical. In Gandhi's own words, 'the Congress claimed to represent over 85 per cent of the population of India, that is to say the dumb, toiling, semi-starved millions...the Congress claimed also by right of service to represent even the Princes...the landed gentry, the educated class... The Congress...claims to represent all minorities.'[84]

In line with this approach the Congress in UP addressed its appeals for support in the campaigns of the 1930s and afterwards to the entire population. Its report on *Agrarian Distress in the United Provinces* (1931) was as concerned with the problems of *zamindars* as with those of tenants. The 'socialist' Nehru called in 1930 for such activity as would 'appeal [to] or inspire the largest numbers or classes of our countrymen'.[85] As regards the proposal for the abolition of *zamindari*, which he had begun to espouse around this time, Nehru declared that those were his 'personal views': the Congress was not committed to them, and they had 'no application to present day politics.'[86] Even in the mid- and late 1930s, when the Congress movement supposedly took a leftward turn, the provincial Congress continued to addressed itself to *zamindars* and *kisans* alike, urging universal, 'national' support for the Congress.[87]

Table 4.4
Classification by Subject of Nationalist Literature Seized in Mathura (1930) and Allahabad (1933).

	Mathura: Seizures under 1930 Ordinances	Allahabad: seizures for 1933 alone under Indian Press (Emergency Powers) Act, 1931
(1) No. of leaflets, etc.	1,640	10,474
(2) No. of different titles	52	60
(3) General nationalist	25	21
(4) Congress circulars, bulletins, etc.	4	17
(5) Concerning peasants	12	13
(6) Concerning boycott of foreign goods	2	3
(7) Concerning boycott of intoxicants	–	1
(8) Concerning the census	3	–
(9) Concerning students	3	1
(10) Concerning volunteers	2	–
(11) Appeal to women	1	–
(12) Appeal for Hindu–Muslim unity	–	3
(13) Revolutionary-terrorist	–	1

Source: Calculated from the titles of seized publications given in UP Police Dept Files 1012/1930 and 1589/1931 (SRR).

An examination of the nationalist literature seized by the Government in two very different districts of UP in the years 1930 and 1933 illustrates the Congress emphasis on a general and undifferentiated nationalist appeal. Although the titles of publications do not reveal much, table 4.4 clearly suggests a preponderance of such appeals over those addressed to specific groups or classes. More than half the unauthorized pamphlets and leaflets that came to the Government's notice fall into this category, over 55 per cent in the case of Mathura and over 63 per cent in the case of Allahabad if we consider columns (3) and (4) alone. The vast majority of the items listed in these two columns broadcast news of civil disobedience in different parts of the country, accounts of meetings and resolutions, exhortations to strengthen one or other aspect of the movement and congratulations for the great nationalist spirit displayed by all. Much of the literature addressed to particular groups also had similar contents.

Some of the collections of patriotic songs contained in such publications also indicate this very broad appeal. It is not uncharacteristic that one such anthology should begin with the invocation, 'Bande Mataram, Sat Siri Akal, Allah-o-Akbar'.[88] Nor is it surprising that the song popularized by Bhagat Singh, 'Mera rang de basanti chola,' reproduced in numerous tracts and handbills, should carry in each different recension additional verses reflecting the local colour of the struggle in terms of the regional, sectional and sectarian interests involved in it.[89]

The themes of these songs illustrate the very wide range of nationalist concern. A pamphlet entitled Bijli, published in Gorakhpur in 1930,[90] contained songs on 'Flag salutation', 'Khadi', 'Non-violent war', 'Memories' (of the greatness of India's past), 'Give the nation its salt', 'Martyrs of India', 'Jawaharlal Nehru', 'Man' (describing the need for nationalist pride and courage in any real man), 'A lackey of imperialism', 'Students' (an appeal), 'Foreign cloth merchants' (an appeal), 'The Civil Disobedience Movement', 'The peasant,' 'Swadeshi' and 'The two sons of India' (Hindus and Muslims). In the same year Baburam Pengoria, a well-known Congressman of Agra, wrote and published a collection of songs entitled Bharat ki Rashtriya Alha, or 'The Patriotic Ballad of India'.[91] Its preface read: 'In view of the satyagraha being launched, this book is written to help readers understand the past, present and future of India... In this book is related the history of the total destruction of India. Any number of tears that may be shed over this [history] will be insufficient.' His songs covered such subjects as India's past, prices old and new, Lord Clive and other colonial rulers, 'The baseness of the fair [skinned]', 'Thoughts on the dumping of British goods in India', 'Atrocities against weavers', 'India's present history', 'Income-expenditure', 'Service in the courts' (a song which gave the wages earned by different levels of the judiciary in India) and 'The condition of the peasants.'

'Why are we fighting?' asked a Congress paper which started publication in April 1930. Its answer will serve as a final example of the Congress's broad, nationalist appeal. The fight, it said, was for the 90 per cent who were poor, the kisans who 'produce the grain and then yearn for a morsel and a rag'. 'Why is their condition so terrible?' it asked further, and answered 'Because we don't have *Swaraj*'. The remaining 10 per cent of India's people included handicraftsmen, traders and service people. The former used to be more prosperous than their counterparts in any other country before the coming of the British, and they exported beautiful manufactured goods, the paper declared. Now, it lamented, only raw materials were produced in India, and even they had to be exported for manufacturing purposes; the British had opened enterprises in their own country and ruined India's manufacturers. The educated had also suffered, it added. If they were unable to work on the land they paced about the cities looking for employment. For every vacant post there were thousands of applicants. 'The chief reason for this war [Civil Disobedience] is to rid the country of this pitiable condition.'[92]

Thus the Congress sought to hold the balance even between competing groups in the society and to speak for every section of it at the same time. Yet the prominence it had attained by the end of the 1920s as the country's principal political party, and its oft-repeated claim to be the voice of the underdog, obliged the Congress to take a stand on every major question affecting any important section of the populace. It is in this light that we can comprehend Gandhi's 'Manifesto to the *kisans*' of UP and his simultaneous 'Appeal to the *zamindars*' of the province, issued in May 1931, when the economic crisis caused by the Depression was at its worst and the situation in many districts extremely tense, and the Congress itself was bound by the Gandhi-Irwin 'truce'. These messages had a distinctly dual aspect. Together they derived from the philosophy of the mutuality of interests between contending classes in rural society. But lest this should appear irrelevant to the agitated peasant, the 'Manifesto' went further. It dealt with the specifics of action that cultivators might take:

> The Congress expects every tenant to pay as early as possible all the rent he can, and in no case as a general rule less than 8 annas or 12 annas as the case may be. But just as even in the same district there may be cases in which a larger payment is possible, it is equally possible that there may be cases in which less than 8 annas or 12 annas can only be paid. In such cases I hope the tenants will be treated liberally by the Zamindars. In every case you will see that you get against payment a full discharge from your obligation for the current year's rent.[93]

Both landlords and the Government were to complain later that the publication of the 'Manifesto' did nothing other than to encourage the total non-payment of rent by tenants.[94] The Congress leadership itself was not unaware that this was the likely result.[95] But in the circumstances they had to go at least that far, while appealing at the same time for the maintenance of non-violence and a spirit of give and take.

This narrative should have indicated that there were several issues on which the task of mobilization was undertaken in rural areas and that there were groups other than those included in the undifferentiated category of *kisans* whom the Congress sought to mobilize. It could not therefore afford to plunge hastily into *satyagraha* on a sectional issue. 'Somewhat contrary to my own expectations,' wrote George Lambert, acting Governor of UP in 1929, 'comparatively hard times in the villages have not led so far to a development of agrarian agitation.'[96]

VII

Commitment to a conscious avoidance of divisive issues and class-war, which amounted in the circumstances to a commitment to the *status quo*, had momentous consequences. I deal with this subject in a later chapter.[97] Here it may be well to try and assess the effectiveness of the nationalist mobilization and of the UP Congress's 'umbrella' approach in the 1930s and 1940s.

Before the Civil Disobedience Movement of 1930–1 was three months old, the Governor of UP remarked on how it had succeeded:

> ...beyond our expectations in arousing very deep sympathy among every class of Hindus... Every District Officer with whom I have talked has been much impressed with the fact that *even those whose interests are affected by the agitation*, such as landowners or Government servants, have some kind of sympathy with the object of the agitation though not necessarily with its precise manifestations or methods. There is even among very well-meaning people a kind of pride in the persistence and sense of solidarity it has shown.[98]

A P Hume, at the time in Roorkee in Saharanpur district, commented on the 'very widespread, well-organized and intense' agitation for the boycott of foreign cloth, on the picketing in small towns like Jwalapur,

and on the way in which an arrested picketer was escorted by something of a triumphal procession to the courts where he might be gar-
landed to the accompaniment of shouts of '*Inquilab Zindabad*' and
'*Mahatma Gandhi ki jai*'. His assessment of the situation was this:
'One may say that the mass of the people do not know what they want
or what is good for them... They may not know what they want but
they want "it" just the same.'[99]

A survey in early 1932 indicated that of the 2,004 Civil Disobedience
prisoners held in five gaols surveyed by the UP Government, 1397 were
'petty tenants or labourers', 145 shopkeepers, 53 students and the
remaining 409 'a sprinkling of beggars' and people in 'miscellaneous
occupations'.[100] We have mentioned earlier the part played by students
and youth generally in the Congress campaign and have referred to the
sympathy and financial support of the business community. From such
groups the movement had clearly spread out to envelop important
sections of the agricultural population, among whom the Congress had
concentrated its efforts at mobilization after the initial months of Civil
Disobedience in 1930. The vast majority of *satyagrahis* in the early 1930s
came from the villages. They represented a broad spectrum of rural
society, excluding only its uppermost segments.[101]

The last category in the 1932 official survey mentioned above was
that of 'beggars' and people in 'miscellaneous occupations'. A large
number of these are likely to have been artisans; weavers in particular
were greatly influenced by the Congress's *khadi* programme. Small
peddlers and hawkers, personal servants and other odd-job men also
appear to have taken some part in the movement.[102]

There is in addition certain evidence of lumpen-proletarian elements
volunteering for Civil Disobedience. 'Congress was, at the time of the
census, employing and paying as volunteers many who would otherwise have been unemployed', reported the UP Census Commissioner in
1931.[103] Earlier Motilal Nehru had called for the removal of 'undesir-
able volunteers'[104] proof enough of the penetration of anti-social, *goonda*
elements into the ranks of Congress activists. The presence of a large
'floating' population as well as the availability of substantial finance
might also help to explain the strength of the Civil Disobedience movement in cities like Kanpur and Agra. These elements were noticed again
in the campaigns of the 1940s.

Nevertheless it is easy to exaggerate the attraction of the pittance paid
to Congress volunteers and of the scarcely edible gaol food[105] for those
who were sent to gaol and not simply beaten up and dumped on a highway.

The available evidence regarding the Congress's long-term volunteers suggests that they were chiefly men from lower or middle income groups in the villages and from the commercial and service sectors of the towns who needed a subsistence allowance while away from their normal sources of livelihood. Moreover, if Kanpur and Agra were notable for their large 'floating' populations and strong financial backing for the Congress campaign, they were notable also for the intensity and scale of nationalist propaganda. Is it unreasonable to assume that this had a major impact on the unemployed as on other sections of the population, particularly at a time when the everyday life of the cities provided ample evidence of the aloofness and arrogance of the foreigner?

Active work in the organization, and volunteering for *satyagraha* constituted the highest level of commitment to the Congress programme. But there were many, less committed or more vulnerable, who were sufficiently influenced by Congress propaganda and activities to demonstrate their support in other ways. Rural notables in various places gave their foreign cloth to Gandhi for burning.[106] Numerous municipal and district boards controlled by commercial and landed groups flew the Congress flag, closed their offices and schools to support nationalist demonstrations and celebrations, and promoted the campaign for the boycott of foreign cloth.[107] In districts throughout UP, Bar and Mukhtars Associations resolved to wear *swadeshi* cloth (as far as possible *khadi*) and to boycott British goods including, in one instance, 'British' newspapers that opposed the nationalist movement.[108]

Such activities increased manifold once the Congress formed the ministry in the province in 1937. But they were by no means insignificant before that. In Lucknow, as noted earlier, a non-Congress municipal board closed its schools to support the boycott of the Simon Commission. In Allahabad where local networks and connections had caused the defeat of Jawaharlal Nehru when he sought election to the chairmanship of the municipality in 1928, the board reminded its teachers in April 1930 of the pledge they had taken in 1924 to wear nothing but *khaddar*:[109] a significant comment on the limitations involved in studying a countrywide struggle in terms of local connections alone.

UP's Liberals – mainly prosperous professionals with a sprinkling of landlords and businessmen in their ranks – for all their Rai Bahadurships and Knighthoods, supported the call for a newspaper boycott of the Simon Commission after police action against anti-Commission demonstrators in Lucknow in 1928. They followed this up with wholehearted backing for the Congress's campaign against foreign cloth.[110] Besides the Liberal papers, *The Leader* and *Bharat*, lent strong support to the Congress for much of the late 1920s and 1930s, speaking out against Government repression and highlighting Civil Disobedience activities. UP Liberals were also prominently associated with the Congress's Harijan uplift programme.[111]

Congress leaders recognized the value of non-Congress support. During the Civil Disobedience campaign of the early 1930s, for example, they called upon their workers to co-operate in the matter of boycotting foreign cloth with people 'who may not be interested in other items of our programme' and to set up special, multi-party committees.[112] Agra provides a good example of how such multi-party efforts could work. Here Rao Krishnapal Singh, a prominent landlord and a Liberal member of the provincial legislative council, was president of the Foreign Cloth and British Goods Boycott Committee. Other members of the committee included a Liberal advocate, Rajnath Kunzru, and a number of mill-owners and businessmen, not all of them members of the Congress. The same people, with the exclusion of Krishnapal Singh and Kunzru and the addition of a few other businessmen and lawyers, again not all Congressmen, made up the Finance Committee responsible for the collection of funds for Civil Disobedience.[113]

In May 1930 Motilal Nehru singled out Krishnapal Singh for an expression of gratitude for all that was being done to make the Congress struggle a success in Agra.[114] Non-Congress sympathizers were not simply participating in the boycott of foreign cloth, which might be considered peripheral to the Congress programme at this time; Krishnapal Singh was standing by at village Jarar when tenants protested against oppressive measures taken by their landlord and police arrived to subdue them.[115] He and others like him provided food and shelter for Congress volunteers, as well as the essential funds. Their social standing and influence even in government circles, prominent *rais* and public men as many of them were, proved to be valuable assets. Men of lesser status and wealth made their own contribution too. Landlords often donated a few bags of grain to provide food for Congress volunteers. Poorer villagers in Agra adopted their own system of chutki whereby each family set aside a little grain daily for the feeding of *satyagrahis*.

Agra was of course exceptional in the strength of its Congress organization, which was greatly aided and sustained by the strong 'second line' support described above. But support of a similar kind could be found in other districts throughout UP. We have noticed a striking demonstration of this in the course of Gandhi's tour of the province in 1929. It was evidenced also by the considerable impact created by the low-caste 'dummy' candidates set up by the Congress in the UPLC elections of October 1930. The Congress reportedly dominated the elections in the districts of Meerut, Banaras, Dehra Dun, Fatehpur and a part of Bulandshahr, and in the cities of Banaras, Agra and Lucknow. Seven of its 'dummy' candidates were returned, including a sweeper, two Doms and two Gadariyas.[116] More charming corroboration of the extent of 'second line' support may be found in the claim made by a Congress worker of Gorakhpur, at the other end of the province from Agra, that the *chutki* system was the invention of his district's Congress leader, Baba Raghavadas.[117]

The aggressive anti-imperialist programme and propaganda of the Congress thus gained a widespread following for the nationalist movement in UP. Yet in all the lists of Congress workers, of *satyagrahis* and of active sympathizers after 1930, one section of UP society is conspicuously under-represented: this fact is all the more remarkable when the record is compared with that of the years 1919–22.

'Muslims continue for the most part to hold aloof from the Congress', the UP Government reported in August 1930. 'The Aligarh Muslim university and other Muslim educational institutions have so far not been affected by the Congress agitation. Successful Muslim counter-demonstrations have been held at Cawnpore, Lucknow and other places.'[118] In the catalogue of UP 'freedom fighters' felicitated subsequently by the Government of independent India there are few names of Muslims who went to gaol for civil disobedience during 1930–3, 1940 and 1942, and these are mostly men like T A K Sherwani, Rafi Ahmad Kidwai and Manzhar Ali Sokhta, Congress leaders in their own right and usually men who had close links with the Nehrus.[119]

A scrutiny of the lists of Civil Disobedience prisoners in Allahabad between 1930 and 1933 illustrates the point very well. Two independent lists give the number of political prisoners as 679 and 655.[120] The total number of Muslim names found in the first list is nine, all of men jailed in the first phase of Civil Disobedience in 1930–1. Eight of these were from the city of Allahabad and of them three were established local Congress leaders. According to the second list five Muslims went to Malaka district gaol in the period 1930–1. Four were from the city, two of them local Congress leaders and a third – whose address is given as 'Congress Office, Allahabad' – presumably a Congress employee. Three more Muslim names are found among those convicted in 1932. Two were of city men, one a recognized leader who had been to gaol in 1930 as well.

In 1932 the UP Government surveyed the political prisoners held in a camp gaol at Lucknow which was open from early January to mid-May that year, and those held in the district jails of Lucknow, Bareilly and Faizabad who had been arrested between December 1931 and 1 November 1932. The proportion of Hindus among the prisoners was as follows:[121]

> Lucknow Camp Gaol – 1,721 out of 1,735, i.e. 99.2 per cent
> Lucknow District Gaol – 755 out of 765, i.e. 98.7 per cent
> Bareilly District Gaol – all Hindus
> Faizabad District Gaol – 135 out of 140, i.e. 96.4 per cent

The Faizabad figure is especially significant since this gaol was set apart mainly for students arrested in the course of the Civil Disobedience Movement. That even Muslim students at college and school hesitated to join forces with their Hindu colleagues in the Congress campaign is a telling comment on the alienation of the Muslims at this time.

It should be added that the position in UP replicated a countrywide pattern. The 1932 sample survey, conducted simultaneously in several provinces, revealed the overwhelmingly Hindu composition of the satyagrahis. The variations were minor, from 89 per cent Hindus (and Sikhs) in one Punjab gaol and 91 per cent in Delhi, to over 99 per cent in the Central Provinces and Bihar and Orissa. Only the North West Frontier Province defied the pattern: here the 1,500 persons jailed for civil disobedience between December 1931 and December 1932 were all Muslim except for five Hindus and two Sikhs.[122]

The techniques of mobilization employed by the Congress go some way towards explaining how this state of affairs came about. For a fuller explanation, however, it is necessary to take a closer look at the changing relationship between Muslims and the Indian National Congress.

The Alienation of the Muslims

The extent to which Hindus and Muslims inhabited socially – and politically – separate spheres in pre-British, or indeed in nineteenth and early twentieth-century India is an open question, though the situation obviously varied from one region to another. It is clear that events like the cow-protection agitations and the Muslim revivalist movements in northern India in the nineteenth century encouraged the growth of a consciousness of religious community and tended to breed suspicion between Hindus and Muslims at the lower as well as the upper levels of society.[1] But it is equally clear that political separatism of a more abiding kind, the mutual hardening of attitudes between the two communities and the loss of faith by each in political leaders hailing from the other, are all part of a subsequent scenario.

Recent research has suggested, convincingly, that the declining (or threatened) position of certain Muslim elite groups had much to do with the beginnings of this political separatism.[2] The constitutional arrangements made by the British in India, it has been shown, were of particular importance in furthering the process.[3] It is also possible, in this light, to see the Nehru Report of 1928 as the point of rupture between Hindus and Muslims. The argument might even be extended to explain some of the more important developments related to the protracted negotiations between the British Government, the Congress and the Muslim League, leading up to the partition of the sub-continent. Indeed, the scramble for the loaves and fishes of office and tensions arising from an apprehension on the part of elite groups of a setback to their own interests had much to do with the frustration and bitterness of those final years of British rule.

What such an analysis does not explain is how these 'threatened elites' gained the popular support that they did and why common

Muslims, no less than their elite leaders, came in most provinces to stand apart from the Congress as early as the 1930s. The general Muslim aloofness from the Civil Disobedience campaign of 1930–3 stands in sharp contrast to the participation of masses of Muslims in the nationalist agitations of 1919–22 in many parts of India. The reversal requires a proper historical explanation, all the more because vast numbers of both the communities had a great deal in common at the grass-root level of their social existence.

The UP experience suggests that an important part of the explanation lies in the manner of political mobilization. Some of the methods adopted by the Congress leaders not only during the Non-Cooperation Movement but also for subsequent electoral and agitational campaigns served to heighten communal consciousness. The British administration sought to strengthen its own position against the growing power of the nationalist movement by encouraging separate Muslim organization. These factors helped to give rise to a situation in which public acts of communal strife became all too common, and the latter – especially Hindu-Muslim riots, an example of unconscious propaganda by deed – did much to spread mutual fear and suspicion among ordinary Hindus and Muslims.

II

In an earlier chapter we have noted the emergence of a powerful Muslim organization and the launching of a widespread agitation on behalf of the Turkish Khalifa as a part of the Non-Cooperation Movement.[4] These developments brought about a Hindu reaction in the form of an emphasis on the need for counter-organization and for purification and protection of the Hindu community. In 1923 Swami Shraddhanand launched a movement for the re-conversion of Malkana Rajput, Gujar and Bania converts to Islam in western UP. In the same year a well-attended session of the Hindu Mahasabha at Banaras adopted the Arya Samaj's *shuddhi* (purification) programme and called for the 'reclamation' of untouchables.[5] This encouraged a mushrooming of *shuddhi* and *sangathan* (unity) organizations among the Hindus, matched by a corresponding growth of *tabligh* (propagation) and *tanzim* (organization) bodies among the Muslims. In certain areas these communal movements very soon became highly organized and potentially explosive.[6] Agra city, for instance, was divided into several sections for purposes of Arya Samaj activity, each under the local leadership of a *samudai bhikshu* (literally, community mendicant). The weekly Samaj meetings and their counterpart, the congregations at the mosque each Friday, indeed came to be the most regular political gatherings in Agra.[7] The escalating communal organization and propaganda led to a considerable tension between the communities and a spate of Hindu–Muslim riots in the mid-1920s (see table 5.1).

Table 5.1
Communal Riots in UP 1923–7

Division	1923	1924	1925	1926	1927
Kumaun	1	1	–	–	–
Meerut	4	3	–	1	3
Rohilkhand	4	6	3	1	4
Agra	2	–	1	–	3
Jhansi	–	–	1	–	1
Allahabad	1	1	–	8	6
Banaras	1	1	2	1	3
Gorakhpur	–	1	–	2	2
Lucknow	2	5	3	2	4
Faizabad	2	–	3	1	1
UP Total	17	18	13	16	27

Source: Prepared from the statements of communal riots for the relevant years, in UP General Department File 438/1927 (SRR.). These refer of course only to what the Government regarded as major outbreaks.

Congress activities had contributed in no uncertain way to the development of this situation of tension and recurrent conflict. Madan Mohan Malaviya and other Hindu nationalist leaders were prominent in the Hindu Mahasabha's *shuddhi* campaign from the very beginning; Malaviya himself had presided at the Mahasabha session, which adopted the programme. What was still more remarkable was that in the electoral campaigns of the mid-1920s the secular wing of the Congress did not lag far behind the spokesmen of other political groups in appealing to overtly religious sentiments for the sake of immediate electoral gains. An examination of the campaigns leading up to the local board elections of 1925–6 and to the 1926 elections for the central and provincial legislatures shows this clearly.

Groups led by Madan Mohan Malaviya and Motilal Nehru clashed in both these elections. As suggested earlier,[8] the Non-Cooperation

Movement marked a turning point in the contest for leadership between these two Congress leaders. Until then Nehru had none of the local support and influential connections that Malaviya had built up through his Hindi work, Seva Samitis and Kisan Sabhas. In 1920 Nehru had expressed his disappointment at the fact that Gandhi relied more on Malaviya's advice than on his own.[9] Non-Cooperation changed all this. Nehru organized new Kisan Sabhas, took part in a variety of other public activities and went to gaol, while Malaviya concentrated on petitioning the Government for a Round Table Conference. In 1923, with the campaign of Non-Cooperation at an end, Nehru and the Bengal leader C R Das set up the Swaraj Party, which was able to use both the organization and the prestige of the Congress. After Das's death in 1925, Nehru became the unquestioned leader of the party, and the adoption of the party's programme by the Congress added to his stature. He became Gandhi's attorney, as it were, in political matters. The positions that he and Malaviya had held at the beginning of the decade seemed now to have been reversed.

Malaviya kept out of the Swaraj Party although it espoused the approach to the 1919 constitution that he had originally advocated.[10] He could not openly oppose the party in the provincial elections of 1923 when it was riding the crest of a popular wave, but he did support some Liberal and independent candidates against it. Over the next few years the aura surrounding the Non-Cooperation Congress declined and there was also a growing disillusionment with the Swarajist programme.[11] The Malaviya group then vigorously opposed Nehru and his followers in the local elections of 1925–6 and in 1926 organized the Independent Congress Party (or ICP)[12] to contest the provincial and central assembly elections against the official Congress (or Swaraj) party controlled by Nehru.

In the build-up to these elections Hindu communal propaganda was an important part of the Malaviya offensive. In Allahabad, for example, the question of Hindu religious processions playing music before Muslim mosques became the centre of political controversy in the years 1923–6. Friction on this issue in 1923 was followed by a riot during the Ram Lila in 1924 and increasingly acute Hindu–Muslim differences before the Dasehra festival in 1925.[13] At this point the district administration intervened. But certain Hindu leaders refused either to guarantee that their Ram Lila procession would be over by sunset or to stop playing music if the procession was still on the road. The Muslims agreed to close 15 out of the 17 mosques on the route if only the processionists would pass silently by the other two. This proposal was also rejected. Ultimately the District Magistrate issued an order under Section 144 of the Criminal Procedure Code prohibiting public gatherings of more than five persons. The Hindu leaders then called off the procession altogether. A riot was averted but Hindu–Muslim relations in the city took a turn for the worse.

The 'music before mosques' controversy raged throughout 1926, easing only after the elections at the end of that year. Holi in February 1926, the Rath Yatra processions in July and the Ram Lila celebrations in October saw Hindi–Muslim quarrels once again. The Government took a decision to enforce 'established local custom' throughout the province but in Allahabad, as elsewhere, Hindus and Muslims differed in their views of what the established custom was.

On both the Hindu and the Muslim sides there were some leaders who were willing to compromise. During the first half of 1926 Motilal Nehru, Kailash Nath Katju and others tried to get leading Hindu *rais* (notables with landed or commercial wealth) such as Lala Sanwal Das Khanna and Lala Kanhaiya Lal to reach some agreement with the Muslim leaders, 'traditional' as well as 'modern', such as Maulana Vilayat Husain, Zahur Ahmad and Badruddin. In May the Muslims withdrew every condition except that the playing of music should be stopped outside mosques for five to ten minutes at the time of the evening prayer.[14] Like the very reasonable terms of 1925 these too were rejected, probably for the same reasons as those of 1925.

The Malaviya group appears to have been behind much of this Hindu intransigence. In 1924 a Unity Conference in Delhi had reached an agreement on the question of 'music before mosques.'[15] But the Allahabad Hindu Sabha, controlled by Malaviya's men, had nullified any conciliatory move by declaring that they would not be bound by the decisions of the conference. After the 1924 riot in Allahabad, when Purushottam Das Tandon and Zahur Ahmad toured the city in an effort to restore normality, they were welcomed and helped by the leaders of most localities; in the *mohallas* dominated by Malaviya's followers, however, they were met with a volley of abuse and threats to Ahmad's life. The District Magistrate noted also that the Malaviyas were the most inflexible when Hindu and Muslim leaders met to consider the situation after the riot.

In 1925 the narrowly 'political' dimension of the problem became clearer, with elections to the local boards due in December. 'To a very large extent,' wrote the Commissioner of Allahabad division, 'the whole movement has been political, with a view to its result on the coming elections.'[16]

This intransigence continued in 1926, the year of the elections to the provincial and central legislature. At the end of September that year the Allahabad authorities, having failed to get Hindu and Muslim leaders to come to terms, again imposed restrictions on processions. This was the occasion for renewed acrimony on the part of some Hindu leaders. Among them was Madan Mohan Malaviya who presided over a protest meeting attended by 10,000 Hindus. 'Meeting invites attention...' he telegraphed the Governor, 'to deep and universal pain which said attitude [of the authorities] has caused Hindus.'[17]

Much the same kind of propaganda occurred in other places, and in 1926 Hindu communal concerns provided most of the ammunition for the assault on the Swaraj Party. Motilal Nehru was denounced for being 'anti-Hindu' and 'pro-Muslim' and, indeed, a 'beef-eater' who wished to legalize the slaughter of cows in all public places.[18] Shyamlal Nehru, a nephew of Motilal, carried this attack to its limit, using the death of his mother in the course of the election campaign to coin the slogan:

Mai meri mar gayee
gai meri mai hai
(My mother is dead,
The cow is my mother)[19]

It was in 1926, too, that the Malaviya group established the communal Hindu campaign on an organized basis at the provincial level. At a UP Hindu Sabha meeting in April 1926 Malaviya strongly backed the proposal that the organization should support those candidates in the elections who would promise to safeguard Hindu interests. The Hindus had for too long given way to the Muslims, he said, and it was time they learnt to protect themselves.[20] In August he and his lieutenants in the UP went a step further. They supported a move by the Hindu Sabhas of the province to set up election boards. These would not nominate their own candidates but support candidates nominated by others who were prepared to sign the Hindu Sabha pledge binding them to abide by the decision of either the majority of Hindu members in a legislature or the all-India or provincial Hindu Sabha. In August 1926 Hindu Sabhas of both the Agra province and Awadh set up such a board.[21]

If until then the Malaviya group had been able to use the Hindu Sabha organization informally, it was now able to do so more fully and openly. In August Krishna Kant Malaviya, nephew of Madan Mohan and his right-hand man throughout the election campaign, issued a notice on behalf of the Hindu Sabha to all candidates seeking election from UP to the central and provincial legislatures. They were to submit to him their names and a statement of their political opinions if they desired Hindu Sabha support in the campaign.[22]

ICP electioneering in the districts showed how close was the party's association with the Hindu Sabha. On 1 October 1926, to take one instance, Lajpat Rai, Gauri Shankar Mishra, a prominent Congress leader of Allahabad, and Raghava Das arrived in Azamgarh to campaign for the ICP. They were taken out in a procession through the town and presented addresses by the municipal board, the Hindu Sabha and the Arya Samaj. There was a public meeting in the evening at which Lajpat Rai and others asked for votes for the ICP and especially for G D Birla, the party's Legislative Assembly candidate for the Banaras and Gorakhpur divisions 'to whom Hindus owe much'.[23]

As it happened Motilal Nehru and his Swarajist colleagues themselves gave way under this communal pressure in the end and adopted something of a Hindu communalist position. They had begun the campaign with a clear avowal of a secular policy, arguing that the rights and interests of the two communities were identical and that the Congress stood for complete freedom in matters of religion and for the protection of all religions from the alien bureaucracy.[24] They had strongly opposed Hindu Sabha involvement in the elections. Sampurnanand, a Swaraj Party candidate for election from Banaras and a man with close Hindu Sabha connections, declared that, while the Hindu body performed a vital role in the sphere of social and religious affairs, it had no reason to enter into 'politics', for the Congress could, and would, protect the interests of all – Hindus as well as Muslims.[25] There was at the same time a move on the part of some prominent Swarajists to dissociate themselves from open Hindu Sabha connections. As late as June 1926 Jyotishankar Dixit, at the time a secretary of the PCC and of the provincial Swaraj Party, resigned as secretary of the UP Hindu Sabha to define his position unambiguously.[26]

But changes occurred as the communal temperature rose. In June the Congress Working Committee, while resolving that a Congress initiative for the abolition of separate electorates should come only after Hindu and Muslim legislators reached agreement on the issue, conceded a free vote to Congressmen on motions introduced on this subject by non-Congress legislators. Before long Dixit and Gauri Shankar Misra, another of the four secretaries of the UP PCC, crossed the floor and joined the ICP; and other UP Congress leaders became involved in a fight against the notion of a Hindu–Muslim *entente* as a plank of the Swarajist programme.[27]

Gradually, Motilal Nehru himself came to work along similar lines. In Bihar he manoeuvred successfully to get the Hindu Sabha to adopt the entire list of candidates nominated by the Swaraj Party. Then he set out to do the same in UP. The plan was to capture the annual conference of the provincial Hindu Sabha by using a provision in the Sabha's constitution whereby any 20 Hindus in a local area could elect delegates to the conference. Swarajists who had been closely associated with the Hindu Sabha such as Sampurnanand and Anandi Prasad Dube were put in charge of the operation, and money was allocated for the purpose. Unfortunately for the Swarajists, their plot was discovered. The Malaviya group, which controlled the Hindu Sabha, filled the conference with its own men. The Secretary of the Swaraj Party wrote forlornly of the dishonesty of the old office-bearers who refused entry to anyone suspected of Swarajist sympathies and enrolled as members anyone who would vote for them, 'students from Banaras Hindu University and men from different districts', as he put it.[28] Nehru's hopes were dashed to the ground; and by a final touch of irony the Agra provincial Hindu Sabha and the Malaviya men controlling it formed an election board to 'protect Hindu interests' at the very meeting at which the Swarajists had planned to capture the Hindu Sabha and have their nominee elected as president.

In the months immediately preceding the elections in December 1926, the Hindu aspects and the Hindu contacts of the Swaraj Party were further activated. There were urgent calls from various quarters for the services of campaigners like Swami Satyadeva. When some Banaras *sannyasis* issued a manifesto criticizing the Malaviya party, Motilal Nehru arranged for its widespread distribution.[29] The Swaraj Party now became 'as good a Hindu body as one could want'[30] and Nehru himself 'a true Hindu'.[31]

Nehru's performance at a crowded election meeting in Pratapgarh in November 1926 reveals the extent of the shift in Swarajist tactics.[32] The chief point in Nehru's speech here was far from being communally divisive. He denigrated C Y Chintamani, the editor of *The Leader* and the Liberal candidate from the Pratapgarh constituency, for being opposed to Gandhi's Non-Cooperation Movement. Moreover, as a minister in the UP Government at the time, Chintamani had helped 'the miserable Aman Sabhas' (the 'peace councils' established by the UP Government to combat the Non-Cooperation Movement) and the police in their effort to check the Indian nationalist movement. He was aware, Nehru went on, that Madan Mohan Malaviya and Raja Sir Rampal

Singh, *taluqdar* of Kurri Sidhauli, were urging the local people to support Chintamani. But this, he said, was astonishing in view of the fact that in 1923 Malaviya had publicly condemned Chintamani's actions as a minister. As still another black mark against Chintamani, Nehru pointed out that, despite many years of residence in the province, this 'Madrasi' gentleman could not understand or speak the local language. If they were going to elect Chintamani, he said, 'they might as well elect a European or for that matter a Chinaman as their representative'. This was getting nearer the communalist temper of the times but not, as the questions revealed, near enough.

Three questions were put to Nehru after his speech. Why had he not joined the Hindu Sabha? Had he indeed prevented Lala Sangam Lal Agrawal, a Swarajist member of the UPLC, from moving a resolution relating to 'music before mosques'? What had he done to help Hindus over the Allahabad Ramlila episode? Nehru spent a long time justifying his position on these matters. Regarding the 'music before mosques' resolution he argued that it would only have handed over to the British the decision on whether music could be played in one region or another:[33] 'My advice as a lawyer is that no individual or community is entitled to interfere with processions taken along the public thoroughfares with or without music.' About the Allahabad Ramlila, he said that, though he himself had been in high fever and unable to participate, he had supported the Ramlila Committee's move for a *satyagraha* provided that there were 5,000 volunteers. On the other hand:

> Malaviyaji made long applications to the Collector, Governor and Governor-General to which he received curt replies and this ended the great fight which Malaviyaji had undertaken to protect the right of the Hindus to take out their Ramlila procession. Now I put it to you to say in whose hands those rights are safe, in the hands of those who stand by them at all risks or those who depend on long petitions and are satisfied with short answers rejecting them.

These were not far from the words of a Hindu enthusiast and for the moment they won loud and prolonged applause. But the adoption of a sectional Hindu appeal, however briefly, played into the hands of communalist Hindu and Muslim leaders and lent credibility to everything that they said about the Congress.

To make matters worse the Congress leadership appeared to draw indiscriminately upon support from all quarters in their efforts to mobilize support for campaigns of agitation as well as for elections. The help of rabidly communal Hindu bodies like the Arya Samaj and the Hindu Sabha was openly accepted in the period leading up to the Civil Disobedience Movement of 1930 to 1931. Well organized and extremely active, these associations contributed substantially to a quick and successful Congress mobilization. But the fact is that the new cooperation was even more counter-productive than the Hindu slant of a part of the Congress propaganda noticed in the last chapter. Coming as it did after a period of growing tension and conflict between the two communities, it was a grave shortcoming in a movement that aimed at keeping the Muslims on its side.

At the local level the Congress–Hindu link could be purely coincidental. The Arya Samaj and the Hindu Sabha had been prominent in propaganda for the uplift of untouchables after the Non-Cooperation Movement. Gandhi and Lajpat Rai's Lok Sevak Mandal had also taken up this work. For the ordinary townsman and villager there was no way of distinguishing their work from that of the Hindu organizations.

The experience of Bhainsa Bazar, a village in Bansgaon *tahsil* in Gorakhpur district, illustrates this. In November 1929, Ganesh Prasad Pandey, secretary of the *tahsil* Congress committee, wrote of the excellent organizational work done in the village. A Village Service Association had been established and it ran a girls' school, a library, an infirmary, a publications division and a music society, among other things. The Hindu Sabha and the Congress had been in the village for quite some time, often working together, as Pandey noted. There were now plans to open a Khaddar Bhandar for *khadi* propaganda, and to start a fortnightly magazine, *Gram Sevak* ('Servant of the Village').[34] It is clear from Pandey's account that at this level Hindu Sabhaites and Congressmen formed, for all practical purposes, a team working for a common cause. They might indeed have been the same people – and in the 1920s they often were.

There were, however, even more flagrant examples of association between the Congress and communal Hindu institutions. The use of religious fairs and festivals for nationalist mobilization has been mentioned earlier.[35] In January 1930 the Kumbh Mela at Allahabad, a great 12 yearly bathing festival, became an occasion for propaganda in favour of Civil Disobedience. Several nationalist meetings and processions were held. *Sadhus* and *sannyasis* were prominent in these, among them Baba Raghavadas, the Gorakhpur Congress leader; and calls to free the country from servitude were bolstered by references to the '75,000 cows slaughtered daily' and by comparisons of British rule with the reign of Aurangzeb.[36]

In 1929 and 1930, various branches of the Arya Samaj and the Hindu Sabha issued statements supporting the Congress move towards Civil Disobedience.[37] Congress leaders sometimes took the initiative themselves and sought support from such Hindu organizations. When the official Congress decided to revive and strengthen the nationalist volunteer corps in 1928–9, the Agra Provincial Hindu Sabha was also taking vigorous steps to improve volunteer organization. The Sabha decided to establish physical training centres in different parts of the province. Six *svayam sevaks* were sent to the famous Hanuman Vyayam Pracharak Mandal in Amrawati (Berar) for training. The Hindu Mahasabha appointed Harihar Rao Deshpande to help in the physical training programme of the Agra provincial Sabha. In January 1929 a physical training centre was established in Gorakhpur. Deshpande toured several UP districts – Gorakhpur, Basti, Azamgarh and Meerut – propagating the scheme. Later physical training camps, where *lathi*-play was practised and the use of spears and knives taught, were started in different areas: in Pratapgarh, a camp financed and run by the Raja of Kalakankar, in Jalaun and Ghazipur, at the Kashi Vidyapith in Banaras and the Kumbh Mela in Allahabad.[38] The moving spirit behind this programme was Narmada Prasad Singh of Allahabad. He was a prominent Hindu Sabha man, general secretary of the Agra provincial branch in 1929. But he was also a well-known Congressman, member of the UP PCC in 1925–6, a leader of the Malaviya group in the Allahabad Congress in 1926 and 1927, shortly to be 'dictator' of the Handia *tahsil* Satyagraha Committee (this being the *tahsil* where the Allahabad Congress concentrated its initial efforts at Civil Disobedience) and subsequently secretary of the Allahabad DCC.

Yet more striking evidence of Congress association with the Hindu Sabha physical training efforts was to come. In August 1929, Sri Prakasa, then general secretary of the PCC, Narendra Deo, an important Congress leader working in Banaras and secretary of Jawaharlal Nehru's Independence for India League, Nand Kumar Deo Vasishht, secretary of the UP Congress Volunteer Board, and Birbal Singh, another prominent Congressman from Banaras, visited the Lajpat Physical Training Camp at Ghazipur. Impressed by the organization of the camp and the training imparted, they published a statement welcoming the idea of training the youth to work together as a disciplined force and declaring that the provincial Hindu Sabha had filled a big gap by taking up this work. The statement added that if the district boards in different areas took advantage of this Hindu Sabha programme a sufficient number of physical training instructors would soon be ready and the physical training scheme could expand.[39] This was not the kind of message calculated to reassure Muslims, even if it contained a reference to the presence of 'two Muslim gentlemen' in the camp. Coming from such exalted quarters in the Congress, it probably caused still greater consternation among Muslims and greater distrust of the 'Hindu' party.

III

British administrators, who wished to wean away Muslim (and indeed any other) support from the UP Congress at this time, added a certain amount of direct encouragement to such ill-considered Congress propaganda and activities. Hailey, taking over as Governor of the province in August 1928, saw his immediate task as that of helping 'landlords' and 'Muslims' to organize and express themselves – in support of the British.[40] For this purpose he regarded the Nehru Report as a heaven-sent opportunity, 'for it presents their [i.e. the nationalists'] ideas in a concrete form'. In the UP he pointed out:

> ...we should probably have 12 or 15 million voters, mainly tenants, so that the landlords would be ousted from general constituencies and at the same time reserved seats would disappear. As for the Mussalmans, they would be far worse off than at present. I am afraid that I have already been guilty of impressing these facts on both parties.[41]

In the following years the provincial Government's courting of Muslims increased. On its behalf the Nawab of Chhatari, an influential Muslim landlord of Bulandshahr district, Home Member of the Government and acting-Governor of the province for a short while in 1928 (and again in 1933–4), tried to persuade the Khilafat leader, Muhammad Ali, to make an announcement against a civil disobedience movement until the results of the Round Table Conference were clear. Efforts were also made to get the *ulema* to pronounce against Civil Disobedience. Chhatari was responsible for a meeting of the Tausih Jamiat-ul-ulema-i-Hind at Kanpur in May 1930 that strongly opposed the current campaign of agitation.[42]

At this stage, when the Civil Disobedience Movement had attained a quite unexpected success, the administration went further in its efforts to win over the Muslims. Noting that UP Muslims were extremely agitated by the Sarda Act (which raised the minimum age at which girls and boys could be legally married to 14 and 18 respectively) and that even a level-headed, loyal *zamindar* like Chhatari pressed for its amendment, Hailey urged New Delhi to change the law; 'I am so impressed by the necessity of retaining Muslim opinion on our side.'[43] Ultimately the idea of an amendment to the Sarda Act was not accepted but it was made clear to Muslims generally that prosecutions for breaches were unlikely.[44]

A similar thought process led Hailey in the last week of May 1930 to order an enquiry by a sessions judge into police action against demonstrators in Lucknow. He saw Muslims adding to the barrage of complaints and noted their dissatisfaction at the magisterial enquiry that had been ordered. 'A danger arose', he explained, 'that the Muslims of Lucknow who had hitherto held aloof from Civil Disobedience would join in with the Congress as a kind of protest.'[45]

From the Government's point of view it was imperative that 'every legitimate effort' be made to prevent the Muslims at large from supporting the Congress movement. The provincial Government itself went so far as to give financial assistance to the UP Tanzim Committee, an organization led by Shaukat Ali and a number of traditional Muslim leaders, which did much to arouse masses of Muslims to organize and defend themselves against the Congress.[46] At the district level official efforts to secure and maintain Muslim opposition to the Congress were often equally brazen. 'Action is being and had already been taken in a quiet way', reported the Commissioner of Allahabad division in May 1930.[47] A Muslim journalist of Kanpur, one of the districts in the division, described his experiences rather differently. 'The Collector tried to throw nets around me', he said. 'He tempted me with everything including title, Honorary Magistracy, and service. A very big Hindu Officer of the province...offered me Rs 150 p.m., besides travelling expenses, for delivering in the villages of Cawnpore district only four speeches against the Congress, every month.'[48]

I V

It is true that much of the activity described in the preceding sections was focused on elite political leaders. Yet it had a direct and powerful influence on masses of Hindus and Muslims, especially in the towns, heightening the sense of separate needs and interests and often leading to situations in which violent clashes occurred, which led in turn to greater fear and suspicion. An examination of one of the worst examples of such violence in UP during the inter-war period indicates the importance of several of these factors as well as the enormous impact that such violent outbreaks could have.

The scene for this 'riot' in Kanpur in March 1931 appears to have been set by the protracted Gandhi-Irwin negotiations culminating in the 'truce' agreement of 5 March 1931. While the calling off of mass protest and the terms of the Gandhi-Irwin Pact caused disappointment in certain quarters represented in the upper echelons of the Congress leadership by Jawaharlal Nehru and Subhash Chandra Bose, to the majority of Congressmen in the districts and towns the pact appeared as it was painted by their leaders – a great victory; their colleagues came out of goal, their newspapers resumed publication and the nervousness of the police and officials boosted their self-confidence. Large numbers of Muslims were on the other hand somewhat perturbed by these developments. Many of them worried about the threats that they, in company with the police and other 'collaborators', now received from Congressmen. Others noticed that, for all their loyalty, Muslim leaders had not even been consulted before the Gandhi-Irwin Pact was signed.[49] The tension between Hindus and Muslims in the towns, which had been sustained by Muslim abstention from Civil Disobedience, increased further.

The repercussions were felt immediately in a number of places. A serious communal disturbance had already occurred in Banaras on 11 February 1931. According to the District Magistrate, 'the release of the members of the All-India Congress Committee...coming as it did on Independence Day [26 January], was regarded by the people generally as a great victory for Congress.'[50] Congress activities, which had been on the wane for some time, were now revived. Picketing was one of the most important of the renewed activities and among the shops picketed in Banaras was that of a well-known Muslim cloth merchant, Aga Mohammad Jan. The picketers themselves were all said to be 'Hindus'. On 10 February they assaulted some customers making their way to the shop. The police made a number of arrests, but that evening Mohammad Jan was shot dead in a lane while on his way home from his shop and fighting between Hindus and Muslims broke out.

After the Gandhi-Irwin agreement communal clashes broke out from 15 to 17 March in the city of Agra and from 14 to 16 March in two villages in the Mirzapur district on the border with Shahabad district in Bihar. In Agra one Muslim was killed and several members of both communities were injured. The old quarrel over 'music before mosques' provided the immediate provocation. Official intervention saved the situation on 15 March when Muslims objected to a Holi procession playing music outside a mosque. The next day a crowd of Hindus attacked a Muslim wedding party and a Muslim crowd retaliated by attacking another Holi procession despite police warnings. Further rioting occurred on the seventeenth; Hindu students and a teacher of St. John's College quarrelled with a group of Muslim butchers who then attacked them, and other groups joined in as the fighting spread.

In Mirzapur a large mob of Hindu villagers massacred seven Muslims. The scene was a village, Manchi, 12 miles east of Police Station Pannuganj in *tahsil* Robertsganj. A haunch of venison sent by a Muslim *zamindar* to a Muslim tenant and believed by the Hindu villagers to be beef was what caused the outbreak. For some reason an armed police guard did not reach Manchi until 16 March, two days after the attack. On its arrival it found fresh violence occurring in the village of Raiya, six miles from Manchi. The *zamindar* had absconded. The assailants then went in search of his men, and followed them to a Brahman's house where they had taken refuge. Allegedly the former had now acquired firearms and another four Muslims were killed and two injured. There was no evidence of any political motive in these riots. But their timing is possibly significant: they may have been a reflection of a growing communal animosity that was spreading apparently even to some rural areas.

What is relevant for my present purposes is that the events in these different places affected Kanpur, a 'difficult' city at any time and by 1930 one noted for its volatility. It was the fastest-growing city in the province and easily the most overcrowded. The municipality of Kanpur, minus the cantonment, had nearly 220,000 people in 1931 (150,000 of them Hindu and a little over 65,000 Muslim) and a population density of 22,000 per square mile, compared with 1,300 in Lucknow. Slums covered three-quarters of the city, and in parts of it population density was several times greater than the average for the city as a whole.[51]

A large part of Kanpur's population was made up of recent immigrants. In 1931, 414 of every 1,000 persons counted in the city were born outside the municipality. The 'unsettled' nature of much of the population could be gauged from another fact: it had the lowest proportion of women to men among the cities of UP, 696 to every 1,000 in 1931. In addition Kanpur attracted what the Government described as 'men with reasons to disappear.'[52] It had more than its fair share of the *goonda* and *badmash* groups that abound in any large city and are often in the pay of wealthy men and willing to perform a range of services for the money. Some of them engaged in cocaine smuggling, trade and gambling, which often led to other criminal activities.

Business and industry dominated the economic and political life of the city. As has already been noted, the First World War provided a considerable stimulus to these activities. The exceptional demand for leather goods during the war brought great prosperity to the Kanpur tanneries. The cotton and woollen industries also expanded rapidly. Hand weaving increased with the decline in imports and the glass industry grew with the officially promoted effort to capture the local market from imported Austrian glass and bangles.[53] The post-War depression in trade and industry had a relatively less adverse impact here. In the course of the 1920s 26 new factories were registered in Kanpur under the Indian Factories Act;[54] and the high prices and stable conditions of the period helped the men of industry and commerce to further enrich themselves and consolidate their position.

To a large extent those who thus accumulated wealth were Hindus, though Muslims also had their share in two limited but fairly lucrative fields – the leather trade and haberdashery.[55] As it happened, however, even those Muslims who had some place in the commercial and industrial life of the city proved to have less luck than their Hindu fellows. The leather trade, which had expanded substantially to meet the needs of the armed forces, inevitably slumped after the War. The closing down of several tanneries at the end of the war meant especially severe distress for Muslim (and untouchable) mill-workers.[56]

Another group to suffer was the handloom weavers, among whom again Muslims predominated. The expanding textile industry cut into their market in the 1920s. In addition the sharp decline in prices on account of the World Depression at the end of that decade considerably reduced the purchasing power of large masses of the rural population. In these circumstances the handloom industry was extremely hard-pressed. The weavers survived, contrary to a popular belief about the fate of Indian handicrafts: in the period under study they still produced thirty per cent of the cloth bought in UP. But their survival, in pretty poor conditions, depended on the mercy of the moneylender, who more often than not was a Hindu.[57] Thus the economic fluctuations of the 1920s and 1930s, which made men and women of all castes and communities in UP more amenable to political persuasion, also made important groups of Muslims feel especially deprived. Some of them were even led to believe that their loss was the Hindus's gain. So the Muslim politicians who spoke in terms of the defence of Muslim interests from Hindu domination found a more ready audience.

Another factor of importance in the political life of Kanpur was the presence of major social and educational institutions. The Arya Samaj had been active here since before the foundation of the Congress. At the turn of the century it claimed a membership of 977 in Kanpur district. In the first decade of this century the Samaj began running a free night school, converted soon after into a day school, and a public library. Even in that period some of its activities had brought it into conflict with groups of Muslims. In the decades that followed the membership of the Arya Samaj in Kanpur continued to increase,[58] and with the onset of the *shuddi* movement in the 1920s Muslim suspicion of its activities intensified. About this time many of Kanpur's educational institutions also began taking an active interest in militant politics, communal as well as nationalist. Among these were the Dayanand Anglo-Vedic College, an offshoot of the Arya Samaj, and Christ Church College. The former was particularly active: of the 13 UP men among the 24 accused in the Lahore Conspiracy Case in 1929, for instance, 8 were ex-students of this institution.[59]

The outcome of all this was a very strong Congress campaign in Kanpur in 1930. The availability of substantial funds helped the Kanpur Congress organize its forces. From the city's student population came recruiting agents, 'shock troops' and, not least, great enthusiasm. Finally, though the workers did not participate in the movement as a class, proletarian and lumpen-proletarian elements contributed substantially to swelling the crowds at public meetings and demonstrations.

By the second half of 1930 the Civil Disobedience agitation in Kanpur had assumed considerable proportions and had begun to get aggressive. There were reports of harassment by Congress volunteers of buyers as well as sellers of foreign cloth and intoxicants of any kind. The police judged the movement to be more firmly established here than in any other UP city and expressed the fear that Congress raj might 'swamp' the place.[60]

This potentially dangerous situation in Kanpur was made even more inflammable by the open hostility of the leading local Muslims to the Congress. In 1926 Dr Murarilal Rohatgi and other Congress leaders of the city had joined the local Hindu Sabha in an effort to gain control of it. Their subsequent claim that they had been unenthusiastic about the objectives of the Sabha[61] made little difference. Association with organizations like the Arya Samaj and the Hindu Sabha which had been active for most of the decade in virulent anti-Muslim agitation over the question of 'music before mosques' and the right to sacrifice cows, was enough to condemn them in the eyes of many Muslims.

There was also a growing feeling among the Muslim politicians of Kanpur in the latter half of the 1920s that municipal affairs were being conducted increasingly on communal lines in a manner unfavourable to the minority community.[62] So widespread was this feeling in 1929 that Murarilal Rohatgi, then president of the TCC, could not secure a single Muslim vote in his contest for the chairmanship of the municipality against Hafiz Halim, a wealthy and respected Muslim of the city with no great political standing. The point was driven home further when Dr Abdul Karim, joint secretary of the TCC, resigned from his post on the occasion of this contest.[63]

In 1928 and 1929 Shaukat Ali and the Tanzim Committee were active in Kanpur, preaching against the Congress. In 1929 they established a breakaway Tausih Jamiat-ul-ulema-i-Hind there to counter any pro-Congress pronouncements from the Jamiat-ul-ulema-i-Hind at Deoband and thus to strengthen their campaign.[64]

All this, following hard on the heels of the communal propaganda and clashes of the preceding years, affected the Kanpur Muslims at large. 'There is no general disposition on the part of the Muslims to give up their attitude of aloofness from the [Civil Disobedience] movement,' said a report on the city in May 1930. Muslim shopkeepers in Kanpur deeply resented and sometimes openly opposed Congress picketing of their foreign cloth and liquor shops. Muslim Congressmen trying to make public speeches in the city were 'howled down' while Muslim communalists were 'listened to eagerly'.[65] In January 1931 Muslim leaders refused to cooperate with Congress leaders in organizing a condolence meeting on Muhammad Ali's death, and two separate meetings were held. The fairly well attended Muslim meeting, presided over by Hasrat Mohani, to condole the death of Motilal Nehru in the following month cannot be regarded as a significant gesture pointing in the other direction. For, barring this one instance, the Muslims on the whole abstained from the processions, meetings and above all the massive *hartal* sponsored by the Congress on this occasion, which halted tramway traffic in the city for 13 hours. 'When pressed to close their shops, some made references to the reluctance of Hindus to take part in the condolence meetings for Mr Muhammad Ali.'[66] Communal animosity had gone so far as to affect even the politics of public mourning.

News of the Gandhi-Irwin agreement compounded the feelings of fear and frustration among Kanpur Muslims. Against this background the execution of Bhagat Singh, Rajguru and Sukhdev in Lahore was a torch to a powder keg. Events connected with these executions followed a perhaps predictable pattern. On 7 March 1931 a meeting held at the Marwari School and attended mainly by students called for Bhagat Singh's release. On 21 March, when it became known that the petition of mercy on behalf of Bhagat Singh had been rejected, a procession was taken out with 500 people, which increased, according to the Government, to 1,500 as it rolled on. There was a partial *hartal* too. In these Muslims did not join. Such abstention, occurring as it did in the wake of the communal disturbances at Banaras and Agra, was clearly a warning signal. For Kanpur had experienced two major communal riots within the past two decades. The demolition of a part of the Macchli Bazar mosque on Meston Road had provoked a violent flare-up in 1913, and the pressure to obtain Muslim participation in a nationalist demonstration in 1927 had caused a riot which kept the city in turmoil for two or three days.[67] But the local administration had obviously learnt little from these events and no special precautions were taken.

On the morning of 24 March 1931, news of Bhagat Singh's execution was received in Kanpur. Congress messengers went out at once to proclaim a *hartal*. There was much excitement. Students broke windows in shops and offices and the police intervened. About 2 pm a quarrel arose on Meston Road between some Hindu Congressmen who urged a *hartal* and some Muslim shopkeepers who objected to closing their shops. The quarrel led to a fight and the congregation of a large crowd of Hindus and Muslims on the spot. *Lathis* and brickbats appeared and general rioting broke out, to rage on for several days in different parts of the city.

It is unnecessary here to trace the course of these events in any detail. It would be useful, however, to examine the way in which the rioting spread and to identify as far as possible the elements involved in it. In Kanpur as elsewhere, young men and students were prominent among those calling for a suspension of business and other forms of protest against the execution. Other participants in the riot in its early stages were petty shopkeepers, vendors, their servants, *ricksha* pullers and other groups associated with the market in an Indian city. The industrial labourers were at work in the mills until about 6 pm on 24 March.

By that time the riot had attained the utmost virulence. There was no evidence of 'criminal' elements participating in any significant number to start with, but several sources suggest that they contributed greatly to the persistence and spread of the trouble.[68]

The riot engulfed entire *mohallas* with great rapidity after its outbreak and it became impossible to tell assassins and instigators from innocent victims or, indeed, Hindus from Muslims among those who were killed or wounded.[69] All that is clear is that the residential areas of the 'respectable' escaped the fury. After the big clashes on the first day on the spacious Meston Road and at the crossing of Meston Road and Halsey Road at Moulganj, the fighting shifted to the less accessible 'dark evil-smelling lanes [where] the passage of light is impeded by projecting balconies and upper storeys'[70] and where crowds of *gwalas, julahas, riksha-walas*, bangle-sellers, peons, millhands, and unemployed immigrants from the villages, were to be found. Areas like Coolie Bazaar in the heart of the Indian quarter were the scenes of some of the greatest disturbances.[71] On the second and third days of the violence there was evidence of large numbers of volunteers arriving from other places to strengthen one side or the other. Thousands moved in the reverse direction, fleeing from the city to the countryside.[72] Others, unable or unwilling to move, remained – praying for their own safety and sometimes attacking and killing those who might endanger it. Anticipating the train to Pakistan, the *ekka* from Bangali Mahal was ransacked and its passengers massacred.

Concentrated in the *mohallas* around Meston Road and Moulganj on the first day, rioting intensified that night and spread very rapidly during the next two days to all parts of the city proper – Sadar Bazaar, Patkapur, Colonelganj, Sisamau, and even to the two outlying portions of the city which lay in the Civil Lines area, Gwaltoli and Parmat. On 28 March, when officials noticed signs of improvement in Kanpur city, incendiarism spread to adjacent villages on the other side of the river Ganga from Gwaltoli. By then, however, the authorities had reasserted their position and generally reestablished the rule of 'law'.

In the course of the investigations following the riot, every class of witness – European businessmen, Muslims and Hindus of all shades of opinion, representatives of the Indian Christians and the Sikhs, officers of the municipal board, the British secretary of the Upper India Chamber of Commerce (who was also in administrative charge of the fire brigade), Indian officials and even army officers – complained about the indifference and inactivity of the police. There were reports that officials had told some of those who sought police assistance and protection to go and ask Gandhi for help. A Kanpur businessman who was also active in the Congress expressed the opinion that the authorities did not take immediate steps to quell the riot 'because they were displeased with the businessmen for helping the Congress activities and they wanted to show that without the help of the authorities they cannot protect their lives and properties'.[73] A meeting of Hindu merchants as well as the Congress committee enquiring into the occurrence laid the entire responsibility for the riots at the door of the local administration.[74]

The UP Government's Commission of Enquiry also found the actions of the Kanpur District Magistrate culpable. It censured him for his hasty withdrawal from the Meston Road area, not far from the place where the Macchli Bazaar mosque and the Teli temple stood opposite one another, in spite of the availability of a police force nearby. This very spot had been the scene of the 1913 riot, and in 1931, as the Commission observed, 'it was the news of the burning of the temple and the mosque that caused the sudden fury of passion which swept the riot out of control and carried it with unprecedented speed out into the farthest quarters of the city.' It was the opinion of the members of the Enquiry Commission that the Magistrate could in all probability have saved both from being burnt, had he acted somewhat differently.[75]

One must not exaggerate the significance of what was obviously a case of cold feet, the failure of the man on the spot. In Banaras and Agra the district officers, Owen and Darwin, were commended by local opinion for their action at the time of the riots.[76] Yet it is not without significance that nationalist organs, Muslim as well as Hindu, had frequently remarked during the mid-1920s on the reluctance of the Government to intervene to stop Hindu–Muslim clashes.[77] And in view of the dimensions attained by the Kanpur riot of 1931 and its deleterious effects it is also important to note that, while the District Magistrate left the disturbed area in fear before 4 pm on 24 March, troops (stationed nearby) were not called in until 5 pm and did not reach the scene of the rioting until after 6. Nor was there any evidence during the next two days of Government firmness in putting down miscreants or in enforcing orders prohibiting gatherings of more than five people. The District Magistrate and others acknowledged that the crowds melted away at the first sight of the military or the police. Yet during the three days from 24 to 26 March, while the riot raged, there was not a single case of police firing and the total number of arrests made was one, five and two respectively, excepting the arrests made in one special raid by a

Deputy Superintendent of Police in Colonelganj on 25 March. By contrast in the smaller Kanpur riot of 1927 nearly 250 arrests were made within the first 24 hours – to good effect.[78]

The direct losses resulting from the riot were severe. The Government estimated the number of killed and injured as 290 and 965 respectively. The Congress put it higher at 400 and 1,200. In addition the latter reported 500 buildings gutted, including 23 mosques and 37 temples, for which alone the damages were worth no less than five lakhs of rupees; the loss of movable property worth at least Rs 20 lakhs by loot and destruction; and a 'general exodus' and the 'utter dislocation' of business and normal life.[79]

The mills that closed on 25 March did not begin to reopen until the 29th. It was only then, too, that there was any abatement in 'the constant shouting at night which had tended to keep up a state of panic'[80] – 'Allah -o -Akbar!' or 'Din! Din! Din!' from the Muslim quarter, 'Jai Sia Ram!' or 'Har Har Mahadeo' from the Hindus. All this while wild and terrifying rumours flew about the city and beyond. The press, the post and the railways carried news of Kanpur far afield, swiftly and, as usual, in exaggerated form. Muslims elsewhere were perceptibly affected by the terror experienced by their Kanpur brethren as well as by their sense of isolation and insecurity.[81] There were reports of further atrocities committed against Muslims in the rural areas around Kanpur and of a chain reaction of fear and suspicion. Significantly, while on 6 April 1931 the city of Kanpur was reported quiet (though Hindu bazaars had not reopened), panic still prevailed in other parts of the district.[82]

Hafiz Hidayat Husain, BA, Bar-at-Law, CIE, a distinguished lawyer of Kanpur, member and leader of a so-called 'centre party' in the provincial legislature, a strong supporter of the Simon Commission and a delegate to the Round Table Conference in London, expressed a reaction that was widespread among educated Muslims of UP at this time. 'The butchery committed on the Cawnpore Moslems', he wrote to a Muslim leader of the Punjab:

> ...is unthinkable in the present age. 32 Mosques have been destroyed at least. 300 Moslems, most of these decrepit old men, women and children, have been either massacred or burnt to ashes... Not one Moslem has been left in Mohallas which are predominantly Hindu... The Police was most callous. Khan Bahadur Ghulam Hassain is the Deputy Superintendent in charge of the city. He refused to give any aid to the Moslems who were

marooned... There was no government, settled or unsettled, in Cawnpore for three or four days. Even now no Moslem is safe. The prosecution is being managed by Sirdar Bahadur Kishen Singh [a Sikh] and no Moslem is free from anxiety, he may be arrested at any time. Hindus are being let off by the Hindu Judge on bails of 10,000/-in murder cases while bail of 40,000/-is asked from the Moslems so that we are undergoing the greatest imaginable privations. I do not think the Nawab of Chattari can help you or us much, for in the Council the Finance Member [a British official] deals with Communal questions.[83]

Here was an educated man who had worked closely with the British expressing loss of faith in the British ability to protect Muslims and their interests. Only a Muslim, the Nawab of Chhatari, could provide the necessary protection, but he was unfortunately powerless. The note of despair was clear. For masses of Muslims in Kanpur and elsewhere there could be but one lesson in all this: unite and organize to resist Hindu, and Congress, domination.

In Kanpur city itself the effects were to last very long. Hindus and Muslims showed greater reluctance than ever before to live as neighbours in the same localities.[84] For years afterwards Hindu clerks and businessmen made it a point to bypass Muslim *mohallas* on their way to work,[85] and *vice versa*. And as if to assert with a vengeance a sectarian identity reinforced by common suffering, Muslim festivals were celebrated in the months after the riot of 1931 with greater fervour than in previous years. Tens of thousands of Muslims turned out, many of the teams of youths among them bearing arms and everyone joining in the resounding shouts of '*Allah-o-Akbar*'.[86]

Muharram ceremonies at the end of May 1931 passed off peacefully everywhere else in UP but brought serious disturbances in Kanpur. There were reports of Muslim threats to Hindu shopkeepers and of the throwing of beef and bones into Hindu houses and temples. Four days before the end of the Muharram period a dispute arose over a signboard strung up across the road outside the office of the local Gandhi Seva Samiti. The question of whether this was a 'new' or a 'traditional' obstruction on the path of the Muharram procession developed into a major conflict and led to police firing, in which three or four people were killed and several injured.

A month later, when the Chehlum was observed, the signboard controversy was still unresolved. The question of whether the *tazias*[87] should in any case be buried aroused heated argument and agitation among the Muslims. A Young Men's Muslim Association came into being in Kanpur at this time. It was decided that the *tazias* should not be buried or moved from where they stood and the Association made arrangements to guard them. The curfew ordered in Kanpur at the time of the Muharram disturbances remained in force until the Chehlum. Restrictive orders under Section 144 of the Criminal Procedure Code were re-imposed before the Chehlum.[88] It was an index of the communal tension, which had come to characterize 'normal' life in the city.

Ten years afterwards, the Government of UP still felt justified in describing Kanpur as 'the most communal place in the province', and Jinnah, visiting the city, was met at the station by some 50,000 Muslims shouting not only '*Allah -o -Akbar*' ('God is Great') but also '*Pakistan Zindabad*'.[89]

V

The communalist propaganda and activities of the 1920s, the attitude of 'non-interference' (and on occasion the active aid) of the British administration and the outbreak of Hindu–Muslim rioting took its toll not only in Kanpur but all over UP. 'Swarajism' had become synonymous with the betrayal of just and legitimate Hindu interests, according to *The Leader*.[90] 'Our politics are really growing absolutely impossible,' wrote Govind Malaviya, son of Madan Mohan but something of an apostate – a close associate, if not a follower, of the secular and 'radical' Jawaharlal Nehru:

> You will have learnt of the shame which the whole country was put to [in 1926] in the form of precautions against communal outbreaks on the occasion of the Bakr-id. All this was done and yet disturbances did take place at various places. It drives me mad. I don't know if I had the opportunity to tell you when you were here that I was losing my patience and was fast becoming a Hindu Sabhaite – but I may tell you that I am a full-fledged one now.[91]

Still more telling is the evidence of a public meeting in Allahabad in May 1926. Here a poor and unknown but angry *sonar* (goldsmith), Kedar Nath, aroused the audience to a frenzy as he upbraided Motilal Nehru for insisting on Hindu–Muslim unity and declared that it was

Hindu cowardice that led to the abandonment of the Dasehra celebrations in the city in the previous year.[92]

The growing Hindu feelings against the Swaraj Party were reflected in the results of the elections of 1925–6. The Swarajists suffered such heavy losses that Motilal Nehru spoke of 'a disaster' and 'a veritable rout', and seriously considered retiring from politics altogether.[93] In 1923 the Swarajists had gained control of the municipal boards in a number of important towns, including Allahabad, Lucknow and Kanpur. Now the Malaviya men rode roughshod over them in these and other places. In the UPLC the Swarajist strength declined from 29 after the 1923 elections to 20 after 1926.[94]

The course of events in two Awadh constituencies illustrates how decisively the wind had turned against the Swarajists since 1923. Then Jaikaran Nath Misra had successfully contested the UPLC election from the Rae Bareli (non-Muslim rural) constituency on a Swaraj Party ticket. A split among the *taluqdars* of the district helped him. Raja Jagannath Baksh Singh of Rehwan had stood as an independent candidate, but partly because of ill feeling between his group and that led by Raja Rampal Singh of Kurri Sidhauli, and partly because of Rampal Singh's nationalist sympathies, the latter had supported Misra. By 1926 the position had changed. The Swarajists no longer commanded the respect of the Non-Cooperation Congress. In addition, the protection of Hindu interests was a principal campaigning issue. Raja Viswanath Saran Singh of Tiloi, one of the richest *taluqdars* in the district, decided to enter the contest this time and quickly gained the support of *taluqdars* of both parties.[95] Later he appears also to have adopted the ICP label. Against such a combination a Swaraj Party candidate would have been lucky not to lose his deposit.[96]

The election to the central legislature from the Faizabad Division (non-Muslim rural) constituency proved more tumultuous. Gauri Shankar Mishra, the lawyer Congressman of Allahabad who had been active among the *kisans* of Awadh in the early 1920s, was first given a Swaraj Party ticket for the seat. In July 1926 the situation changed dramatically. Nehru came to know that Kunwar Rananjay Singh, heir to the *taluqdari* estate of Amethi in Sultanpur district, wished to contest the Faizabad election. At the same time it was discovered that Mishra had received some money from the Malaviya party and consented to work as their secretary. Nehru and the Swarajist secretary, Sitla Sahai, now concluded that Rananjay Singh was 'in every way preferable' to Mishra. 'The Taluqdars will help him, Raja Rampal Singh and his party may also like this selection of ours. He is therefore a sure and self-paying candidate.'[97] Rananjay Singh however declined the invitation to stand as a Swaraj Party candidate, choosing to contest under the ICP label instead.[98]

The events that followed the Non-Cooperation Movement, and the unprincipled adoption of communalist positions by even the most secular of Swarajists, had far-reaching consequences. At the end of the 1920s and in the first years of the 1930s public attention was diverted away from electoral contests and the Congress was extremely cautious in its handling of communally inflammable areas.[99] Consequently the frequency of Hindu–Muslim riots declined from the high proportions it had attained in 1923–7, though some major outbreaks still occurred as at Kanpur in 1931. Thus the public acts of strife, which contributed so greatly to the growth of feelings of 'separatism' and antagonism between the communities, were now less in evidence. But appearances were deceptive. The consequences of eight years or more of propaganda and mobilization on religious, sectional lines were not to be so easily undone. Communal feelings had hardened and large numbers of Muslims in UP were now distrustful of Hindu leaders and indeed of Muslim leaders associated with the 'Hindu' Congress.

It was precisely because of the growing fears of masses of Muslims and the general demand for securing the interests of the community first, that the Nehru Report of 1928 assumed such great importance in the eyes of the entire Muslim political leadership, and even nationalist Muslim leaders found it difficult to participate in Congress activities in the years afterwards. 'Some of those very Muslims who...[had] in the recent past contributed to a considerable extent to the greatness of Congress...now arrayed themselves among its enemies,' wrote Motilal Nehru.[100] Thus Shuaib Qureshi, a prominent Khilafatist and Congressman and member of the committee that produced the Nehru Report, wrote a dissenting minute challenging some of its basic premises; and Shaukat Ali, the elder of the famous Ali Brothers, president of the UP PCC as recently as 1925–6, came to be considered the leader of the opposition to the Nehru Report in 1928. Immediately after the Congress decision in favour of Civil Disobedience at Lahore in December 1929, T A K Sherwani and Khaliquzzaman, two of Motilal Nehru's closest followers in UP, resigned from the AICC on the grounds that the Viceroy's 'Dominion Status' declaration of 31 October 1929 deserved greater credit than the Congress had given it.

The actions of several important Muslim politicians reveal the quandary in which nationalist Muslims found themselves at this juncture. Among these were Sherwani and Khaliquzzaman who were both persuaded to accept the new Congress position as the party moved towards another round of militant anti-British agitation. But Muslim leaders like them were no longer entirely comfortable in the Congress. Khaliquzzaman even accepted the position of 'dictator' of the banned national Congress during the Civil Disobedience Movement, but wore the 'crown' rather uneasily for three months. He was a member of the central Congress Parliamentary Board in 1934, but was increasingly concerned about the need for a separate organization of the Muslims. After 1935, he cooperated with the socially conservative and politically reactionary Raja Ali Ahmad Khan of Salempur to revive the UP Muslim League. After 1937, he came to be seen – and certainly saw himself – as one of the most important lieutenants of Jinnah not only in UP, but in the country as a whole.[101]

The 'extremist', Hasrat Mohani who had clashed with Gandhi as early as 1921 when he demanded that the Congress's goal of swaraj should be defined as 'complete independence', provides another example of Muslim ambivalence towards the Congress in later years. He rejected the Nehru Report out of hand. While he supported the idea of an All-Parties' Conference to frame a constitution for India, he also insisted on a settlement of Muslim claims first. In 1929 he was prominent in the sectional Muslim struggle against the Sarda (Restraint of Child Marriages) Act, which Muslims (and indeed orthodox Hindus) considered to be an unwarranted interference with their religion.[102] At the same time he was enthused by the 'rising spirit' of the Indian youth and the growing opinion within the Congress in favour of 'complete independence'. In November 1929 he resigned his membership of the Jamiat-ul-ulema-i-Hind, Kanpur, to make his nationalist commitment clear.[103] He played an active part in the campaign of Civil Disobedience that followed, doing his utmost to persuade his Muslim brethren to join in the struggle. After 1937, he became a powerful propagandist for the Muslim League and an outspoken defender of Muslim interests. Yet all of this jostled with his long-standing advocacy of 'complete independence', and his commitment to 'socialism'; and the idea of the division of the country – when it developed – added further elements of discomfort.

The stand taken by Maulvi Riyasat Husain, a prominent local leader of Rae Bareli serves to illustrate the point further. Here too communal and nationalist feelings are seen to co-exist uneasily. Founder and organizer of the Madrasa Rahmania in Rae Bareli, Riyasat Husain was drawn into the Khilafat and Congress agitation and spent a year in prison. By 1922 he was a recognized leader of the Congress in the district. In the troubled communal situation of the following years, however, he drifted away from the main line of Congress activities. In the late 1920s he spoke at mosques and public meetings on specifically Muslim questions, urging the defence of Muslim rights including the right to decide on the age of a Muslim child's marriage.[104] He must be counted among those who had come to feel that Muslim interests must be protected from the threat of non-Muslim attack and encroachment. Yet the Civil Disobedience Movement, the Government's response to it and growing anti-British feelings in Rae Bareli again brought the anti-imperialist in Riyasat Husain to the fore. In May 1930 he was elected president of the local TCC. Throughout that year and later he appears to have worked for the success of the movement in the town, supplying Congress volunteers with food and urging Muslims to join the Congress.[105]

It is evident now that such efforts on the part of the Muslim leaders still sympathetic to the Congress proved to be of no avail in turning the tide of communalism in UP. The support of a few 'traditional' Muslim leaders, and the *fatwa* issued in April 1930 by the Jamiat-ul-ulema-i-Hind at Deoband declaring the Salt Tax to be 'impious',[106] did little to reduce the increasing suspicion of the Congress in Muslim circles. The extended wrangling at the Round Table Conferences in London on the most appropriate safeguards for Muslims in a future constitutional arrangement, and Congress indecision afterwards appear to have deepened the rift.

One indication of this came with the next round of elections in the mid-1930s. Muslim Congressmen of long standing now showed extreme reluctance to contest elections as Congress candidates. As Khaliquzzaman explained, 'The Communal Award being there, the elections were to be on the basis of separate electorates and as such I was fully convinced that Muslim candidates on the Swaraj Party ticket would have no chance.'[107] Rafi Ahmad Qidwai and other leaders thrown up by the Civil Disobedience Movement now shared the feeling that no Muslim candidate put up by the Congress could win an election fought on the current basis.[108] The opinion was well founded. Not a single Muslim standing as a Congress candidate was elected in UP in February 1937.

Qidwai himself was trounced in the Gonda district (northeast) Muslim constituency by a little known Lucknow lawyer, Ghulam Hasan Butt, who stood as an independent candidate. Qidwai was a prominent lawyer and *zamindar* from Bara Banki district. From 1926 to 1929 he had been secretary and whip of the Swaraj Party in the Legislative Assembly of India, having won the single Muslim seat allotted to the rural areas of Awadh. During the Civil Disobedience Movement he was one of the chief organizers of the no-tax campaign in Rae Bareli and other Awadh districts. He was shortly to be minister in the first Congress Government of UP. Yet in 1936, in a part of Awadh he knew well, Qidwai obtained only 1,525 votes against Ghulam Hasan's 4,104 and the 3,659 votes polled by another Independent, Abdul Qadir Khan.[109] It was striking evidence of the way in which the Congress had lost credibility among wide sections of the Muslims.

VI

The broad mass of Muslims in UP, drawn into the nationalist political arena for the first time after the First World War, thus developed a noticeable distance from the Congress movement within the space of a decade or so. By the 1930s Congress leaders appear to have become well aware of the pitfalls surrounding their position. There was now an insistence in the upper echelons of the leadership on the adoption of a completely secular approach, although at the local level a number of important concessions continued to be made to the communalist Hindu position and to communalist Hindu organizations.[110] At the higher levels the leaders strove manfully to maintain peace between Hindus and Muslims. Their anxiety to prevent clashes on the occasion of religious festivals and other public demonstrations was obvious,[111] and both the Government and the Congress commissions enquiring into the causes of the Kanpur riot of 1931 remarked on this.[112]

In the early 1930s the leaders of the Congress appear to have taken a conscious decision to minimize Civil Disobedience propaganda and activity in areas with a high proportion of Muslims in the population, in order to avoid inflaming communal passions. The pattern of arrests in Allahabad district certainly suggests this (see Table 5.2). It is perhaps not without significance that the smallest number of *satyagrahis* came from the *doab* region where there was a concentration of large Muslim-owned villages. *Tahsil* Chail, for which this was especially true, and *tahsil* Manjhanpur had been the scene of major disturbances in the early 1920s when Kurmi and Ahir tenants rose up against their Muslim landlords. What were basically agrarian conflicts assumed a communal aspect, as Bayly has pointed out in his study of the district, and the Kisan Sabhas therefore began to avoid the area.[113] It appears that in 1930–3 the Congress too adopted the same policy – and this non-involvement with the Muslim population may have been a factor contributing further to the negligible participation by Muslims in the Civil Disobedience Movement.

Table 5.2
Allahabad District Political Prisoners, 1930–3 (Classified by *tahsil*)

	According to:	
	Swatantrata Sangram ke Sainik	*Malaka Gaol List*
The City	179	245
DOAB		
Allahabad or Chail *tahsil* (minus City)	15	13
Sirathu *tahsil*	10	10
Manjhanpur *tahsil*	19	12
TRANS GANGA		
Phulpur *tahsil*	34	38
Soraon *tahsil*	97	55
Handia *tahsil*	87	51
TRANS YAMUNA		
Bara *tahsil*	43	47
Karchana *tahsil*	82	83
Meja *tahsil*	113	100
Tahsil not known	–	11
Total	679	655

Source: Calculated from the addresses and police stations given in *Svatantrata Sangram ke Sainik* for Allahabad district and 'Malaka Gaol List' (Collectorate, Allahabad) respectively. The discrepancies between the two sets of figures arise chiefly because the 'Malaka Gaol List' mentions the police station where an arrest occurred, not that of a prisoner's home. Obviously many of those arrested in the city of Allahabad were villagers from neighbouring tahsils who had gone to the city for demonstrations or public meetings.

At the provincial and national level, the Congress leadership chose at this time to underplay the problem of communalism, to paper over the cracks, and to argue that conflicts between Hindus and Muslims arose only because of the alien presence and that the departure of the British would lead to the disappearance of such strife. There was not a single reference to Hindu–Muslim relations in the resolutions passed by the numerous meetings of UP Congressmen between 14 June 1931 and the end of December 1934.[114] The reactions of the national Congress leadership to the Communal Award of August 1932, again, indicated the extreme difficulty of their position. A small group of Congress leaders, Malaviya among them, condemned the Award in no uncertain terms. They broke away to form a Congress Nationalist Party calling for total opposition to the Communal Award and declaring that 'the nation is greater than the Congress'.[115] The official Congress, however, publicly resolved that it neither accepted nor rejected the Award. Gandhi's fast against the granting of separate electorates to the untouchables, followed by the Poona Pact between representatives of the untouchables and other political leaders, touched on a crucial aspect of the Award and led to an important amendment in it. But the Congress was not now able to say anything about separate electorates and reservations for Muslims. Its initial prevarication and later shamefaced acceptance of the Communal Award earned it little credit among Muslim leaders.

An alternative approach, embodied first in the Muslim Mass Contacts campaign of 1937, and then in the refusal to compromise with 'communal' elements (as they were described) in the formation of the first Congress ministry in UP, as well as in a new emphasis on an 'undiluted' nationalist agenda, miscarried in a similar way. In 1933–4 Jawaharlal Nehru began a frontal assault on the communalist position, accusing communal parties of being 'blissfully ignorant' of the hunger and unemployment among the masses including the lower middle classes. 'The Muslim masses', he wrote, 'are probably even poorer than the Hindu masses, but the 'Fourteen Points' [put forward by Jinnah in 1929 as the minimum demands of the Muslims] say nothing about these poverty-stricken Muslims.'[116]

After the 1936–7 elections, in which the Congress succeeded beyond all expectations in the non-Muslim constituencies of UP but fared poorly in the Muslim ones, Nehru and others decided that such words must be matched by action. A Muslim Mass Contacts programme was then launched under the direction of the Muslim socialist, Kunwar Muhammad Ashraf. I argued in the first edition of this book that this campaign offered too little too late. Others have suggested that it petered out after a promising start because of opposition from various right-wing elements and a more general inability to sustain momentum; or that it failed to get off the ground altogether because it was just not seen as being important enough. After its thumping electoral victory in 1937, it has been said, the opinion that the Congress could, and should, go it alone, increased in strength – and with that an underestimation of the strength of Muslim feelings.[117]

This new belief in the undoubted correctness of its political position may have contributed to the Congress's refusal to accommodate the Muslim League when it came to ministry making after that election.[118] Leaguers who had fought the election in a spirit of cooperation with the Congress, as partners in an informal alliance against colonial rule, were now told that they could join the ministry in UP only if they renounced their membership of the Muslim League and pledged total allegiance to the Congress programme. The same sense of arrogance probably had something to do with the adverse propaganda that the UP ministry, like its Bihar counterpart, generated for what were dubbed its 'anti-Muslim' policies and actions.

The record on all these issues is still unclear. There were certainly instances of the promotion of Hindi, and of local appointments and decisions that appear to have gone against Muslim aspirants in these provinces. There was also a recrudescence of communal strife during this period, including two serious riots in Banaras and Kanpur in 1938 and 1939. On the whole, however, the performance of the UP Congress ministry compared well even in these areas with that of other (Congress and non-Congress) ministries. Indeed, Muslims in the province benefited from several new policy intitiatives, and fared well in the matter of appointments to public service.[119] Be that as it may, the Congress was not able to present its own efforts and achievements in a particularly favourable light, and a general Muslim sense of grievance against the party increased, especially following the publication of the Pirpur and Sharif reports and the intense propaganda that followed in their wake.[120]

Jawaharlal Nehru admitted in 1939 that the Congress leadership had failed to check the spread of anti-Congress feelings among the Muslim masses. Mushirul Hasan concurs. 'After two and a half years of Congress rule,' he writes in an assessment of this period, 'Muslims were profoundly embittered.'[121] Yet, if there was widespread Muslim disillusionment with the Congress by this time, there was no great evidence yet of mass enthusiasm for any Muslim political party. Recall that men like Chowdhry Khaliquzzaman, or the newcomer, the Raja of Mahmudabad, who worked for the revival of the Muslim League from 1936, still saw the Congress and the League as partners, and that the two parties adopted a broadly similar nationalist platform in their election campaign: and in Bengal, the Muslim leadership of the Krishak Praja Party, soon to be assimilated into the Muslim League, adopted an even more radical agrarian programme than the Congress.

Recall too that the Muslim League did not perform very impressively at all in the elections of 1936–7. It obtained a bare 4.4 per cent of the Muslim vote, and won no seats in the North-West Frontier Province, 2 out of 84 reserved seats in Punjab, and 3 out of 33 in Sindh. Even in UP, where the Congress and the League worked in a kind of informal alliance and the Congress had left League candidates unopposed in most constituencies, the League won only 28 of the Muslim seats: as many as 11 of the rural Muslim seats went to the landlords' National Agriculturists' Party and others to Independents.[122] The Bijnor by-election, held in October-November 1937, showed the continuing uncertainty of the relative standing of different parties even in the now polarized political situation. After a tough campaign in a contest that was seen as a major trial of strength, and in which major leaders of both the Congress and the Muslim League took an active part, the Congress candidate Hafiz Muhammad Ibrahim, who had resigned from the Muslim League to join the Congress and become a minister in the Congress government, won with a massive 77.6 per cent of the Muslim vote: the Muslim League candidate obtained the remaining 22.4 per cent.[123]

It is perhaps not wrong to suggest that it was the UP Muslim land-lords, along with a few disillusioned Muslim professionals of the older generation (like Khaliquzzaman) who carried the 'separatist' Muslim League flag in UP into the late 1930s and early 1940s. As many of the older Muslim political leaders of Khilafat times died or faded away, new political elements had emerged – among whom, as among younger Hindu political activists, a composite nationalism remained the dream – and the Left was fairly well represented. Indeed, Aligarh Muslim University, later seen as the arsenal of the Pakistan movement, reflected these political tendencies strongly.[124] It was the formal support of the more deeply-rooted, and in the end more significant, Muslim political leadership in Punjab and Bengal that carried the day for the Muslim League in the mid-1940s: and then, with growing enthusiasm for the Pakistan idea and for Jinnah as the leader of all the subcontinent's Muslims, large numbers of younger Muslim men and women, from Aligarh Muslim University and elsewhere, joined the campaign against the Congress.

VII

In retrospect, if an unthinking 'Hindu' slant in the propaganda and activities of the Congress accounted for part of the problem of growing alienation among Muslims, an equally intractable part of the Congress predicament was that the all-inclusive, nationalist appeal of the party did not allow for any variation between the highly differentiated interests of the sections of the population to which it addressed itself. For a long time in the 1920s the Congress leadership resorted to rather general, at best mildly reformist appeals in its effort to mobilize the Indian 'nation'. There was a single identifiable enemy, and only one long-term goal in the fight for which support was to be sought from all possible quarters. In the 1930s, when it was becoming clear that the absence of a differentially formulated policy had contributed particularly to the emergence among the people of a deep and growing chasm on communal lines, the Congress could still do no better than to try to wish away the problem.

The reluctance of the UP Congress to act decisively on the recommendations of the Congress Committee of Enquiry into the Kanpur Riot illustrates the dilemma. This Committee called for 'a more complete scheme of Swaraj…[to] convince Hindus and Muslims alike that the Congress strives impartially for the moral and material good of all, and does not favour any one community or section at the expense of another, Hindu or Muslim, landholder or tenant, capitalist or labourer'. More specifically, it advocated the establishment of a Standing Congress Board to work for Hindu–Muslim unity; the disqualification of any member of a communal organization from election to any Congress committee; the exposing of the policies and methods of communal leaders; the abolition of separate electorates; and the acceptance by Hindus and Muslims respectively of cow sacrifice and music-before-mosques.[125]

Excepting the first, these recommendations would have proved very difficult indeed for the Congress to implement, even if it had so desired. The abolition of separate electorates was unacceptable to most of the Muslim political class. The proposals regarding cow sacrifice and music-before-mosques were unlikely to find support among the general body of ordinary Hindus and Muslims. It was not until December 1938 that the Congress Working Committee barred elected members of Congress Committees from holding elective positions in the Hindu Mahasabha and the Muslim League, which were now declared to be communal organizations.[126] Even so, the ban was not extended to ordinary members of these two parties. The Congress appeal to all comers prevented such a move, just as it had prevented any clear-cut choice between the interests of *kisans* and those of *zamindars* in the agitations of the early 1920s and early 1930s and in the election campaigns of the mid-1930s.

The fact is that any 'more complete scheme of Swaraj', to use the Kanpur Riot Enquiry Committee's phrase, would have required taking a stand wherever there were clashes of interest between Hindu and Muslim, landholder and tenant, mill owner and labourer. That was precisely the problem that the Congress was up against – and it was a problem that was complicated further by the conditions of the Depression, when the UP Congress had either to let down a suffering tenantry or be seen to work against rent-receivers. Even the limited Congress campaign on behalf of tenants at various junctures in the 1930s had been given a communal colour by Muslim landlords and publicists. At the Round Table Conferences and later, the Congress was accused of stirring up the Hindu tenants against Muslim landlords of the province in particular.[127]

However, if fear of unfortunate 'communal' repercussions was one reason for the hesitant approach adopted by the Congress to agrarian problems in UP at this time, yet another was the fundamental conservatism of the party, arising to a large extent from the very sources of its financial support and the social background of its leadership and cadres. This conservatism, together with the institution of separate electorates and the restricted franchise that gave to the propertied classes a considerable weightage in the electorate, had contributed to the Hindu sectarian bias in the political appeals of the Congress in the 1920s. In the years of the Depression, when large masses of the rural population were in great distress, as well as later in the 1930s and 1940s when widespread agitation developed among the lower castes and classes, the same conservatism led the UP Congress to canvas support on every front, to seek to reduce sectional discord among its potential followers to a minimum, and to avoid taking sides as long as possible when the clash of interests developed into open conflict. The consequences turned out to be no less momentous than those of the Congress stance on the communal question.

6

Mass Mobilization

There were significant differences in the pattern of mass participation in the campaigns of agitation launched by the Congress at different times during the last three decades of British rule in India. An obvious contrast between the Non-Cooperation and the Civil Disobedience Movements, for instance, was that the former was largely an urban event, organized and conducted by townsfolk, whereas the latter was in many areas much more of a villagers' campaign – even if the villagers often went to the towns to shout slogans and court imprisonment.

Among the factors responsible for this difference was the experience of the earlier campaign. The agitations of 1919–22 had not only instilled a new pride in large numbers of Indians and popularized *satyagraha* as a powerful technique of anti-imperialist agitation; they had also indicated that the road to *swaraj* was going to be a long one and that the Government could be iron-handed in putting down what it considered as dangerous opposition. This must go some way towards explaining 'the weariness of the middle-class elements' noticed in different parts of the country at a fairly early stage of the Civil Disobedience Movement.[1] It may also provide part of the explanation for the remarkable decline in Congress membership between the time of Non-Cooperation and that of Civil Disobedience, though as suggested above[2] more methodical calculations and increased checking by the AICC and the PCC were probably responsible for the smaller claims in the later period.

Again, Congress leaders in several provinces were fully aware by the beginning of the 1930s that the success of the nationalist movement depended upon winning the support of the masses in the villages. This awareness probably helped to shift the centre of gravity of the Congress campaign at this time. Certainly (as Chapter 4 has shown) there was a sustained effort in UP in 1930–1 to carry the Congress message to the rural areas. Above all, however, the marked rural orientation of the Civil Disobedience Movement of 1930–3 appears to have come about owing to its coincidence with the world Depression. Jawaharlal Nehru acknowledged this:

> The Civil Disobedience movement of 1930 happened to fit in unbeknown to its own leaders at first, with the great world slump in industry and agriculture. The rural masses were powerfully affected by this slump, and they turned to the Congress and civil disobedience. For them it was not a matter of a fine constitution drawn up in London or elsewhere, but of a basic change in the land system, especially in the *zamindari* areas.[3]

However, the implications of this acknowledgment have never been fully appreciated. What it suggests is that economic conditions and the independent actions of hard-pressed 'apolitical' men and women did much to shape the course of one of the most important nationalist campaigns of agitation and, consequently, of the nationalist movement as a whole. The following pages should show that this was true at least in UP in the 1920s and 1930s.

It must be emphasized, however, that this was by no means a simple case of disparate local grievances being piled on to an opposition bandwagon. As we have already noted,[4] there were particular reasons why a variety of complaints and agitations should have been channelled into a specific political movement. Many of the grievances stemmed from the crisis in world capitalism, of which the Indian economy was now so much a part that an event like the Depression affected even poor and middle peasants deep in the countryside. Many complaints were addressed directly or indirectly to the alien rulers of the country: at the least, people expected the administration to take steps towards alleviating their distress in times of hardship.

Finally, the very presence of the Congress as the principal nationalist party with an organizational network spread over large areas of the subcontinent was a stimulus to mass patriotic action. The fact is that UP was not only a province of 'notoriously bad, harsh landlords',[5] rackrenting and ill-treating their subordinates, but also of Harcourt Butler, the British Governor who was given an honoured place in the Awadh *taluqdars'* fraternity.[6] This, and the belief that the Congress was the 'poor man's party', contributed to the rise of strong *kisan* agitation at the time of the Non-Cooperation and the Civil Disobedience Movements.

II

The view that the Congress became a *kisan* party after 1920 must be set against the evidence of Congress leaders holding down the Oudh peasants' revolt of 1920–1 once it threatened social disruption.[7] Jawaharlal Nehru wrote of his discovery of 'a whole country-side afire with enthusiasm and full of a strange excitement',[8] when he and other nationalists from Allahabad went to southern Awadh in the summer of 1920. That visit occurred when 200 peasants of Pratapgarh, participants in the *Kisan Sabha* movement in Awadh, had marched to Allahabad and demanded that nationalist leaders come out to see their conditions and support their struggle. It was in this way that a somewhat reluctant Nehru was led to his 'discovery' of India; he was, in his own words, 'thrown almost without any will of my own, into contact with the peasantry.' That visit to the villages 'far from the railway and even the *pucca* road...was a revelation to me.' What surprised Jawaharlal was 'our total ignorance' of the rural areas; no newspaper ever carried reports of agrarian questions or events in the villages. 'I realized more than ever how cut off we were from our people and how we lived and worked and agitated in a little world apart from them.'[9]

Nehru was amazed that such a major agrarian struggle 'should have developed quite spontaneously without any city help or intervention of politicians and the like. The agrarian movement was entirely separate from the Congress and it had nothing to do with the Non-Cooperation that was taking shape.'[10] This was an accurate assessment, for long before the involvement of nationalist leaders from Allahabad, the Kisan Sabha movement in Awadh had gathered momentum. Rure, the village in Pratapgarh District where the first local *sabha* had been established, was the centre of the movement in the initial months of its life. During this time, 100,000 peasants were reported to have registered themselves with the association, and there were said to be as many as 585 *panchayats* functioning in Pratapgarh District alone. With the development of urban nationalist support, the movement advanced swiftly to engulf large parts of Pratapgarh, Rae Bareli, Sultanpur, and Faizabad Districts and smaller areas elsewhere. Its strength may be judged from the numbers of peasants reckoned to have turned out for different kinds of demonstrations: 40,000 to 50,000 to press for the release of Baba Ramchandra from the Pratapgarh jail in September 1920, 80,000 to 100,000 for the first Awadh Kisan Congress held in Ayodhya (Faizabad District) in December 1920.

By December 1920/January 1921 the peasant movement in Awadh

had entered another phase. What began as a limited agitation among Kurmi and other middle caste peasants, mainly tenants-at-will and sub-tenants with small holdings, for an improvement of status and a re-laxation of unduly oppressive demands by landlords' agents, had developed by this time into a powerful movement, involving peasants of many different Hindu and Muslim castes, which called into question the entire structure of *zamindari* and, by implication, colonial author-ity in the region. The phenomenal expression of this was a campaign for the non-payment of taxes; open attacks on landlords, moneylend-ers, and the police; and the demand that was once or twice voiced for distribution of land to the tiller. Not long after these militant protests of the Kisan Sabhas had been suppressed in southern Awadh, the move-ment burst forth again in a slightly different form in northern Awadh, and peasants began to come together in Eka associations.

Congressmen and other urban nationalist leaders were not greatly in favour of these autonomous demands and tactics of the Awadh peasantry. Hence Jawaharlal's comment on Baba Ramchandra, that 'remarkable person' who had taken a most prominent part in organizing the Kisan Sabha movement in Awadh:

> Having organised the peasantry to some extent he made *all man-ner of promises* to them, vague and nebulous but full of hope for them. He had *no programme of any kind* and when he had brought them to a pitch of excitement he *tried to shift the responsibility to others*... Ramachandra continued to take a prominent part in the agrarian movement for another year and served two or three sen-tences in prison, but he turned out later to be *a very irresponsible and unreliable person*.[11]

By the early 1920s Congress leaders had acknowledged that the peasants must form 'the bulwark of the nationalist movement'.[12] For all that, peasant agitation was for these leaders still something of a journey into the unknown at this time. Lack of experience of peasant struggle, however, less easily accounts for the leadership's reactions a decade later, when they were fully aware that the success of the nationalist movement was dependent upon peasant support, another severe economic crisis struck and peasant unrest and agitation again arose in UP. Yet, an analysis of the progress of the Civil Disobedience Movement in different parts of the province, which reveals substantial popular participation in the campaign (and the importance of local initiative in bringing this about), reveals also the severe limits within which the Congress wished to restrict its mobilization of 'the masses'. Both these aspects are amply illustrated by the experience of Agra and Rae Bareli, two districts that were to the fore in the civil disobedience campaign.

For UP Agra was a fairly 'advanced' district. It had once rivalled Kanpur as an industrial centre and still had prosperous industries in its headquarters city and in Firozabad town. It was also an important centre of commercial activity and, with its good educational facilities, one of the most 'literate' districts in the province.[13] The prosperity of some of its urban sectors did not, however, extend to the district as a whole. Bordering on the Rajasthan desert, Agra was drier and less densely populated than districts further east or north:[14] the average rainfall was 26 inches per year, the density of rural population 590 per cultivated square mile. Wheat and barley were the major *rabi* (spring) crops. The chief *kharif* (monsoon) ones were bajra and jowar and the scarce rainfall allowed little cultivation of rice. The acreage under cotton was declining in the late 1920s while that under sugar cane increased significantly, especially after the sugar industry was granted protection in 1931.

The district had only a handful of really big landowners and a wealth of small landlords and rich peasants, nearly two-thirds of them resident. In addition, the majority of tenants held occupancy rights. Yet it would be misleading to conjure out of all this the picture of a haven of contented yeoman peasants. The topography of Agra, the path of its rivers and the uncertainty of its canal irrigation system made its agricultural conditions very uneven. In parts of the district, especially the *tahsils* south of the Yamuna, cultivation was not a very profitable occupation and the majority of tenants and peasant proprietors were in debt. In the half-century before 1930 something like 20 per cent of the land had passed into the hands of moneylenders,[15] an index of the precarious position of many of its smaller proprietors.

Again the district had, for Agra province, a relatively high proportion of statutory and non-occupancy tenants. These occupied a quarter of the cultivated area. There was also a large percentage of high-caste tenants and 'peasant proprietors' who did not touch the plough: out of a total of 800,000 acres of holdings, Brahmans and Thakurs alone held 300,000, that is 37.5 per cent.[16] As a consequence there was a significant incidence of sub-letting. In general both non-occupancy tenants and sub-tenants met a high rental demand, as we have already noticed.[17] This meant that in years of scarcity or low prices large numbers of peasants in the Agra villages came under heavy pressure. Yet few of them were so completely under the thumb of their overlords or the agents of their overlords as their counterparts in Awadh districts like Rae Bareli.

Rae Bareli was better provided for than Agra in terms of rainfall and fertility of the soil. The average annual rainfall was 38 inches, and only on two occasions between the settlements of 1897 and 1929 had it been much below 25 inches, whereas in Agra in dry years the rainfall could be as low as 15–18 inches or less and unevenly distributed over the district into the bargain. This difference in rainfall accounted for differences in the cropping pattern of these districts in two respects. One was the cultivation of rice on a larger scale in Rae Bareli. The other was the relative immutability over time of the cropping pattern in this district, compared to fairly major changes in the acreages under different crops in Agra during the first three decades of the twentieth century.[18]

Despite these advantages in natural resources, however, Rae Bareli appeared poor in comparison with Agra owing to the density of its rural population (over 990 persons per cultivated square mile), the low level of urban development and literacy and, above all, the concentration of its land and wealth in a very few hands. *Taluqdars* held no less than three-fifths of the district and in 1929 there were 44 estates paying annual revenue of Rs 5,000 or more. In the single *parganah* of Dalmau, which was particularly prominent in the Civil Disobedience campaign, 228 out of 295 *mahals* were held by *taluqdars* and the rest by *zamindars* and coparcenary communities. The largest *taluqdari* estate in the *parganah*, Khajurgaon, covered 88 *mahals*, and there were many others that extended over 10 or more.

Moreover, estates in southern Awadh had been in a settled condition longer, and were therefore more compact and secure than those in the rest of the province. This led to far greater control by the landlords and their agents. Thus in the quarter-century preceding the second settlement of Rae Bareli district, the *taluqdars* substantially improved their position. The sub-settled area[19] declined owing chiefly to the ejectment of sub-settlement holders by *taluqdars*. There were also a disproportionately high number of mortgages in coparcenary and sub-settled estates and land held by underproprietors. 'Taluqdars are the principal buyers of land in the district,' wrote the Settlement Officer. 'After them, but with a long interval, come the large Brahman moneylenders, the small Baniya *mahajans* and the professional classes.'[20]

The privileges of other groups on the estates were also reduced. There was a rapid all-round increase in rents and a general levelling of rates.

The greatest increase occurred in Salon *tahsil*. Since the position of the Rajput notables had not been well established here at the time of British annexation of Awadh in 1856, rent-rates had been lower than elsewhere in Rae Bareli. Hence there was a felt need to make up for lost ground. The gap between rents paid by Brahmans and Rajputs and those paid by lower castes was narrowed. In the early 1880s it was also found that Rajput and Brahman tenants held less land than they had done earlier, and that they were served more ejectment notices than tenants of other castes. The landlord no longer needed to keep the Rajput soldier on the estate to fight for him or the Brahman priest to legitimize his rule, and he saw no reason to let out land at concessional rates to men who would probably be less subservient than their lower caste, or better still, untouchable brethren.[21]

Ejectment notices were only one of the means by which the *taluqdars* asserted their authority. They fought too against the registration of the rights of subordinates, whether recently acquired or of long standing. For similar reasons most of them were 'systematically opposed to any improvements...being carried out by the tenants'.[22] Where permission to make improvements was granted it was usually done after a *bazdawa*, i.e. a relinquishment by the tenant of any claims to compensation for the improvement.[23] The fear of the accrual of new rights may also explain the reluctance of landlords to have wasteland reclaimed. Rae Bareli had a smaller proportion of land under cultivation and a larger area of cultivable waste than other districts in southern Awadh. Yet, according to the Revenue Department of the UP Government, the *taluqdars* preferred 'rather to have old lands improved [cf. above evidence] and rent raised than to have new land broken up.'[24]

Taluqdari dominance in Rae Bareli, then, made for a low level of security for the subordinate classes in the district. Occupancy tenants held only 1.5 per cent of the area of the district, while 72 per cent was in the hands of men with no occupancy rights. The rents paid by this mass of unprotected tenants had shot up in the period of high prices after the First World War (see table 6.1). So much so that, in the opinion of the Governor of UP, 'there were many cases where they were most distinctly high and can only have been collected in ordinary times with a good deal of pressure...there must be a large number of individual cases in which rents have in recent years been worked up to figures so high that I should not have cared to have quoted them publicly'.[25] In addition the levying of illegal cesses continued, the Awadh Rent Amendment Act notwithstanding. The report on the third settlement of Rae Bareli district in 1929 observed that the *nazrana* system existed 'with very insignificant exceptions, in all taluqdari and single zamindari estates, and has begun to spread also to coparcenary estates'. The average *nazrana* paid by that stage was the equivalent of two year's rent for admission to a holding, and the equivalent of one year's rent for readmission.[26] Sub-tenants generally bore an even heavier burden, in terms of demands for cesses and services – and they constituted a slightly higher proportion here than in Agra district.[27]

Table 6.1
Index of Prices, Rents and Revenue in UP, 1916–34
(Average 1901–5 = 100)

Year	Wholesale prices	Rents (stable tenants)	Rents (ordinary tenants)	Land revenue demand	Agricultural wages
1916	160	111	121	104	120
1917	158	111	122	104	–
1918	200	111	125	104	–
1919	258	109	128	104	–
1920	243	113	133	107	–
1921	258	114	134	108	–
1922	236	115	137	108	–
1923	182	117	139	108	–
1924	187	118	142	108	–
1925	220	119	144	109	–
1926	230	120	146	109	–
1927	217	120	146	109	–
1928	213	120	146	109	–
1929	218	120	165	110	180
1930	162	121	166	111	–
1931	112	121	165	112	–
1932	119	120	162	112	–
1933	114	121	161	112	–
1934	103	121	161	113	120

Source: B R Misra, **Land Revenue Policy in the United Provinces Under British Rule** (Banaras 1942), 260–1; **Agricultural Prices in the United Provinces**, Bureau of Statistics and Economic Research, UP, Bulletin No 1, (Allahabad 1937), 51–2.

It is significant, however, that in spite of the erosion of the rights of ex-proprietors and other privileged groups on the Rae Bareli estates, and in spite of the fact that the rent-rate of the district generally was high even by Awadh standards, there is little evidence of resistance to the demands of the landlords until well into the twentieth century. It was observed at the turn of the century that for the previous twenty years the revenue from the district had been realized 'with the greatest of ease'; that 96.7 per cent of the rental demand had been met on average; and that the only source of any trouble had been some *pattidars* of Salon *tahsil* who had never formed part of a *taluqdari* estate.[28] What this suggests is that an explanation of peasant movements in such areas in the nineteenth and twentieth centuries simply in terms of a disjunction between the realities of power in rural India and the political structure established by the colonial administration – meaning, for Awadh, a persistent tension between so-called 'area controllers' and 'village leaders'[29] – is misleading. Conditions varied significantly even within the limited area of Awadh; 'village leaders' in Rae Bareli at any rate appear to have been in no position to challenge the authority of the absentee landlord. The evidence regarding the social origins of the peasant rebels of the 1920s and 1930s and the orientation of their struggle suggests too that interests other than those of 'village controllers' played a large part in the movements at this time, even if the village notables took the initiative at certain stages.[30] It is necessary, therefore, to take account of the intervention of new factors in this period that served to exacerbate a variety of existing tensions in the villages of southern, central and eastern Awadh, the districts of the *doab*, Kumaun and a few other areas which were the scene of rural protest.

At the end of the 1920s, there was a catastrophic fall in the price of food grains after more than a decade of high prices, during which rents and cesses had been increased and the upper rural classes had grown accustomed to substantial profits from the produce of the land (table 6.1). 'Nothing like the chute of prices in 1930–31 had been observed before in provincial history,' a UP government official observed.[31] 'The prices were reduced to half in about a year's time. No other period of such short duration in the history of Indian prices shows such a violent change', commented another.[32]

Men with fixed incomes and urban dwellers generally benefited from the new situation, though factory workers suffered some retrenchment. Regarding agricultural labourers, official opinion was that 'thanks, partly to the increasing purchasing power of money, partly to rural custom, wage-earners have certainly suffered little loss, certainly far less than their employers.'[33] We have seen, however, that rural custom was no bar to the imposition of new burdens by the upper classes upon the lower. In the matter of wages too the statistics suggest an all-round decline at this time. Interestingly, for labourers who were paid in kind there appears to have been a greater decline than for those who received their wages in cash: here even the increased buying power of money was inconsequential.[34] In addition, in some areas there was a reduction of job opportunities on account of the straitened circumstances of employers and increased competition from petty tenants forced to relinquish their lands. One reflection of this was a perceptible increase in the movement of people from the villages to the towns.[35]

Nevertheless, landless labourers, paid mostly in cash by the 1920s, living at subsistence level and having minimal contact with the market, probably experienced less change in their circumstances than various other rural classes. The bigger landlords, substantial rural *mahajans* and town-based *sahukars* were of course affected by the difficulty of collecting dues and arrears. In most cases, however, they had enough savings and credit to tide them over the crisis. Smaller *zamindars* and *pattidars* and upper-caste rent-receivers were badly hit; they liked to maintain a life-style befitting their 'status' and were often the groups most heavily in debt.

The worst sufferers almost certainly were tenants and subtenants with smallholdings. This included the majority of the large body of non-occupancy tenants in Awadh and the mass of depressed peasants who scraped a living from the soil in the eastern-most divisions of UP. Of the 'typical' cultivator in these areas, an official wrote as follows in 1933: 'At the present time he owns fewer cattle than he did; he has sold or pawned his ornaments freely; his reserves of hoarded silver are much reduced; his crops have not only fallen in value, but for four years past have been indifferent; and in many cases he must have lost his most important subsidiary asset, namely his *jajmani*.'[36]

This comment took note of a second factor that adversely affected the position of peasants and landowners in UP in the late 1920s. Insufficient or unseasonal rain played havoc with the crops in many areas and caused widespread hardship. The drought of 1928 produced a disastrous shortfall in food production all over UP and there were considerable fluctuations in the amount of agricultural produce in the years that followed.[37]

A statement of actual results in the *rabi* of 1930 and the *kharif* of 1931 helps to indicate the severity of the problem. For the *rabi* of 1930 there was a decrease of 8 per cent in the cultivated area of the province as a whole. But the cutback was greatest in Agra division, as much as 37.6 per cent. In Awadh the area sown actually increased by 10.5 per cent and the result was a record harvest of wheat, the best since 1921.

The *kharif* of 1931, on the other hand, suffered from heavy rains in October which destroyed the standing crop in many parts of UP. Agra was one of the two districts where the calamity was widespread; here the Government was constrained to make a flat revenue remission of four annas in the rupee.[38]

In normal circumstances the bumper *rabi* of 1930 would have led to a definite improvement of living conditions in Awadh, if only for a while. Coming with the slump in prices, however, the larger crop did little to ease the situation of the majority of the peasants. Agra suffered doubly, with a reduced output accompanying the decline in prices. Added to this there was an increase in the demand of revenue and, in many cases, of rent consequent upon a revision of settlements in certain districts. Agra and Rae Bareli were among these. In Agra there was a small increase in the revenue demand, Rs 117,000 or 5.5 per cent. In Rae Bareli the increase was greater, Rs 218,000 or 12 per cent,[39] and this was quickly passed on to the lower classes.

III

Economic changes of this kind seriously affected the well-being of large numbers of people in the villages of UP and prepared the ground for the intensity of rural agitation during the Civil Disobedience campaign. But there were other factors of importance, too, in determining the shape and course of political developments. Crucial among these were the actions of the Government, peasant resistance of varying degrees, and the organization and propaganda of the Congress in different areas.

In Rae Bareli, for example, there were reports of stirrings among the peasantry as early as 1928–9 – quite independently of any Congress initiative.[40] An important reason for this was the enhancement of rents and illegal cesses that followed the enhancement of revenue at the new settlement, just when a series of poor seasons had culminated in the drought of 1928–9. Officials did take some notice of the unfavourable agricultural situation, postponing the introduction of the new revenue demands. But the Government was unwilling, and to some extent unable, to do anything to restrain the landlords from raising rents and other cesses, which was the immediate cause of peasant discontent.

Official measures to deal with the crisis of the Depression proved to be even more unsatisfactory and offered little relief to the poorer peasant groups. At the time when the *kharif* of 1930 was harvested, the Government expressed the view that 'the extent and duration of the fall in prices [are] still uncertain'.[41] Hailey asserted, as late as May 1931, that neither sugar nor rice had been affected by the slump[42] – statistics to the contrary notwithstanding. The Government sanctioned a remission of Rs 10 lakhs in the revenue due from the province as a whole for the *kharif* of 1930, on the simple condition that landlords observe the law in the matter of rental remissions. This brought little relief to tenants, especially in Awadh, where the landlord was obliged by law to remit only twice the amount of revenue remitted and in practice often refused to do even that. Perhaps because of the presence of stronger and more autonomous bodies of tenants, Agra landlords tended on the whole to comply better with their Tenancy Act, which required a remission of rent in the same proportion as Government's remission of revenue.

By March 1931 it had become apparent, even to the Government, that the slump was more than 'a passing phase'. Officials now worked out a scheme that gave rent relief to statutory tenants, in both Agra and Awadh, and to occupancy tenants who had obtained their rights within the preceding twelve years, i.e. to the tenants whose rents had risen sharply with the post World War I price rises. The aim was to bring their rents back 'roughly' to the level of 1915 and to make a proportionate remission of revenue for both Agra and Awadh landlords. Thus a total of Rs 60 lakhs of revenue and Rs 207 lakhs of rent was remitted for the *rabi* of 1931.

By mid-1931 the defects of this second government scheme were obvious. It became clear that the stable tenants also needed some relief. So, obviously, did the cultivating proprietors who had earlier been granted no remissions on the ground that they received little or no rentals and hence suffered no loss in terms of income from rents. Besides, it was now acknowledged that prices had fallen to the level of 1901, not 1915. This created a new problem. It was feared that revenue remissions based solely on the amount of rent remitted would, if rents were brought down to the 1901 level, lower the land revenue far below the 1901 figure and result in bankruptcy for the provincial government.

Ultimately the Government decided, following the proposals of a Rent and Revenue Committee appointed by the UPLC in July 1931, that rents should be remitted after reference not only to the fall in prices between 1928–9 and 1930–1 but also to the actual enhancement of rents between 1900–1 and 1930–1. There were two other important conditions. First, no rent was to be reduced below the 1900–1 level. This meant the absence of any relief for the many occupancy tenants in

Agra whose rents had not risen in the 30 years before the Depression. Secondly, no remission of rent was to exceed more than eight annas in the rupee. The total rental remission calculated by this method for the new agricultural year, 1931–2, amounted to Rs 412 lakhs – though of course there was no way of ensuring a just distribution.[43]

The manner of revenue remission, however, did not, in any case, follow the wishes of the landholders in the UPLC – 'the elected representatives of the agriculturist classes' (in the Government's phrase)[44] who dominated the Rent and Revenue Committee. Instead of making a remission of revenue directly proportionate to the remission of rent, as the latter desired, the Government first calculated 40 per cent of the actual reduced assets of landowners:[45] this gave a revenue remission of Rs 74 lakhs for UP. To this the Government added Rs 38 lakhs to cover the greater loss of rents in older assessed or lightly assessed districts and, importantly, to give some relief to cultivating proprietors. The final result was a remission of Rs 108 lakhs. With only minor modifications this scheme of remissions was maintained in the following years.

A principal drawback in all the government measures to adjust rents was the failure to take any account of *nazrana* and other illegal cesses. The districts of Awadh and parts of Agra, chiefly in Gorakhpur division, suffered badly from this. The absurdity of the Government's approach is evident from a comparison of the remissions forthcoming in Agra and Rae Bareli districts for the years 1930–1 and 1931–2 (1338 and 1339 *Fasli*).

Table 6.2

Remissions in	Agra	Rae Bareli
Kharif 1930	Rs 119,453 revenue. Proportionate remission of rent.	–
Rabi 1931	Rs 340,764 revenue. Rs 1,047,000 rent.	Rs 208,052 revenue. Rs 560,191 rent.
Kharif 1931	4 anna remission of revenue owing to destruction of crop. Proportionate remission of rent.	Not applicable
Kharif 1931 and *Rabi* 1932	General remissions of rent and revenue based on the proposals of the UPLC's Rent and Revenue Committee.	

While the revenue due from these districts was only slightly greater in the case of Agra, and the percentage of land held as *sir* and *khudkasht*, that is, not rented out but retained for the landowner's personal cultivation, was higher in Agra than in Rae Bareli, Agra tenants (and landowners) received far greater relief than their Rae Bareli counterparts until the last quarter of 1931. The latter obtained no remissions for the *kharif* of 1930 since the Government was of the opinion that rice prices had held up. In the *rabi* of 1931 the rental remission for Rae Bareli was just over half that granted to Agra, in accordance with their respective rental situations on paper. The Government's later and more carefully calculated measures to bring relief to the agricultural population still refused to consider the question of unrecorded rents in allocating remissions for the tenantry. In addition, the inefficiency of local administration[46] and the greed and power of intermediaries meant that even the sanctioned remissions were not available in full to the tenants – and in this respect too those in Awadh generally suffered more than their opposite numbers in Agra.

Given the Government's handling of the crisis it was not surprising that an explosive situation soon arose in southern and central Awadh. But acute economic privation and the insufficiency of remissions were only part of the reason for this: otherwise there was no reason why tension should not have been as great in other parts of UP and especially in the rest of Awadh. The peculiar landlord–tenant relations of the area and the experience of earlier struggle made their own contributions to the development of conflict.

As we have noted southern Awadh was the scene of the unprecedented *kisan* agitation of 1920–1 that constituted a substantial part of Jawaharlal Nehru's discovery of the 'real India'. The *taluqdars* had only reluctantly agreed to the Government's amendment of the Awadh Rent Act immediately afterwards. Subsequently they had done everything they could to strengthen their positions even through the provisions of the new law. Faced with the prospect of another powerful peasant agitation in 1930–1, they were determined to prevent any further erosion of their authority, and the provincial Government did all it could to support them. Agents of the landlords and the Government used force freely in the effort to exact dues and obtain the submission of peasants. The Government's special concern for the *taluqdar* was also reflected in the fact that, in the calculation of the revenue remission in the latter half of 1931, the loss of *nazrana* had been taken into account. Consequently in certain Awadh districts, and in certain villages and *mahals* in Agra, the amount of revenue remitted actually exceeded the amount of rental remission.[47] Such official actions did more than a little to exacerbate the situation in Rae Bareli and other districts.

In a number of these districts the successes of the 1920–1 agitation, and the continued presence of famous peasant leaders such as Baba Ramchandra, proved to be an important source of inspiration for the discontented peasantry. By contrast most districts in Agra province had no recent example of successful peasant resistance. Nor was there quite the same tension here between pampered landlord and insecure tenant as existed in Awadh, though there were signs of growing strains after the passing of the Agra Tenancy Act of 1926.[48]

A final factor of significance in the development of agitation in different areas was the strength of the local Congress organization and the extent of its propaganda. It was for political as well as for economic reasons that numerous districts in UP reached crisis point in the winter of 1930–1, resulting in a widespread and well-publicized 'no-tax' campaign. Rae Bareli and Agra were among the districts where this campaign was strongest, and a detailed examination of rural agitation in the two districts reveals the difference that the Congress presence made, in more than one way, to the nature and quality of the agitation.

I V

The renewed burst of Congress activity in 1928–9 after the hiatus of the mid-1920s affected Agra and Rae Bareli in common with other districts. In Agra the strong city Congress organization and special organs such as the Hindi weekly *Sainik*, published by the district Congress leader, Sri Krishna Dutt Paliwal, facilitated the Congress's task, of propaganda and mobilization. The nationalist effort made rapid advance, especially after the visit of the Simon Commission to Agra and other cities in UP in November and December 1928. Agra Congress leaders also made a concerted bid to extend their influence in the villages.[49] In Rae Bareli nationalist organization was not so strong, but Congress propaganda in the district received a boost when settlement operations and poor seasons created unrest among sections of the peasantry.[50]

After the decision of the Lahore Congress to go ahead with a campaign of civil disobedience, Congress workers in UP turned their attention increasingly to the villages. In both Agra and Rae Bareli there was much talk of *swaraj*, the boycott of foreign cloth, *kisan* unity and the need for greater loans and remissions. In Rae Bareli appeals for the non-payment of rent and revenue increases were also heard.[51] Sometimes little known local men went further and advocated the total withholding of taxes, including rents,[52] a fact of some importance, as we shall see presently. When Gandhi began his march to Dandi, salt and Gandhi became major issues of agitation. In October 1930 the UP Congress officially launched a 'no-tax' campaign. From then until the end of the Civil Disobedience Movement, except for the period of the 'truce' from March to December 1931, the non-payment of taxes was perhaps the most important part of the Congress programme in the province.

In Agra the success of the salt *satyagraha* in small towns and large village centres such as Shahdara and Runkata and the decline of mass agitation after the arrest of important district leaders in April 1930 revealed the far-flung influence of the district Congress organization and the importance of Congress initiative in bringing about local demonstrations. The involvement of significant numbers of landlords, village officials and rural schoolteachers in the campaign also indicated the success of the Congress effort to gain support from all classes.[53] The penetration of such elements into the village-level Congress organization, and the very efficiency of the Agra Congress machine, which ensured control by the leadership, impeded the development of anti-landlord struggle. This is clear from the pattern of popular agitation in the district after October 1930 to which we shall turn presently.

In Rae Bareli the movement advanced rather differently. The 'economic' aspect of mass agitation was more evident from the start. As early as April 1930 the local Congress was forced to abandon some of its chosen centres for the salt *satyagraha* and soon afterwards this *satyagraha* was shelved altogether concurrently with the decision to lay more 'stress on the economic side.'[54] The arrest of the handful of known Congress leaders in the district certainly led to some decline in rural protest, but more notably it made for a clearer focus for the substantial political propaganda and agitation that continued in the villages.[55] In June the 'dictator' of the district Congress, Kalka Prasad, intensified the picketing of village liquor shops and extended 'no-rent' propaganda coupled with promises of smaller rents under *swaraj*. His arrest for these activities led to a complete hartal in 'a few small bazaars' (as the Intelligence Department put it),[56] a reflection of his considerable following in parts of the district. On 19 August 1930, to take another instance of Rae Bareli's peasant protests at this time, *kisans* in the Mustafabad circle practised civil disobedience by grazing their cattle on fields belonging to local landholders. Intelligence officials acknowledged that 'no district leader was present'.[57]

In the period after October 1930 the differences in the nature of popular agitation in Agra and Rae Bareli, and also the conflicting interests of 'responsible' Congress leaders on the one hand and local 'militants' on the other, became abundantly clear. Taking a cue from the Bardoli *satyagraha*, the Agra Congress decided on an intensive and concentrated agitation in two villages of every *tahsil* after the PCC Council's authorization of a selective 'no-tax' campaign. City and district leaders who were released in October and November 1930 and *Sainik*, now something like the official organ of the Agra Congress, enthusiastically took up the new task.[58]

The 'no-tax' campaign was inaugurated in villages Barauda and Bhilaoti in Kiravali *tahsil* in December. From there it spread to other *tahsils* and villages. The Congress claimed that altogether 95 villages took part in the campaign and refused to pay taxes,[59] 20 of these in Etmadpur *tahsil*. By February 1931, according to Congress reports, 55 villages in Etmadpur *tahsil* alone had Prabhat Pheris and 50 had their own Bal Bharat Sabhas. In Firozabad *tahsil* 90 villages had National Village Panchayats, and over 200 villages celebrated Independence Day on 26 January 1931. On that day, 68 villages in the district claimed to have more than 200 persons each at their celebrations, and over 1,000 people were reported to have taken part, in every instance, in processions and meetings held in Khandauli, Pinahat, Bah, Okhra, Nagla Ajeeta and other villages.[60]

The evidence suggests that a strong organizational effort lay behind this Congress success. The method of the Barauda–Bhilaoti campaign clearly testifies to this. Well-known Congress workers were posted in the villages in October 1930 to expedite preparations. Jayanti Prasad and Sobaran Singh were sent to Barauda and Muneer Khan to Bhilaoti. On his release from gaol in December after his second arrest, Paliwal inspected the two villages. He obtained written pledges from *zamindars* as well as tenants that they would remain steadfast in the *satyagraha*.[61] After that:

> …from 15 December to 21 December, Agra celebrated Khadi Week. The sixth day, i.e. 20 December, was celebrated as Barauda-Bhilaoti Day in the city. In the morning a flag salutation ceremony, and *kabaddi* matches and other sports were held. In the afternoon, a thousand volunteers and some men and women from Barauda, Bhilaoti took out a grand procession. In the evening a meeting

was held in which Mr Paliwal announced that…because the Gita Week [?] was to end in Barauda-Bhilaoti the next day, a great sacrifice would take place there. In the morning there would be flag songs, until the afternoon religious recitation, and after that the distribution of *prasad*.

On the following day, in spite of the precautions, orders and actions of an alarmed administration, thousands of people congregated in the two villages and 'The *Gita* was read, *prasad* distributed, and speeches made on the non-payment of taxes.'[62]

The next step in this *satyagraha* was the desertion of the two villages. Brutal action on the part of the police – the looting of property, the driving away of animals, and the destruction of crops – seems to have led to this mass exodus.[63] There was no other means of avoiding the forced payment of taxes. Hence small landlords, peasant proprietors and cultivating tenants and labourers left, many of them to live in open fields for a few days before the Congress could provide them with any alternative accommodation.[64] Barauda, a village of Jats whose leader Bhanwar Singh was to become a force in the Civil Disobedience campaign of the district generally, was completely deserted. 'For two months,' says the Congress history of the *satyagraha*, 'even the village dog was not seen.'[65] In Bhilaoti success was less complete and some men paid up their taxes. Even so, 300 out of its 435 inhabitants left the village, returning only after the Congress-Government 'truce' came into force.

The *satyagraha* in Barauda and Bhilaoti showed all the marks of efficient organization and sustained propaganda. Bardoli was an appropriate idea: like Bardoli, Barauda and Bhilaoti were, for the Congress leadership, struggles primarily against the British Raj and secondarily for peasant rights. In the villages that took up the 'no-tax' campaign after Barauda and Bhilaoti, Congress leaders tried to maintain this pattern. It was deemed right to avoid an anti-landlord agitation, though one might become inevitable, as happened in village Jarar,[66] when the landlord openly allied himself with the foreign Government. The major object was to broaden the anti-imperialist movement as far as possible while keeping it firmly under the control of the Congress.

With the signing of the Gandhi–Irwin Pact in March 1931, a change of tactics became necessary. Congress leaders returning 'victoriously' from jail descended on the Agra villages in large numbers.[67] *Sainik* declared that the UP Government had done little for the *kisans* and that the latter should join the Congress to gain redress of their grievances.[68]

The number of rural meetings increased and Congress branches – including *panchayats* and arbitration boards – spread further into the countryside.[69] In one crucial respect, however, the approach of the Agra Congress had changed. Its leaders now said that 'land revenue should not be withheld', while suggesting that 'remissions should be asked for'.[70] They themselves appealed to the Government for substantial remissions, enquired into any reports of the continued non-payment of taxes and helped *zamindars* realize 'reasonable' and 'proper' rents.[71]

In May 1931 the Achal Gram Seva Sangh was established in Agra, following a PCC directive that Kisan Sanghas should be set up in every district. Seth Achal Singh, a prominent local *rais* and Congress leader financed this association. Paliwal became its president and other important Congressmen, including Achal Singh, Chandradhar Johri and Jaspatrai Kapur, joined the executive committee. Among the objects of the Sangh was the distribution of free medicine, the teaching of agricultural reform, health and cleanliness, the education and organization of villagers and the encouragement of a spirit of cooperation among *kisans, zamindars* and all castes and religions.[72] It looked very much as though the Trade Union of Barauda and Bhilaoti had become the Social Service League of Seth Achal Singh.

Henceforth the Achal Gram Seva Sangh guided much of the Congress work in the rural areas of the district. Congress workers preached self-help, collected statistics and of course spoke of the insufficiency of remissions, a complaint that Agra *zamindars* were making at the same time.[73] At a typical meeting in July 1931, the Tahsil Kisan Conference at Achnera, Paliwal who was in the chair spoke of the need to reduce rents, bribes, interest rates and military expenditure, and to increase agricultural produce and government loans which would enable peasants to pay off debts to moneylenders. In addition he compared the action of a Congressman, Achal Singh, who had given Rs 15,000 to help 'peasants who joined the Congress', with that of the British Collector who received a pay of Rs 2,200 every month.[74] In September 1931, Jawaharlal Nehru visited Agra and, while advising local workers to be prepared to renew the struggle at any time, asked them to concentrate for the present on 'quiet constructive work'.[75]

Yet the extreme hardships of large numbers of peasants, which had been the chief cause of the 'success' of the peasant *satyagraha* in Barauda-Bhilaoti and elsewhere, remained. Government officials noted in May 1931 that 'economic distress' accounted for the still slow payment of taxes.[76] A 'Manifesto to the *kisans*', issued by Gandhi in that month, and the open efforts of various provincial Congress leaders to 'champion' the cause of *kisans* in the more troubled districts, gave the defaulting peasants further support in their stand. 'Peasants are taking shelter under Congress instructions and postponing full payment in the hope of more remissions,' the Intelligence Department reported.[77] Unrest among sections of the Agra peasantry was so great at this time that even a strong Congress presence could not always prevent violence. Shahjagarhi in Etmadpur *tahsil*, with 80 registered Congress members among its 97 families, a total of 540 people, illustrated this in a serious clash on 27 June 1931. Villagers resisted an attempt to attach some of their property. The police opened fire, killed 4 persons, injured 14 others and arrested another 16.[78] The DCC then appointed a committee to enquire into the incident, and asked the District Magistrate to nominate two persons to the committee. The officer's refusal played into Congress's hands; the Government was seen to be callous by contrast with the concern shown by the Congress.

Such publicity, however, achieved little. For all its organizational and propaganda efforts the Congress lost much of its influence in the Agra villages during the Gandhi–Irwin 'truce'. The granting of remissions on a larger scale than ever before, as well as punitive measures taken by the Government, such as the initial withholding of remission notices from villages that had taken part in Civil Disobedience and the use of the police force in the collection of dues,[79] played a part in this. But the Congress's own actions substantially contributed to its decline. Having worked large numbers of peasants up to fever pitch in late 1930-early 1931, the Congress had suddenly called off the campaign. What the peasants had gained from the *satyagraha* was not entirely clear. In Barauda and Bhilaoti fields and houses still lay ruined; there was no proper *rabi* crop in March-April 1931, and the *kharif* was not due until the autumn. Peasants in such villages as Shahjagarhi wanted a lead in their fight against tax collectors, more than enquiry committees. The failure of the district Congress to provide this leadership meant a loss of support.

By the second half of 1931 militant Congress propaganda in Agra district appeared to have ceased completely. Congress leaders drifted back to the city. At the end of that year, when Allahabad and other districts decided to renew the 'no-tax' campaign, Agra was found unready for such agitation. 'There was no "no-rent" campaign in Agra after 1931,' a prominent Congress leader of the district recalled later.[80]

Certainly the second phase of the Civil Disobedience Movement proved to be much more of an urban exercise in Agra than the first.[81] Volunteers were still enlisted and some funds collected in the rural areas. There were also occasional 'no-rent'/'no-tax' appeals. Moreover the Intelligence Department reported in May 1932 that the tenants of Barauda had again withheld rents, that some *zamindars* had applied for the realization of rent arrears as arrears of revenue, and that the tenants had therefore removed all moveable property.[82] The district Congress supported this protest to a certain extent. Yet Barauda was a special, isolated case and even in Barauda, as the local *zamindar's* appeal for government help indicates, support for the Congress campaign had declined considerably.

As it happened, the renewed Congress campaign was unable to generate much enthusiasm even in the urban areas. From the last months of 1932, the Congress in Agra began to pool its resources with those of neighbouring districts. In addition the younger Congress leaders resorted to various kinds of 'spectacular' activity in order to create some impact. Apart from the staging of illegal nationalist conferences, they organized 'raids' on confiscated Congress property, the cutting of telegraph and telephone wires, the burning of postal pillar boxes and first class railway carriages, the blowing up of small bridges and the distribution of anti-imperialist leaflets on trains after pulling the alarm-chains to bring them to a stop.[83] The failure of this endeavour was not surprising since the Agra Congress had itself spiked its biggest guns – the mass of supporters in the rural areas – by its actions in 1931.

V

A somewhat similar end was reached in Rae Bareli after a rather more arduous struggle. The peculiarly strained landlord–tenant relations in the district and the striking lack of adequate or timely remissions, especially of rent, made the district easily responsive to a 'no-rent' campaign. Besides, the provincial Congress chose Rae Bareli as one of the chief centres of the Civil Disobedience Movement. Sitla Sahai, Motilal Nehru's lieutenant and Swaraj Party and PCC secretary in 1926, was called back from Gandhi's Sabarmati Ashram in March 1930 to organize the campaign in the district. A party of seven students from Kashi Vidyapith reinforced the local Congress leadership.[84] Other prominent Congress leaders visited the district whenever they could. Jawaharlal Nehru and Sri Prakasa were there in the first quarter of 1930 and Nehru came again during his week out of gaol in October 1930. In the intervening period Rafi Ahmad Qidwai, Ganesh Shankar Vidyarthi, Mohanlal Gautam, Jai Prakash Narayan, Sundar Lal, Nand Kumar Deo Vasisth, Ramakant Malaviya, Birbal Singh and Chandramul Misra visited Rae Bareli, and Misra was arrested for his activities in the rural areas of the district.[85] Qidwai returned to the district in early 1931, and after the 'truce' was signed Jawaharlal Nehru and Purushottam Das Tandon sent special messages to 'the Rae Bareli peasants' congratulating them for their part in the *satyagraha* and urging them to prepare for a further campaign should it be required.[86]

We have seen that during the respite provided by the 'truce' Congress leaders worked to extend their organization in the district.[87] Their success was evidently very considerable. Large numbers of peasants flocked to their meetings: there were 10,000 at one in March 1931. Congress *panchayats* sprang up all over and usurped many of the functions of the police and magistrates. 'National' flags appeared in more and more villages. The hoisting of these flags and a collective contribution of one and a quarter rupees signified the allegiance of a village to the Congress. In certain weeks of May and June as many as 29, 34 and 45 new flags were hoisted in Rae Bareli,[88] and by June, as already noted, officials acknowledged the existence of over 13,000 Congress volunteers in the district and more than a thousand villages flying Congress flags.[89]

The Government observed at this time that Congress workers and volunteers came from 'all classes'.[90] But this appears to have been a slightly mistaken impression. Ordinary volunteers in Rae Bareli included men like Ram Autar, a Brahman teacher in a district board school in Bachrawan who resigned in 1930 to take part in the Civil Disobedience Movement; Asa Din, an Agnihotri Brahman 'cultivator' holding 12.5 *bighas*[91] of land; Thakur Lal Bahadur Singh, probably a rich peasant, who was said to have 'sufficient influence over *kisans* of Nasirabad circle' and Thakur Bhagwan Din Singh, alias Sadhu Bhagwan Das, who lived on charity and wandered all over the district. But many more volunteers seem to have come from less privileged groups. Among them were Amol Das Sharma, a Brahman described by the police as a man of 'low means' who 'knows Hindi', Mahabir Murai, an illiterate member of an 'ordinary *kisan* family' and Sheikh Bhoosanoo Ghosi, an 'ordinary milk-seller and cultivator', to take three examples at random. And it is fairly clear that the masses of men and women who were not regular volunteers but simply participated in demonstrations or other actions of protest also came from the ranks of middle and poor peasants. Though they belonged to a variety of castes and sub-castes – probably the basis of the government assessment that they came from 'all classes' – most of them appear to have been tenants, sub-tenants and cultivators with a little land who paid exorbitant dues and suffered greatly on account of the Depression.[92]

The attempt to force the collection of dues from men who were in no position to pay, and to eject them from their lands as the penalty for non-payment, created almost an insurrectionary situation in the Rae Bareli countryside. In May 1931 grain prices were at their lowest point.[93] Statutory tenants as well as peasants in other tenurial categories had been granted only the most meagre remissions. The advocates of resistance found an appreciative audience in the peasant masses who turned out for demonstrations leading to violence in a number of places.[94]

Gandhi's 'Manifesto' of May, publicized widely in the district, had contributed to the general turbulence. The Government noted an increase in 'disguised no-rent propaganda' and consequently of tension in the rural areas. 'Matters are coming to a head,' it declared, 'owing to the greater pressure exerted by the Congress.'[95] A typical weekly intelligence report of this period referred to the 'no-rent' propaganda conducted by Rae Bareli workers and to the efforts of the revenue staff to realize rents by attachment of property with police help. On 13 June, the report added, a clash occurred at Sheoratanganj and *lathis* had to be used to disperse the crowds. On 16 June trouble arose between Sheo Datt, the president of the Sagona Congress and some *zamindars* of Bilwa Hasanpur. Again, *sadhu* Bhagwan Din squatted on the outskirts of Gullupur village to stop tenants from meeting their *zamindar*. Mohanlal Gautam and others from Allahabad arrived to enquire into recent incidents. The report concluded on a note of optimism: proceedings under Section 12(a) of the Awadh Rent Act had been successful.[96] Here was clear evidence for the Government's charge that the Congress was planning another, more dangerous 'mass' movement and that strong police action alone prevented a conflagration.

A closer analysis of events in Rae Bareli suggests, however, that the Government gave the Congress undue credit. The Congress leadership hardly wished to see the world turned upside down, more especially when there was the possibility of settling important constitutional issues round the conference table. And the great accession of strength to the 'Congress' in Rae Bareli at this time appears to have been largely the fruit of the labours of local 'militants', speaking in the Congress's name but not as 'responsible' Congress leaders would.

When the Congress initially launched its 'no-tax' campaign in October

1930, Intelligence men expressed the opinion that in Rae Bareli rents would in any case be collected with 'the greatest difficulty' and that 'the *kisans*...are likely to accept any Congress suggestion of non-payment of rents'.[97] The Congress decision to encourage men not to pay taxes was aimed of course at strengthening their anti-Government campaign. Accordingly, Rae Bareli Congressmen issued calls for the non-payment of dues, whether rent or revenue.[98] Local militants, little known in Congress circles but closer to those who toiled in the sun, supported this plea sometimes with vehement and bitter attacks against landlords and Government.[99] On occasion tenants took independent action. For instance, all except three tenants of village Surajkunda surrendered their holdings in the winter of 1930–1 as a protest against the enhancements of rent made in 1930.[100]

The Gandhi–Irwin Pact of March 1931 changed the official Congress position. However, it did not affect that of the discontented peasants. Officials observed in March that 'tenants are disposed to withhold payment of rent irrespective of Congress instructions, because in some cases they are unable to pay and in many cases, they are on bad terms with their landlords.'[101] On the other hand, in June and even as late as September 1931, Congress leaders in the district were lamenting the fact that they were unable to give the peasant problem the attention it deserved.[102]

Meanwhile militant 'Congress' propaganda spread in Rae Bareli villages. The evidence suggests that much of this was outside the control of the official Congress leadership. In May 1931 Governor Hailey found it necessary to revise, as unwarranted, the impression he had formed on his return to UP from England, that Congress was violating the Gandhi–Irwin Pact. 'The trouble in many districts is purely economic', he now wrote. Where agitators were responsible for the spread of discontent it was difficult, he felt, to establish that 'responsible' Congress leaders were involved, for the local volunteers might have passed beyond even their control.[103] At the end of June, the Chief Secretary to the provincial Government also remarked on the 'somewhat new factor' of the intervention of 'leading Congressmen' in rural affairs.[104]

The special correspondent of *The Pioneer*, investigating the 'serious aspect' that agrarian affairs in Rae Bareli had assumed after the Gandhi–Irwin Pact, made a similar assessment. 'Taking advantage of the agreement,' he wrote, '...more than ten thousand volunteers, *whose connection with the Congress was not very apparent*, swarmed into the villages to stir up trouble between zamindars and tenants.'[105] His figure was perhaps exaggerated, and his suggestion that volunteers 'swarmed into the villages' was misleading since most of them were local men, but he had sensed correctly a certain gap between these volunteers and the 'responsible' Congress leadership. Rae Bareli's 'responsible' Congressmen and local 'militants' worked along very different lines during the crucial months of March to July 1931, and it appears that the former did much, ultimately with success, to reduce militancy in the rural areas.

After the Delhi Pact Sitla Sahai and his associates followed provincial Congress guidelines strictly. Here, as in Agra and elsewhere, they announced the suspension of the 'no-tax' campaign. But, acknowledging that sections of the peasantry might still have difficulty in paying rents, they suggested that tenants should send applications for relief or grace to the Congress office. Congress workers would then see landowners and officials and try to get rents suspended, remitted or reduced.[106] For peasants who lived at or only slightly above subsistence level in ordinary times, who had suddenly had the value of their produce reduced by half or more and who were still expected – and pressurized – to pay the normal rent, revenue or other demand in cash, this was not an easily acceptable position. There were occasions in 1931 when the Congress leaders' unqualified assertion that rents should be paid, at least in part, provoked loud tenant protest.[107] Congressmen then urged patience. *Kisans*, they pleaded, should strengthen the Congress's hand so as to bring nearer the *swaraj* that would rid them of their grievances. For the time being, however, tenants were advised to pay five or six or eight annas of their rent, a position that Gandhi himself had advocated in May.[108]

In July 1931 some of the bigger landlords of Rae Bareli met under Rai Rajeshwar Bali. They formed a District Landlords' Association, appealed to the Government for further remissions and urged the cultivation of good relations with tenants.[109] In a manner reminiscent of the best of the Agra Congress, 'responsible' Congress leaders and 'responsible' landlords in Rae Bareli had arrived on a similar platform.

Significantly the district's Congress leaders had, since the signing of the Gandhi–Irwin agreement, worked to bring about settlements between landlords and tenants, and where these could be arranged they helped landlords in the collection of rents.[110] Even with Sardar Birpal Singh, the *taluqdar* of Khureti, nicknamed the Dyer of Rae Bareli for firing on unarmed peasants in 1921,[111] and described by the Congress report on *Agrarian Distress in the UP* as 'very harsh before...harsher today',[112] Congress leaders reached an agreement.[113] And efforts to arrange settlements with individual landlords of the district with the assistance of the district administration continued well into the second half of 1931.[114]

The 'militants' spoke a very different language. Kalka Prasad, an active Congressman since the Non-Cooperation Movement, who was managing the Khaddar Bhandar and living in the Congress office at Lalganj when the Civil Disobedience campaign began, became the most notorious of the 'militants', partly because he was one of the most influential among them. 'Kalka Prasad told the cultivators not to pay rent, and naturally has a greater following among the masses,' the Intelligence Department reported.[115] Again, he asked why the Government ordered the police to beat up peasants while it refused to arrest Gandhi for advising the cultivators to pay up only half of their rents and obtain full receipts.[116]

In mid-1931 Kalka Prasad's forthright approach caused a complete estrangement between him and the official Congress leadership. The break came with his threat to picket the house of Rana Umanath Bux Singh, *taluqdar* of the great Khajurgaon estate and a very loyal landlord according to the Government, for alleged oppression of his tenants. Police intervention sent Kalka Prasad into hiding,[117] and it was another month before he was arrested. Meanwhile, the Congress had disowned his actions and suspended him from party membership for a year.[118] When he was finally arrested in September no one in the Congress camp uttered a word of protest.[119]

Earlier Kalka Prasad's election to the presidentship of the DCC – an indication of his extraordinary influence among the cultivators then being enrolled as Congressmen in large numbers – had caused trouble in the Rae Bareli Congress. The election was set aside, and a protracted dispute ensued between Kalka Prasad and Mata Prasad Mishra who was appointed acting president.[120] Nehru visited the district in June and announced that an enquiry committee would be sent to settle the dispute. Kalka Prasad did not participate in Nehru's meetings at this time, nor did his followers welcome the enquiry committee when it came;[121] he himself was in hiding at the time. The result of the enquiry was a foregone conclusion.

It seemed no coincidence that, when Kalka Prasad was striking out on a radical path in opposition to the approved Congress policy in Rae Bareli, Baba Ramchandra, the remarkable leader and organizer of the Awadh *kisan* agitation of 1920–1, should be fighting a similar battle in the UP Political Conference at Mirzapur held on 2–4 May, 1931. Ramchandra condemned as short-sighted and inadequate a resolution calling for the fixing of rents in accordance with the rates of a year when prices were at the level of 1931, and suggested that much more radical changes were required in the countryside.[122] Kalka Prasad, like Baba Ramchandra, had his ears tuned to the 'masses'. Like Ramchandra, he saw the importance of the political struggle launched by the Congress, but only in the context of the peasants' grievances. It was poetic justice that Rae Bareli's own Sitla Sahai should have moved the resolution Ramchandra so bitterly attacked. It was Congress justice that Ramchandra's standpoint should be rejected, and with it Kalka Prasad's.

The middle months of 1931 were crucial so far as popular agitation in Rae Bareli was concerned. Peasant distress and militancy were at their height. Officials and landlords were near their wit's end as to how to collect their dues. There was a vicious circle of peasant resistance, the use of police and other force, further resistance and still greater repression. Congress workers in the *parganas* and *tahsils* of Rae Bareli district saw the brutality of combined Government-landlord action. Some of them wrote of the scenes they witnessed. Even women and children were beaten and tortured by the agents of *taluqdars* and by armed policemen. The police entered houses and forcibly took away food and utensils and anything else they could lay their hands on. There was often no question of issuing receipts for payments, and thus there was no record left to indicate whether the collection represented a part or the entire amount due or – as also often happened – even exceeded it.[123]

Congress leaders at a higher level could not fail to notice the extent of the repression. In their charge sheet against the Government they noted incidents of the terrorizing and beating of tenants in Rae Bareli in July and August 1931. They referred also to the special orders issued by the Deputy Commissioner of the district, aimed at undermining the district Congress organization. Moreover they enquired into allegations of police excesses, such as the firing at Daulatpur, which resulted from resistance to a *qanungo*, and condemned such use of force as 'quite unjustified'.[124] Later in the year the DCC encouraged *kisans* to petition against the insufficiency of the recently made remissions and posted a clerk at the Collectorate to help the *kisans*, who now came there in large numbers. But at no time during the period of 'truce' did they feel able to call for resistance.

Indeed, far from giving a concerted call for organized peasant protest, the official Congress leadership took disciplinary action against men who 'offended against the creed or otherwise misbehaved themselves'.[125] Combined with the continuation of stern government action and the provision for the first time of substantial relief to the Rae Bareli tenant, this served to weaken the resolve of the peasants.

The Intelligence Department observed in October 1931 that all had been quiet in Rae Bareli since Nehru's visit in June.[126] The payment of taxes, had improved. Peasant interest in the Congress had declined; no more than two or three new Congress flags were hoisted in the villages in any normal week in the second half of 1931. The resumption of agricultural operations was partly responsible for these developments. But Nehru's visit also had an impact, for reasons that the Intelligence men did not suspect. They implied that 'outside agitators' fomented trouble in Rae Bareli. The truth, on the contrary, was probably that the 'outside agitators' had helped to bring a volatile situation under control.

Rural agitation was not completely finished, of course. That was not the Congress's intention and, even had it been, conditions in the rural areas were not such as to foster complete peace and quiet. Prices had taken an irrevocable dive. To make matters worse the winter rains failed in 1931–2 and rats destroyed 25 per cent of the meagre crop harvested in Rae Bareli that spring. The monsoon too turned out to be poor: less than two inches of rain fell in the district in the entire month of July 1932. In addition there were problems with rent remissions: corruption at the local level, and 'hopelessly confusing, ambiguous and inadequate orders' from the provincial Government.[127] Finally, many landlords and the Government continued the use of force for the collection of their dues. Consequently there were signs of resistance at various times in 1932.[128] In general however the movement had lost its momentum.

Andrew Parke Hume remarked on how 'extraordinarily quiet' Rae Bareli district was in December 1931. In May 1932 he reported that, of the 22 *tahsils* in Lucknow division, three of Rae Bareli were third, fourth and fifth in order of merit in the year's revenue collections: 'for the centre of the Congress no-rent campaign in the UP...' he wrote, 'this is quite satisfactory.'[129] By July that year 80 per cent of the revenue due from the district had come in and the administration had until September to collect the rest. It was evidence of the brutal efficiency of the Government and the blundering decline of the 'no-tax' campaign.

VI

It is clear that the Congress was unwilling to let Civil Disobedience in the rural areas develop into an anti-landlord campaign. Rather, it continued to appeal to every class in rural society and obtained some success at every level: numerous rich peasants participated in the Civil

Disobedience Movement, and even some big landlords were openly sympathetic.[130] Perhaps the most striking and momentous consequence of this was the decline of peasant resistance in the latter half of 1931. The Government of course played its part in bringing this about with its policy of simultaneous concession and repression. One could expect a colonial regime to protect its interests thus. What is surprising, however, is the amount of unexpected (and indeed unrecognized) aid that the regime received from the conscious actions of an ostensibly 'radical' Congress leadership. The UP Congress *volte-face* on the question of peasant protests following the Gandhi-Irwin agreement was surely one of the more telling episodes in the history of the anti-imperialist struggle – and one of much consequence.

In districts other than Rae Bareli and Agra, too, the patience of dis-contented peasants gave way and violent conflict occurred in the months after the Congress officially withdrew the 'no-tax' campaign in 1931. On such occasions, again, local Congress leaders did their utmost to restore 'non-violence' and keep the situation under control. Allahabad, headquarters of the UP Congress organization and home of such influ-ential 'radicals' as Jawaharlal Nehru and Venkatesh Narain Tewari as well as of older Congress leaders like Motilal Nehru, Sundar Lal and Tandon, provides examples of this kind. Here the pattern of participa-tion in the Civil Disobedience Movement differed markedly between the *doab tahsils* on the one hand and those of the trans-Ganga and trans-Yamuna regions of the district on the other (see table 5.2 on p.124 above). Figures of the number of *satyagrahis* who went to jail from one region or another are not to be treated as conclusive evidence. But other reports indicate that the general picture presented by these figures is accurate enough.

Handia, Soraon and Phulpur and, after them, the trans-Yamuna *tahsils* were the areas of Congress concentration and organization during the early 1930s. Following the decision to start a campaign of civil disobedience, the UP Congress chose Handia, together with Rae Bareli district, for special attention.[131] Already in June 1929 Handia was said to have recruited 1,125 Congress members – when even the city of Allahabad, aiming at a target of 4,000 members, could claim no more than 342. A month later the figure for Handia *tahsil* had risen to 1,850,[132] and in March 1930 it was reported that, while Allahabad city was still not ready for Civil Disobedience, Handia was straining at the leash.[133] Paid workers had been appointed in the *tahsil*, a number of women had been recruited for propaganda purposes, a Congress publicity department was functioning actively. In March 1930 a working committee was appointed for the circle and it was decided that the Allahabad DCC should in future meet in Handia rather than at Allahabad.[134]

The presence of renowned and influential Congress workers who hailed from Handia facilitated the task of mobilization and organization. Among them were Bhuvarji, who had recently returned after spending eight years at Gandhi's Sabarmati Ashram, and Shyam Sundar Shukla, who resigned from his post as a sub-inspector of police to take part in the Non-Cooperation Movement.

These local leaders had their counterparts in other *tahsils* of the district. Earlier on in this narrative we have come across Sheomurti Singh and Tikaram Tripathi of Kotwa and Jamunipur in Phulpur *tahsil*.[135] The same kind of leadership was provided by men like Ram Bharos Malaviya in Bara and Mahabir Prasad Shukla in Meja. Interestingly, Shukla recalled that for some reason Chail and Manjhanpur, two of the *doab tahsils*, had no 'leaders' in the early 1930s[136] – an indication of the 'backwardness' of the *doab* in terms of Congress organization and activity, which is plain from other evidence.

In November 1930, for example, when the DCC inaugurated the 'no-tax' campaign in the Allahabad villages, *Abhyudaya* observed that Handia, Karchana and Meja were well organized and prepared for the struggle. In the remaining trans-Yamuna *tahsil*, Bara, and the other two across the Ganga, Phulpur and Soraon, the work of organization was proceeding apace and the clashes that had occurred with the administration were expected to hasten the process. The *doab tahsils* on the other hand found no mention.[137] In November 1933, again, when the Allahabad Congress selected some areas for renewed propaganda and activity, the *tahsils* chosen were Soraon, Handia, Phulpur and Meja – and not one from the *doab*.[138] Then, as in 1930, officials came to refer to the Handia region as 'the notorious circle of Handia'.[139]

Appropriately enough, the DCC's decision in November 1931 to advise nonpayment of taxes even though the Gandhi-Irwin agreement was still in force, was made public at a meeting in Saidabad in Handia *tahsil*. A short while before that P D Tandon, Venkatesh Narain Tewari, Tikaram Tripathi and other district Congress leaders had admonished a meeting of peasants in Manjhanpur for the fact that no more than 150 men from the *tahsil* had attended the district *kisan* conference at Allahabad in October 1931.[140]

Yet during the period of 'truce' between the Congress and the

Government, it was not Handia or Phulpur or Soraon or Meja but the *tahsils* of the *doab*, and especially Manjhanpur, that came to be considered 'the worst affected area in the district'.[141] There were reports of disturbances from Manjhanpur, Chail, Sirathu, Soraon and even Handia. But agitation appears to have been most intense in the first two.[142]

A number of factors may account for this. The Government's remissions were of course utterly meagre everywhere. In Manjhanpur the 'liberal' remissions of late 1931 brought a concession of little more than three annas in the rupee for a majority of tenants[143] and the situation was no better in many other areas. Even such pittance was not granted to subtenants and tenants on *sir* and *khudkasht*, who remained outside the ken of official concern. And there were a particularly high proportion of such tenants in Chail tahsil. This was probably one reason for the high level of unrest in that region.

More significant, perhaps, was the fact that the Congress appears to have consciously limited its propaganda and activity in the *doab* tract of Allahabad, fearing an outbreak of communal trouble.[144] This may explain the very limited participation of the *doab tahsils* in the Civil Disobedience Movement. It may also have led to greater oppression of tenants and sub-tenants by the landlords and rich peasants of the area, which in turn was what perhaps contributed to the intensity and violence of peasant protests here.

Whatever the reasons, the areas that were most 'backward' in terms of Congress organization and conspicuously inactive in the two phases of formal Civil Disobedience took the lead in anti-landlord and anti-imperialist agitation during the 'truce'. The Intelligence Department reported in June 1931 that Manjhanpur was now 'the centre of activity and the volunteer movement is particularly strong here'. The widespread distribution of 'strongly worded' 'no-rent' leaflets in Chail was one of several indications of the militancy that alarmed the sleuths.[145]

By May there were regular reports that villagers in Manjhanpur *tahsil* were taking matters into their own hands – resisting revenue and police officials, forcing *zamindars* and other village notables to sign the 'Congress pledge', and attacking them by social boycott and even violent means if they refused to do so.[146] On 7 June a violent clash occurred in village Bhatwaria in this *tahsil*, resulting in the death of a *zamindar*, four of his relatives and two servants, all Shia Muslims. The assailants were poor peasants, many of them Lodhs and Pasis. After the riot the Congress appeared on the scene. LawyerCongressmen represented the tenants in what became known as the Bhatwaria Riot Case. In addition the Congress committee conducted extensive enquiries in Bhatwaria, published a report and condemned the *kisans* who had been guilty of violence.[147]

While the Government suspected and accused the Congress of fomenting trouble, here and elsewhere, Congress leaders asserted their innocence and said that they were not responsible for 'no-rent' propaganda at this time, far less for the violence. The honesty of this disclaimer is evident from Congress actions in Agra and Rae Bareli. But Allahabad had a more classic statement of the Congress position in February 1931, when Gandhi visited the city on the occasion of Motilal Nehru's funeral. *Abhyudaya* reported that 80,000 peasants had come to hear Gandhi, who for his part chided them for travelling on the railway without tickets in order to come and see him, advised nonviolence and courage and urged the peasants to wear *khaddar* and abstain from liquor, *ganja*, *hashish* and so on. The matter of rents, debts and arrears was not even mentioned.[148]

Given such a lead, peasants in many places took matters into their own hands and resisted oppression in whatever way they could. Government and newspaper accounts spoke of miserable conditions and agitation among groups of peasants in districts from Farrukhabad to Azamgarh. Violent clashes occurred in several districts where the Congress was not strong enough to bring about 'compromise' solutions and 'discipline' the peasants. In June–July 1931 the situation was considered particularly dangerous in Bara Banki, Rae Bareli, Unnao and part of Allahabad, while in Bara Banki gatherings of armed villagers were commonly reported.[149]

The UP Congress refused at this juncture to lend its support to peasant actions against landlords and the Government. For the peasants this was clearly a letdown. For the Congress too it was a costly mistake. Quite unlike the Civil Disobedience agitation of 1930, the campaign of 1932–3 was limited to the big cities and their immediate surroundings, and here it was mainly the financial resources and strong organization of the Congress that kept the movement alive. Hailey observed in early 1932 that, except in two districts of the Allahabad division, Kanpur and Allahabad, the 'no-tax' campaign 'doesn't exist any more'.[150] A A Waugh, the Settlement Officer of Meerut, put it more pungently: 'When at last Congressmen definitely launched their 'no-rent' campaign in the autumn of 1931, they found, not for the first time, that they had 'missed the bus'.[151]

VII

The Gandhi–Irwin agreement, whereby the Congress had undertaken to refrain from 'political' agitation against the British, was part of the reason for its leaders' reluctance to adopt a progressive stand on the agrarian question in UP in 1931. But other factors too contributed to the generally hesitant approach of the Congress to peasant problems and mass agitation during the period under study. One was the class composition of the party leadership and cadres. The UP Congress counted among its more important leaders a number of substantial landlords, Sri Prakasa and T A K Sherwani being the most prominent among them. And as we have already suggested, small *zamindars* and upper-caste rent-receivers provided the majority of Congress leaders at the district and tahsil level.[152] This is confirmed again by the evidence we have regarding the Congress leadership in Rae Bareli during the 1930s.

Of the four Congressmen of Rae Bareli who have already featured in this narrative – Sitla Sahai, Satyanarain Srivastava, Kalka Prasad and Mata Prasad Mishra – the second certainly earned part of his income from land he rented out and the fourth, a well-to-do cloth merchant and house-owner in Rae Bareli town, probably did so too. Apart from them the names of the district and *tahsil*-level leaders that appear in Congress and police reports include a Brahman *Vaidya* (practitioner of Ayurvedic medicine), a Brahman lawyer, a Baniya merchant, a Kayasth teacher and, significantly, seven Thakurs who derived their incomes chiefly from land. Thakur Mahesh Narain Singh is described as a *zamindar* of five villages, Thakur Bhagwan Baksh Singh as the *zamindar* of Rampur in Maharajganj *tahsil*, paying an annual revenue of Rs 800. Three of the others were smaller *zamindars*, while Thakur Raghuraj Singh owned a buffalo and paid a rental of Rs 39 on his land, which he let out on *batai* (crop-sharing basis), and Thakur Rameshwar Singh is described as belonging to the 'tenant class'. Of the other local leaders mentioned in the reports, I have been unable to trace the background of Thakur Jagrup Singh, Pandit Gaya Prasad Shukla, Pandit Bachan Lal Shukla and Munshi Ambica Prasad Srivastava. Munshi Ram Bharose Srivastava is the sole *tahsil* or district-level Congress leader of Rae Bareli described in the records as an agriculturist of very ordinary means.[153] All of them, without exception, were upper-caste men who would not touch the plough, and we may assume that most of them derived a good part of their income from rents – especially in view of the tangential but suggestive evidence that upper-caste tenants possessed a disproportionately high share of large holdings.[154] It is only to be expected that men from such backgrounds would be neither enthusiastic nor unambiguous in their support for the struggles of the rural poor against the rich, particularly if the conflicts assumed the form of a 'no-rent' campaign.

The dilemma of the Congress was, however, still greater – since as a party it relied on landlords, money-lenders and businessmen, most obviously during elections but also for the major part of its funds at other times.[155] No wonder, then, that the Congress would not speak out against money-lenders, despite the growing realization in the early 1930s that indebtedness was the most important single problem for a large proportion of the peasantry in UP.[156] Neither the UP Congress's report on agrarian distress (1931) nor its resolutions during this period mentioned the problem at all. It was not until 1936 that the party first noted its magnitude, and even then the woes of moneylenders were given attention along with those of the indebted.[157]

Equally the socio-economic demands of the industrial working class found no place in the Congress programme, in spite of the token representation granted to the UP Trade Union Congress in 1929 and the involvement of individual Congressmen with workers in the urban areas. In the industrial towns, even more clearly than in the villages, the Congress showed its willingness to mobilize the working 'masses' on issues directly concerning the British, but not on those affecting the interests of the Indian upper classes.

Thus Harihar Nath Shastri, the labour specialist of the UP Congress, organized protest meetings in Kanpur in August and September 1928 against the Trades Disputes Act and the Public Safety Ordinance, the one seeking to control general and 'wildcat' strikes and lockouts in certain public utility services, the other aimed at expelling from India foreigners who were taking part in the labour movement. In December 1929, again, he organized black-flag demonstrations against the Royal Commission on Labour in India on the occasion of its visit to Kanpur.[158] On other occasions, however, Shastri excelled as a leader of 'compromise'. This is illustrated by his actions in November 1931 over a strike in the Jhuggilal Kamlapat Mills. The strike was the workers' response to large-scale retrenchment. When the employers tried to bring in new hands in order to replace the strikers, the workers resisted and tension mounted. Shastri then appealed to Jawaharlal Nehru to use his influence to win over the employers. At the same time, he sought the arbitration of the Kanpur district administration. He was successful in arranging a compromise, saving for the time being at any rate both the face and the purse of the Congress.[159]

It was not merely its dependence on and links with privileged classes that made the Congress leadership vacillate in its approach to the 'masses'. Much of this was also due to a certain want of clarity in the official Congress thinking about the nature of both Indian society and popular anti-colonial struggle. In part this flowed from the accepted view of the nationalist movement as a multi-class, yet internally undivided and non-contradictory, campaign for the removal of an alien power.[160] There was unanimity about the desirability of *swaraj*, but this was not accompanied by any close analysis of the structure of imperialist domination or of the forces and contradictions within local society. Notions about the task of mobilization to be performed remained somewhat hazy, and the party often moved in two directions at once in response to the pressures of the moment.

The Congress's approach to rural society in UP illustrates the point very well. The Swaraj Party manifesto of 1923 made a confused state-ment about the agrarian structure in this and other *zamindari* areas. Repudiating any suggestion that the Swaraj Party aimed at the aboli-tion of landlordism, it declared that the party 'cannot possibly dream of such madness as to undermine the very foundations of society *as it has existed for hundreds of years* in India by trying to eliminate an important and influential class from it.'[161]

The performance of the Swarajists in the provincial legislature during the debate on the Agra Tenancy Bill in 1926 indicated the extent to which the UP Congress went, with Gandhi, 'one step at a time'. 'Our party has decided today to act as umpires,' declared Mukandi Lal, the deputy leader of the party, 'and we will watch the interests of both the peasant and the landlord, and make an earnest effort to find a solution for the existing friction and conflict of interests.'[162] What followed was a demonstration of adept political footwork through a series of what the Swarajists considered reasonable compromises. The party first combined with the 'progressive landlords' in the Council to defeat the Government: even the Liberal paper, *The Leader*, expressed its dismay when their concessions to the landlords became known.[163] Then it took advantage of the absence of a large body of landlords from the legislature – they had left Naini Tal when proceedings closed for Muharram and were late in returning – to support the Government in amending certain clauses favourable to that class, indeed going as far as to withdraw some of the concessions that the Swarajists had themselves made to the landlords in the first compromise. And finally, in a sequel to the drama on the Tenancy Act, it joined the indignant landlords in forcing the withdrawal of the Government's UP Land Revenue (Amendment) Bill.

The legislation that emerged brought some benefits to small *zamindars*, occupancy tenants and even tenants-at-will. But the real victory, in the eyes of the Congress, lay in the successful outwitting and embarrassment of the Government. In order to achieve this, the party was quite ready to compromise on issues on which it had earlier steadfastly defended the tenantry. William Marris, then the Governor of UP, was bitter but correct in his appraisal: 'The Swarajists profess pro-tenant views, but their only serious aim is to down the Government.'[164]

During the 1930s, the UP Congress continued to appeal for support to the *kisans* as an undifferentiated mass. On many occasions, its leaders addressed themselves to *kisans* and *zamindars* in the same breath. Generally speaking, there was no acknowledgement of the conflict of interests between the different sections of the rural population that the party wooed. Recall Jawaharlal Nehru's disavowal of his 'personal' views on the need to abolish the *zamindari* system: 'Those views have no application to present day politics, and in any event the Congress is not committed to [them]'.[165] It is interesting to set this opinion against the debate in the Communist Party of China in the mid-1920s about the forces to be mobilized in their anti-imperialist struggle and about the nature of the alliances to be sought. 'The greatest adversary of revolution [i.e. the National Revolution, led by the bourgeoisie] in an economically backward semi-colony is the feudal–patriarchal class (the landlord class) in the villages', said Mao Tse-Tung at a critical stage in that debate. It was through this class and its chieftains, the warlords, that the imperialists maintained their domination in the country. Hence, Mao concluded, to overthrow that domination it was necessary to mobilize the peasantry to destroy the foundations of imperialist and warlord rule.[166]

No such analysis rocked the councils of the Congress as it appealed for support to every section of Indian society, rural and urban, during the years of Non-Cooperation and Civil Disobedience. The party's 'socialist' programme was in the nature of a fitting climax to this period of struggle. From September 1933 to April 1934 virtually every meeting of UP Congress leaders urged the drawing up of a 'socialist' programme.[167] At the same time a leading Congressman of the province made it clear that 'socialism' was nothing new, that even a republican form of government meant 'socialism' and that the work of Congress for the uplift of Harijans was one aspect of 'socialist' propaganda.[168] Appropriately, too, in 1934, when the CSP was formed and gained a large number of adherents among Congressmen in UP, the provincial Congress also staked its claims once again to being a landlord-cum-tenant party in the campaign for elections to the central Legislative Assembly.[169]

VIII

The severity of the economic crises of the post-War years – in the early 1920s and the early 1930s – and the independent and 'direct' actions of large numbers of oppressed peasants highlighted the inconsistencies between the claim of the Congress to represent the 'masses' and its aim of winning the support of all sections of the society. At the height of the Depression the UP Congress leadership declined to throw its weight behind the protesting peasants and preferred to work for an amicable settlement between the warring parties and a maintenance of the 'truce'. This was indeed a crucial factor in reducing popular support for the Civil Disobedience campaign. Yet the very steps that led up to the resumption of Civil Disobedience indicated that the independent actions of the peasant masses of UP forced political leaders to reconsider their attitude of blind 'neutrality' and their customary compromises intended to paper over the cracks in rural society which the Depression had laid bare.

The 'direct' and sometimes violent resistance of groups of poor and middle peasants appears to have made its point not only to the Government and the landlords – who hastened to make more remissions and accommodations in the villages – but also to Congress leaders, who now began to take up the peasants' grievances in one place and another, thereby expediting the granting of relief by landlords and the Government. In the Bhatwaria case in Allahabad, militant peasant action drew the Congress leadership into a new region – in order to represent discontented peasants in the courts, as well as to restore order in the area. In Rae Bareli, to take another example, a 'strike' by 500 tenants of the Arkha estate, who stopped tilling their *zamindar*'s field in October 1931,[170] led to immediate intervention by the district Congress. Congress leaders negotiated with the *zamindar* and quickly concluded an agreement, laying down conditions under which land would be leased out to the tenants once again and the tenants could pay a given proportion of rent arrears or postpone payment for a limited period.[171]

Nothing, however, shows more clearly than the case of Anjani Kumar

(Tewari)[172] how a recognized Congress leader could be swept along in the wave of peasant militancy. The son of a police official of Balrampur (Gonda) and himself a lawyer in Rae Bareli town, an active Civil Disobedience worker in his home *tahsil* of Bachhrawan and 'dictator' of the district Congress in December 1930, Anjani Kumar led four or five hundred volunteers to picket the house of the Raja of Sheogarh who had started attachment proceedings against some of his tenants in June 1931. The picketers demanded an apology from the manager of the Raja's estate and announced that the Congress had fined the Raja Rs 1,000.[173] At this stage Anjani Kumar was pulled up by the senior Congress leader of the district,[174] partly because the Raja of Sheogarh had earlier reached an agreement with the district Congress regarding remissions for his tenants.[175] But the action of Anjani Kumar and the peasant volunteers had demonstrable effect. By August this 'militant' had been fully rehabilitated in the Rae Bareli Congress and detailed enquiries were being conducted regarding atrocities in the Sheogarh estate; and the report of the enquiry committee on agrarian distress in UP, published in September, carried a long note on the subject, written by Anjani Kumar himself.[176]

In the second half of 1931, indeed, numerous Congress leaders began to question some of their own basic assumptions regarding the nature of the nationalist movement. Several of them toured the districts of UP, enquiring into and publicizing the peasants' sufferings and Government and landlord atrocities. The pronouncements of the UP Congress on agrarian questions also assumed a more urgent and radical tone. The report, *Agrarian Distress in the UP*, showed a greater inclination than ever before to represent forcefully the position of exploited peasants on big landlord estates, while pointing out at the same time the difficulties faced by various classes of *zamindars* on account of the Government's mishandling of the crisis. There was an increasing number of calls for 'direct action' to right grievous wrongs and bring relief to the peasantry.[177] All this was a response to the new experience of peasant conditions and peasant resistance. The leaders' subsequent act of referring the question of agrarian troubles in UP to Gandhi at the Round Table Conference was a mere formality, seeking sanction for a *satyagraha* which others had started and into which the provincial Congress leadership was reluctantly but surely drawn.[178]

Around this time too a growing number of Congress leaders in UP woke to the need for a long-term solution of the peasant problem.[179] The demand for the abolition of *zamindari* gained popularity and became a regular feature of UP Congress resolutions, together with appeals to wipe out communalism, boycott British goods and so on. In the years that followed the radical trend in UP Congress circles became more marked. We have noticed in an earlier chapter[180] the strong position attained by the CSP in the province and the important work done by the Socialists in a number of different areas. Much of the new drive to mobilize and organize workers and peasants was initiated by a small group of committed Socialist leaders, many of whom, including Mohanlal Saxena, Damodar Swarup Seth, Venkatesh Narain Tewari and Balkrishna Sharma had been prominent in 1930–2 in Congress enquiries and activities relating to the peasantry.

That 'the socialist idea' made some headway during this period is evident from a comparison of the UP *Congress Agrarian Enquiry Committee Report* of 1936 with the provincial Congress's report on agrarian distress in 1931. The 1931 enquiry committee had produced an account of the suffering and ill treatment in the countryside, with no attempt at a serious analysis of the structure of rural society.[181] The 1936 committee faced precisely this latter task and concluded that only the abolition of the *zamindari* system would provide a final solution of the agrarian crisis. Until such a transformation became possible, the Congress was advised to work for a reduction in rent, the exemption of uneconomic holdings from any rent or land-tax, the abolition of all feudal dues and illegal demands, the tackling of the problem of rural indebtedness, and the introduction of cooperative farming.[182] The interests of the landless labourer still went by default,[183] but the problems of poor and middle peasant groups at least appear to have received attention. Rent-receivers of various categories, small landlords and rich peasants had of course been active in the Congress since the 1920s, and they had an important say in the making of Congress policy. These classes were the chief beneficiaries of the 1939 Tenancy Act, the first major piece of agrarian legislation passed by a Congress ministry in UP. But the Act also brought certain tangible concessions for the poorer *zamindars* and tenants in the province.[184]

There was some clarification then of what had hitherto been a hopelessly vague and ill-defined programme. The skeleton of the promised *swaraj* took on some flesh,

> Both…poor landowners and the middle landlords, though often intellectually backward, are as a whole a fine body of men and women…Not so the *taluqadars* and the big *zamindars*, barring a

few notable exceptions. They have not even the virtues of an aristocracy. As a class they are physically and intellectually degenerate and have outlived their day; they will continue so long as an external power like the British Government props them up.[185]

Jawaharlal Nehru expressed a growing body of Congress opinion in UP and outside when he wrote these lines in 1934. The more open and extended anti-landlord propaganda of the middle and later years of the 1930s was also part of the endeavour by the Congress leaders to spell out their notion of *swaraj* in more meaningful terms.

In 1926 Madan Mohan Malaviya and Lajpat Rai had led a revolt against the orthodox Congress position, formed the Independent Congress Party to contest the elections to the central and provincial legislatures, and successfully combined the call for a revision of the Congress programme inside the Councils with the cry of 'Hinduism in Danger'. The official Congress organization (or Swaraj Party), controlled by Motilal Nehru and enjoying the tacit support of Gandhi, suffered heavy losses as a result of individual defections by party workers and legislators throughout the Hindi-speaking region of northern India. In addition, the Responsive Cooperationists of western India allied themselves with the Malaviya-Lajpat Rai party, and the Swarajists of Madras adopted a 'responsive cooperationist' position – favouring the acceptance of office under 'reasonable' conditions. So marked was the depletion of official Congress strength in UP and Bihar that even the secular and allegedly pro-Muslim Motilal Nehru was forced into campaigning on sectionalist Hindu lines. Thus the Swarajists fell into a double-trap. Their Hindu image was newer and less convincing than Malaviya's, and the act of setting themselves up as a Hindu party inevitably lost them support in the Muslim community. The results of the 1926 elections and the events of the following years indicated this.[186]

In 1934 Malaviya and M S Aney, the Hindu nationalist leader from Berar, led another breakaway from the orthodox Congress on the issue of the Communal Award and formed the Congress Nationalist Party (CNP) to contest the central Legislative Assembly elections. But on this occasion the cry of 'Hinduism in Danger' had relatively little impact. There were very few defections from the official organization (controlled at this time by Gandhi with the assistance of Jawaharlal Nehru and others). And there was no sign of this 'wing' of the party being swayed from a secular position by Hindu pressure. On the contrary, many of the leaders of the Congress moved to a stance of aggression against the communalist Hindu (and Muslim) position in 1933–4, while the party as a whole concentrated its propaganda and energies in rather different areas – the programme of Harijan uplift and the debate on mass mobilization along class lines. The question of land and labour had come so clearly to the forefront, indeed, that an important section of the Congress leadership decided to establish another breakaway organization, the Congress Socialist Party, which was to devote itself to activity among the workers and peasants. It was the CSP rather than the CNP that made the largest number of converts in UP in 1934.

That, too, is a measure of the achievement of the belligerent UP peasants in the period between the two World Wars. By fighting against the callousness of an alien government and the greed of the indigenous landlords, they advanced the nationalist movement by one significant step. It was their struggle that made the Congress leadership aware at last, though by no means fully, of the gravity and significance of the peasant question and led them to relate it to the concept of *swaraj*, making it somewhat more lucid and concrete than ever before. The peasants' own 'liberation', however, had to wait. The anti-landlordism of the Congress, when not confused by directly contradictory statements, was still to be matched by action. The sacrifice of the interests of hundreds of thousands of ordinary, illiterate men and women in the villages at moments of severe economic privation, on the ground that these must await the pleasure of 'national' political developments, was not an unambiguous portent.

7

Conclusion

The Congress's spectacular victories in the elections of 1934 and 1936–7, the ability of its central leadership to get the ministries in all the Congress-ruled provinces to resign in 1939 when India was declared a participant in World War II without consultation with the Congress, and its success in launching another widespread and massive campaign against the British presence in 1942, all reflected the significant changes that had come about in the Indian nationalist movement during the years under study. Some of the developments of this period proved to be of a lasting nature. One was the much consolidated and strengthened position of the Congress organization. Nationalist propaganda had intensified, and there was now a wider range of institutions to propagate the message of the Congress and carry it to new districts and new sections of the populace. For a long time afterwards 'defections' were to take place only within the party, and while 'defecting' groups often formed new factions, they were loath to adopt new, non-Congress, names.

Following the increase in nationalist activities among the poorer sections of the society, and in the rural areas generally, in the late 1920s and early 1930s, there was also a growing expression of concern for the social and economic well being of the masses. The 'socialist' claims of the Congress remained in place for a long time after the mid-1930s, and enabled it to steal some of the thunder of left-wing parties.

An abiding concern with the question of secularism, and the call to isolate politics based on exclusive appeals to particular religious communities, dates from the same period and helped the Congress leadership in independent India in its fight against a whole range of communal groupings. The adoption of this secular position – never very clear-cut in any case – came too late, however, to avert the alienation of Muslims at large, especially in the provinces where people of that denomination formed a minority. Between the Non-Cooperation Movement of 1920–2 and the Civil Disobedience campaigns of 1930–3 the Congress lost a great deal of its Muslim support: as it happened, this was never to be fully recovered.

This growing limitation of the Indian nationalist movement – all too obvious in UP by the 1930s – has been widely recognized, at any rate at the level of elite conflict. Other limitations, which flowed from the increasing strength of the Congress position, have been less clearly acknowledged. Perhaps the most important of these was the fact that the very extension of the Congress organization and the efficiency of central control imposed an unprecedented degree of restraint on popular participation in Congress campaigns with regard to the issues as well as the manner of agitation. Again, this is evident from the UP evidence.

A contemporary observation on the peasant protest movement in Pratapgarh in 1920–1 indicates some of the unpredictable consequences of the earlier and more spontaneous involvement of the masses in nationalist politics. 'In this district,' wrote an official, 'at any rate in the first instance, it was a movement of tenants for the amendment of the law. As soon, however, as the agitation was taken up as a political cry, many of the Sabhas or tenants' associations came to be composed almost entirely of landless labourers, who were led to believe that they were somehow in the promised *swaraj* to acquire land and wealth.'[1] There was then a good deal of volatility in the political protests of these impoverished cultivators; and as we have seen Congress leaders strongly disapproved of their tendency to violence.[2] By the time of the Civil Disobedience Movement the stronger position of the Congress enabled its leaders to extend the 'political cry' while ensuring at the same time that the agitation did not develop beyond their control into unruly and potentially violent demonstrations by disorganized mobs and individuals.

The focus of the Congress towards agitation thus narrowed down as it enlarged its organization and area of activity. This had still another dimension. As the developing anti-imperialist struggle came to incorporate some of the basic contradictions of Indian society and thereby intensify the contradictions within the nationalist movement itself, the Congress leadership became involved in a conscious effort to separate what they called the 'political' question (which was: the struggle for *swaraj*) from so-called 'social' and 'economic' issues – the struggle of Hindus against Muslims or caste against caste, of peasants against landlords, and so on. It was the former, they argued, that required immediate and total attention; the latter could wait, for they would 'automatically' be resolved with the coming of *swaraj*.

Precisely because of this separation between politics and economics, or more precisely between economics and one kind of politics, the peasant movement in Awadh in 1920–1 could be seen as having, in its origins, nothing to do with 'politics'. The same was true of Kisan Sabha struggles in the late 1930s: at best these were narrow, economic struggles, at worst 'anti-national'.[3] Much the same kind of analysis came to be made of 'communalism' as well.

Communalism, it was correctly argued, was not a religious but a political problem – a movement promoted by landlords, princes, and other reactionaries in their own, narrow class interests. At the same time it was said to be, for the masses, primarily an economic question, arising from the fact that the Muslims in the country were generally poor and backward compared to the more privileged and in some instances enterprising Hindus.[4] The colonial regime had been responsible for the encouragement of communalism. Under a nationalist regime it would disappear. That was the extent of this political analysis.

Nehru declared in his presidential address to the Lucknow Congress in 1936 that 'the principal communal leaders, Hindu or Muslim or others, are political reactionaries, quite apart from the communal question.'[5] In a note on the sectarian strife in Bihar in 1946, again, he observed that the propaganda of the Muslim League and the Hindu Mahasabha 'did not affect the widespread popularity of the Congress among the Hindu masses so far as the political issues were concerned. But it did produce communal feeling and a tendency among the middle class to criticize the Congress for not supporting the Hindu case as against the Muslim League.'[6] The distinction was significant, and put something of a question mark against the Congress's proposition that communalism was a political problem.

There were a number of efforts to settle the question through negotiations at the top – All-Parties Conferences, talks between Nehru and Gandhi and Jinnah – for communalism was, after all, a 'political' problem. For a short while after 1936, as we have noted, Congress also initiated a Muslim Mass Contacts programme, for communalism at this level was judged to be an 'economic' problem, and the masses had to be educated. There was, however, no longer any question of assigning a primacy to political struggle for the advancement of consciousness and the achievement of radical change in society, with which the nationalist leadership had been caught up for a short time after the

First World War. It was not unlike Nehru's acceptance of the 'science' of Marxism, bereft of its political content.[7]

The leaders of Congress now appropriated for themselves the role of political activists and educators. Gandhi put it succinctly in London in October 1931 when asked whether Indian peasants and workers were doing the right thing in throwing themselves into the class struggle in order to secure social and economic freedom: 'I myself am making the revolution for them without violence.' Asked further what his response would be if the masses, on coming to power, 'decided to put an end' to the landlords and princely classes, he replied: 'The masses at the present time do not regard the landlords and Princes as enemies. But it is necessary to make them aware of the wrong which is being done to them.'[8]

Nehru took a similar position on the question of political initiative in a speech to the Bihar Provincial Students' Conference in 1945. He praised the students for the extraordinary part they had played in the Quit India movement of 1942, but then went on to say: 'I encourage you to have academic discussions on political matters, but warn you against taking the initiative in the political field. You must look for guidance from the accepted political party which is the Congress.'[9] Indeed, this elitist line had been laid down in some areas as long ago as in 1921, with the peasants being asked to give up 'meetings' and 'disturbances' and to leave it to Gandhi to win *swaraj*.[10]

Thus, the experience of popular struggle in the decades between the two World Wars led to a somewhat sharper definition of the social content and objectives of Congress nationalism as well as a correspondingly more cautious political practice. And the 'socialist' statements of the UP Congress were instrumental in eroding the sympathy of the bigger landlords for the nationalist movement, whereas the party's activities during the 1930s led to some disillusionment at the lower levels of agrarian society and in general among progressive people – precisely because the 'socialist' stance amounted to so little.

A reflection of this disillusionment is found in the stories of Premchand. His writing in the 1920s tends increasingly to present a realistic portrayal of current events and problems – communal, cultural and agrarian – and to prescribe 'Gandhian' techniques for their solution. His later village stories, however, indicate a different understanding. 'Pus ki Raat', 'Thakur ka Kuan' and Premchand's classic last novel, *Godan* (1936), are all tales of unrelieved oppression and despair. There is a return to the long-suffering Indian peasant with his belief in *karma*.

Godan's Hori cannot win. His short-lived triumph in obtaining the gift of a cow from the Ahir *mukhia*[11] of a neighbouring village ends in grief: his precious acquisition arouses the jealousy of his neighbours, and his own brother poisons and kills the animal. At the same time Hori discovers that his only son has had an affair with the *mukhia's* widowed daughter and run away leaving her pregnant. Thus shame and new burdens descend on the household. More typically, Hori returns from the sale of his annual sugarcane crop without a rupee in his hand: two of his creditors quickly relieve him of the Rs 120 he gets for it, and there are still other creditors with whom he must settle other debts. To his enraged wife Hori says reassuringly: 'One can get work as a labourer. I will work and we shall eat.' His wife responds: 'Where is there work for a labourer in this village?'[12] Hori's oppressors include the agents of the British administration, but the Congress no longer figures as a saviour.

It thus emerges from the present study that the notion of the Indian nationalist movement as one of unilinear progression is somewhat misleading. It would appear, on the contrary, that as the organization and strength of the Congress increased and the scale of its campaigns widened, the social depth of the movement actually diminished. The fact that more arrests were made during the Civil Disobedience campaigns than during the Non-Cooperation Movement does not detract from the force of this observation. It simply reflects the fact that the Congress was more organized at the beginning of the 1930s than ever before and that the Government dealt with the agitation with a firmer hand, particularly in 1932. In any case the Civil Disobedience Movement evoked in UP and elsewhere a noticeably less enthusiastic response to the Congress appeals for members and volunteers than the call for *satyagraha* had done a decade earlier.[13]

In other parts of the country, such as the Central Provinces, the Non-Cooperation Movement did not have the kind of drive and power that it had in UP. In such areas the relative impact of the later mass nationalist campaigns was greater in extent as well as in social depth.[14] Yet I would suggest that even here the basic pattern of development was the same as in UP and other, older Congress strongholds. As a wider range of social groups consciously espoused the nationalist cause, and as struggles for initiative developed within the movement through crises and conflicts of various kinds, some clipping of the more provocative wings of the Congress became imperative. The numbers involved in its campaigns and even the figures of its membership, generally increased, but the 'catchment area' became narrower. It was a part of the transformation of the Congress from a movement into a party.[15]

II

About the character and mechanics of this particular transformation there is a great deal to learn from the UP experience of the 1920s and 1930s. For most of the economic and political factors that might explain the new departures in the nationalist movement were at work in the province at this time. The air was thick with rumours, promises and expectations of important constitutional concessions, and argument about the merits and flaws of various British gestures in this respect continued interminably and noisily throughout this period. There were crushing economic fluctuations, none more so than the crisis brought on by the Depression, which hit the province harder than any other part of India except perhaps Bengal and the Central Provinces (tied, respectively, by jute and cotton to the vicissitudes of the world market).[16] And these decades were marked by a series of widespread and yet intense political agitations that generated much popular enthusiasm. All this contributed to some significant and altogether new developments in the nationalist politics of UP.

One of the most critical and far-reaching of such developments was the Congress response to the contemporary pressures for a clarification of the social content of its nationalism. As demonstrated in these pages, this response was by no means entirely positive. Confronted with an increasingly articulate urge among the rural masses to harness the power of nationalism in order to knock down some of the obsolete structural impediments to social progress, the Congress leaders shied off and pressed the brakes on any radical action likely to involve a direct conflict between the exploiters and the exploited in Indian society. The manner in which they scaled down their world-transforming promises[17] and postponed any action that would fundamentally affect the structure of society indeed presaged the things to come.

Nevertheless, circumstances forced a certain degree of ideological differentiation – polarization would perhaps be too strong a word for what happened – within the Congress itself. The clear emergence of a left wing within the party was a development of much consequence. It inspired and helped in the formulation of an alternative ideal, though not quite a full-fledged strategy, of political emancipation through social change. And the CSP and the Kisan Sabhas played an important mobilizing role in the 1930s and afterwards. In UP and Bihar this accounted for much of the force of the 1942 revolt, while in the country as a whole it helped to foster the somewhat closely related ideologies of left nationalism and petty bourgeois socialism which were immensely important in the politics of the following decades. Moreover, as the workers' and peasants' movement matured and established itself as an independent force on the national scene, some of the leftist elements were to break away from the Congress and march along another road in the fight for national liberation – the road of scientific socialism.[18]

This historical process of the articulation of the social position and aims of different strands in the nationalist movement was clearly the child of the mass struggles of the period. It was not born in the Council Chamber. To say this is not to deny that Congress policies and, consequently, Indian politics in general, were influenced to no mean extent by the constitutional preoccupations of the leadership. We have already observed, for instance, that the impending constitutional changes inspired some of the institutional arrangements within the Congress in the early 1930s, particularly those connected with the establishment of a Harijan Sevak Sangh and the launching of a concerted Harijan programme.[19]

It is necessary however to maintain a clear perspective on this issue and not to overestimate it as some historians have recently been tempted to do.[20] The new opportunities offered within the framework of the colonial state attracted such elements of the various elite groups as were in a position to benefit from them by virtue of their superior command of material and cultural resources. Since these opportunities were limited, contest for them inevitably increased the rivalries between the elites and sharpened still further some of the existing conflicts of interest between them and the colonial authorities. The leadership of the Congress, too, was involved in these rivalries at many levels of institutional politics, and was able, on occasion, to use its influence among the masses in order to solve in its own favour the contradictions produced by its striving for a larger share of the loaves and fishes of office and other secondary forms of power conceded by the British. This is why nationalist politics came from time to time to acquire the semblance of a constitutional cockfight.

To look upon this as the whole or even the more substantial part of the reality of Indian nationalism is to take a narrow view of history. For constitutionalism hardly explains all the political developments of the period. Even the chasm that began to appear between the Congress and the Muslims by the late 1930s can hardly be understood in terms of a squabble over immediate constitutional issues, although disagreements over separate electorates and reserved seats for various groups had already before this period hardened communal attitudes among the elites. The manner and content of much of the Congress propaganda in the 1920s, dictated more often than not by short-term goals, had tended to play directly into the hands of communalist Muslim and Hindu leaders and the colonial administration, and contributed to political mobilization on a religious sectarian basis. There was little in what the Congress said or did during the period under study to encourage the great majority of the Muslims of UP – workers, peasants, artisans, traders, intelligentsia and other sections of the Muslim petty bourgeoisie – to look beyond their communal identity and acknowledge their status as the oppressed who shared with their opposite numbers among the Hindus a common colonial bondage and exploitation by the worst semi-feudal elements among the indigenous elite of all denominations. What made it impossible for the Congress to win the support of the Muslim masses of UP during the period under study was the failure of its leaders to develop a mass appeal across religious (and caste) lines, itself a product of their reluctance to espouse the basic social and economic demands of the urban and rural poor.

Thus it was not the Congress's – still less, the people's – response to the constitutional initiatives of the British authorities that made up the stuff of nationalism in northern India in the 1920s and 1930s. It was the economic response of an agrarian hinterland of the empire to the crises of world capitalism that constituted its material basis, providing much of its force and determining its major changes of direction. Nationalist energies were drawn from sources sunk deep in the underlying divisions of north Indian society, especially the village society of peasants and agricultural labourers dominated by landlords, money-lenders and tax-collectors. The crises weakened, if they did not altogether dissolve, some of the traditional ties that bound together the upper and the nether halves of this millstone and created the conditions for their mutual recognition as class enemies. It is the explosive impact of this recognition, its uneven pitch and its lapses that made up the true score of the nationalist movement during this period.

III

One final thought on the issue of mobilization. While the presence of the Congress was, without doubt, a major source of inspiration for popular revolt, there seem to have been two different processes of mobilization at work – largely independent of one another. Barauda and Bhilaoti in Agra district and Jamunipur in Allahabad illustrate one of these. In their more or less long-term commitment to the Congress and disciplined response to the call for non-violent *satyagraha*, the men and women of these villages reveal the influence of extended propaganda and organization. The actions of the people of Bhatwaria, also in Allahabad district, and of many parts of Awadh, however, reflect a different experience. Peasants in these places did not receive quite the same guidance from recognized Congress leaders. Instead they appear to have appropriated the slogans of self-help and *satyagraha, swaraj* and (in due course) socialism, and interpreted them by their own lights.[21]

The UP Congress's own account of developments in Bara Banki district in 1931 shows how the Bara Banki peasant stepped forward and took the lead in the struggle after the Congress and the Government had agreed to a truce when the agrarian crisis was at its worst. A three-man committee was sent by the UPCC to make detailed enquiries in June-July 1931 when, as we have noted,[22] gatherings of armed villagers had become common in the district. Their impressions bear quotation at some length. One complaint made by local landlords and their agents against 'Congress' workers, they recorded, was that:

> …many of them did not act according to the directions given by the local Congress leaders but preached a general non-payment of rent and they further preached that the tenant was the owner of the land and he could do whatever he liked with it, plant gardens, sink wells and build houses thereupon without seeking the permission of the zamindar. All this was, of course, in defiance of the legal rights of the zamindar and very much to his distaste. This complaint may have been couched in a language of exaggeration but again we have no doubt that attempts have been made to spread ideas among the peasantry about their having rights in the land which the zamindar is at the present moment not willing to concede. One Congress worker specifically asked by us as to what he told the tenants as to the Congress message, said that he told them that the land was a gift of God. It belonged

to the tenant and the zamindar equally and had it belonged to the zamindar, he would have been in a position to take it away. Another cultivator who was a Congress worker said to us that he said to the peasants that they should retain for their own subsistence and that of their families as much as was necessary and pay whatever remained to the zamindar…but…we must add that no instance of any retaliation on the part of the tenants among whom the Congress workers have been working, towards the zamindars were brought to our notice and nonviolence has been observed on their part…

It seems to us that it is absolutely necessary that clear and definite instructions should be given to all the Congress workers in the villages as to the attitude which the tenants should be asked to adopt towards the zamindars in the matter of payment of rents and other cognate matters. *Kisan Sabhas* have been organised but without definite programme, and unless properly led might do more harm than any good. We also regret to note that in our extensive tour through the Bara Banki District we found that use of *khadi* was little in evidence nor were any *charkhas* being plied in the villages.[23]

We have in these statements a clear indication of the fact that the Congress organization was poorly represented in Bara Banki. Its insignia – the *charkha* and *khadi* – were missing from most parts of it. And it is evident that the participation of the peasants in the anti-imperialist campaign did not come about because of any kind of direct encouragement or special prodding by a propaganda machine. The happenings in the Bara Banki villages were not only a departure from the methods of the Congress – with peasant demonstrations often assuming a violent form. What was perhaps more frightening from the Congress point of view was that the peasants, under the banner of the Congress, were deviating from the thrust of the Congress programme. In the name of fighting the Raj, local workers were propagating the slogan of land to the tiller which was directly opposed to the message of Congress nationalism.

That the involvement of the official Congress organization of the district was minimal was directly admitted by the UPCC investigators: 'the local Congress Committee was not strong in numbers nor does it seem to have been well-supported by the educated classes in the district, [but] the tenants flocked to it and *on their invitation* a number of meetings were held in the interior and the Congress Committees organised'.[24]

This process of self-mobilization by the peasants was indeed a feature of many of the most famous mass campaigns and demonstrations of the 1920s and 1930s. The leaders of the Bhatwaria tenants, with whom the landlord Mohammad Jawwad negotiated on 7 June 1931 before the clash in which he and six of his party lost their lives, were two Lodhs, Narain and Sallahi – illiterate, low-caste peasants, unconcerned with universities, local boards or even Gandhian *ashrams*. Two men from neighbouring villages who arrived with other peasants to strengthen the hand of the Bhatwaria rebels, perhaps better fit the traditional image of the rabble rouser from outside; and it is they who were described in the court proceedings that ensued as the chief instigators of the trouble. Yet one of them, Gayadin, a Brahman who succumbed in jail to injuries sustained during the riot, is not considered important enough to be mentioned in the long list of 'freedom fighters' and martyrs so laboriously drawn up by the Congress Government of UP to mark the Silver Jubilee of Indian independence. The other, Nand Kishore Jaiswal, is the only participant in the Bhatwaria action to find his way into this list. He is described in it simply as 'an enthusiastic worker who was involved in the famous no-rent campaign in Bhatwaria'. There is no reference to any other 'Congress' connection or to any earlier or later jail sentence for participation in Congress activities.[25]

The violence at Chaura Police Station in Gorakhpur, known to history as the 'tragedy' of Chauri-Chaura, which became a large part of the argument for calling off the Non-Cooperation Movement in 1922, proves on examination to have a background of a somewhat similar leadership and organization. On 4 February 1922, between three and four thousand peasants from the surrounding villages were involved in a demonstration outside Chaura Police Station that led to a battle in which the incensed peasants killed 23 policemen and *chowkidars*, injured several others, plundered Government property and burnt down the Police Station. The demonstration was organized by a handful of nationalist volunteers who had been insulted and beaten by the local Sub-Inspector of Police three days earlier for the attempted picketing of meat and fish and liquor shops at a bi-weekly *bazaar* held in the neighbourhood. And the demonstrators had planned, on 4 February which was the next market day, to extract an apology from the Sub-Inspector and then go on to picket the *bazaar* in order to bring down the price of fish and meat or, failing that, to stop the sale of these commodities and of intoxicants altogether.

It was only three weeks before these happenings that Niaz Ahmad, *alias* Hakim Arif, whom the Sessions Judge of Gorakhpur described as 'a leading non-cooperator', organized a Circle Committee at a meeting held in this area. Nazar Ali was appointed President of the Circle, Lal Muhammad, Shikari and Bhagwati *bania*, Secretaries, and Ramrup *barhai* an officer, and later Nazar Ali obtained the services of an ex-army man, Bhagwan *ahir*, as drillmaster. And, as the votary of justice observed on the same occasion, 'the Circle at once showed very great activity'. The tremendous enthusiasm generated within a short time is evident from the actions of the thousands of depressed peasants, described in the court proceedings as coming mainly from 'the lowest strata of society', who defied the powerful local representative of a powerful Raj – shouting, when the police opened fire, that Mahatma Gandhi was working miraculously in favour of the peasants and turning the bullets into water.

All of the office-bearers of the Circle Committee mentioned above, except Bhagwati *bania*, and a man called Mahadeo were present at two meetings on 1 and 2 February which decided on mobilizing forces against the Sub-Inspector of Police. They and five other unnamed men who attended the second of these meetings were described as the 'officials and ringleaders' of the agitation. Yet it is remarkable that none of them was capable of writing the letter that they decided to send to neighbouring volunteer associations; they had to employ a boy of 11 called Nakched to transcribe five copies of a letter for them.[26] Here, indeed, we have a striking example of leadership by illiterate peasants from the bottom of the social hierarchy[27] and autonomous mobilization by the rural poor for anti-British agitation.

Evidence from other parts of India also provides instances of peasants taking the initiative to organize themselves and indeed guide the Congress in the course of the struggle. David Hardiman's researches have shown how in Kheda district in Gandhi's own Gujarat, during the period 1917–34, various peasant groups mobilized themselves over and over again and took the initiative for protest action, demanding and receiving acquiescence or support from a reluctant urban nationalist leadership only at a later stage.[28] Jacques Pouchepadass, Arvind Das and others have argued the same case convincingly for Champaran in 1917, the scene of Gandhi's earliest triumph in India. In Pouchepadass's reading the 1917 movement appears as a 'traditional' resistance movement similar to those that had broken out periodically in the district since the 1860s, and local leaders were responsible for calling Gandhi in. Bringing forward Gandhi's name as the authority for every act of rebellion they instigated, they drew the peasants into illegal or violent forms of resistance that were quite distasteful to Gandhi, even though he could not too overtly repudiate them. All this constituted what may be called the 'internal face' of the movement, which extended far beyond the scope of initiative of the intelligentsia.[29]

This internal face of popular nationalist campaigns deserves study in its own right. The actions of peasants in Bhatwaria and Chauri Chaura cannot be explained in terms of an aberration in the freedom struggle, a failure on the part of the masses to imbibe the spirit of Gandhism sufficiently well, though this is precisely how the Congress leaders and elite historians have always represented it. Rather, it must be recognized that there was an alternative stream of popular politics within the Indian nationalist movement. For all their criss-crossing and mutual imbrications, this stream was different in character and approach from the stream of elite politics represented by Gandhi and the Congress. It was not bound down in the same way by legalism or constitutionalism. It often showed evidence of horizontal mobilization cutting across lines of faction and caste. And in the period of struggle against foreign rule it appears to have been marked by a fight for a more fundamental transformation of the colonial regime – with the masses attacking their local overlords as well as the agents of an alien Raj who together upheld an obsolete and oppressive social system.[30]

Through recognition of these different streams of politics, it may be possible to arrive at a better understanding of the strength and complexity of the nationalist movement after the First World War, and of why, for example, the Presidencies lost their place as the leaders of the movement from this time. As the contradictions of colonialism became more evident and the anti-imperialist struggle matured, the inter-meshing of the two streams of politics became more frequent and the question of links between the two crucial. Where these were forged successfully a powerful nationalist campaign developed. In Gujarat a devoted Gandhian leadership responded to the needs of a discontented Patidar peasantry (composed mainly of rich and middle peasants) with whom they had close social links, to lay the foundations of effective agitation. In the backward, landlord-dominated provinces of UP and Bihar elite nationalist leaders who had no secure urban base and little experience of mass politics, proved willing to reach out to the rural areas and were carried along at least some distance by the waves of popular unrest.

It is our contention, moreover, that these uprisings of the people at large – the violent protests in Lahore and Bombay and Delhi in 1919, peasant revolt in the Godavari and Vizagapatnam agency in Andhra Pradesh from 1922 to 1924, forest *satyagraha* by tribals in Central India in 1930-1[31], and so on – had a considerable impact on Indian politics in general and the Congress in particular. If the experience of Gujarat, UP and Bihar, the home grounds of Vallabhbhai Patel and Jawaharlal Nehru and Rajendra Prasad, is anything to go by, it may turn out to be truer for the country as a whole that it was the popular masses who brought an increased militancy and 'radicalism' to the Congress, rather than a militant and radical Congress which took politics to the people and armed them with the necessary initiatives for anti-imperialist struggle after 1917. Whether or not such mass protests and demonstrations had much direct influence on the reform of elite institutions or the policies of the British, they constitute an important part of the totality of Indian politics and the Indian nationalist movement. To neglect this, to concentrate on the Gandhian or Congress stream of nationalism and to treat the popular actions as an abnormal outgrowth, peripheral to a study of the development of the Indian nation, is to present a very distorted picture of the history of the times.

One of the best accounts of a phase of the nationalist struggle, Sumit Sarkar's study of the Swadeshi Movement in Bengal, makes the important point that the nationalist leaders of the first decade of the twentieth century were unable to break through to the peasant masses. Commenting on the nationalist movement as a whole, Sarkar describes as modern India's greatest tragedy 'the failure to intermingle the currents of national and social discontent into a single anti-colonial and anti-feudal revolution.'[32] There is a recognition here of the existence of different levels of political consciousness and activity which evidently never merged altogether. But this is not simply a case of failure on the part of the elite nationalist leaders to exercise an initiative in one particular area. A good deal more is involved in this innocuous omission. The evidence from the period between the two World Wars points to the presence of two streams of nationalism which often crossed and influenced one another, but continued by and large to flow in their separate courses. There were several instances of their coming together but also many indications of a struggle for initiative as expressed negatively in the efforts of the Congress leadership to control and, if necessary, suppress the stream of popular politics.

In Bengal, where the structure of agrarian society produced a crisis at least as acute as that in UP in the 1920s, 1930s and 1940s, popular protests were championed by isolated Gandhian workers in certain districts[33] but struck no responsive chord in the main body of the provincial Congress leadership. Here, the opposition of the Congress to popular demands in the rural areas was manifestly calamitous in the long run; for the force of the peasant movement was diverted into the swelling currents of communalism.[34] As it happened, the responsiveness of the Congress leaders proved to be strictly limited in UP too.

The Congress electoral victory and the formation of a popular Congress ministry in 1937 had generated tremendous enthusiasm all over UP. One result was an outburst of intense and continuous agitation among peasants and industrial workers, and other groups, for the setting right of long-felt wrongs. Regarding labour disputes, for instance, the authorized Congress account of this period of national government in UP noted that there had been 'a sense of suppression and immediately on the advent of the Congress Ministry disputes between capital and labour began and continued in one form or the other throughout...Labour, held down for so long sometimes failed to realise the true implications of civil liberty [sic].'[35]

By the end of the decade, however, the provincial Congress had done much to bring popular nationalism under control. The party that emerged out of the experience of civil disobedience, widespread election campaigns and ministry formation was far more sophisticated but not a great deal more progressive than before. For it developed a more self-conscious conservatism in the form of support for social stability and insistence on measured and 'orderly' progress, even as it declaimed ever more radical slogans. One is tempted to say that the 'poor man's party', as the new generation of Congress leaders described it in 1920, had become a rich peasants' party by 1940. Thus Congress nationalism became increasingly irrelevant to the predicament of men like Premchand's luckless peasant Hori, and what survived of initiative and agitation among the mass of the peasantry had to search elsewhere for inspiration and leadership.

The immediate nationalist aims of the Congress have long since been achieved. The protests of masses of the labouring poor, in towns and villages, played no small part in that achievement. What the latter had gained from the success of the nationalist movement is a question that many like Hori were still asking in the decades after 1947. The nation, for them, was yet to come to its own.

Glossary

accbutoddhar	uplift of untouchables.
bazdawa	agreement by which a tenant relinquished all claims to compensation for any improvement on his or her land.
bhaiyachara	brotherhood, community jointly holding an undivided estate.
bigha	measure of land, 5/8 of an acre in much of UP.
doab	land between two rivers (used in this book for the land between the Ganga and Yamuna, unless otherwise specified).
jajmani	conventional right of a priest, potter, cobbler, barber, etc. to perform his respective duties on ritual and other customary occasions for particular individuals and families, who are his *jajmans*.
kharif	monsoon crop.
khatauni	village accountant's register of rights in land.
khudkasht	a proprietary cultivator's holding which is cultivated by him.
mahajan	private banker, trader, frequently a money-lender.
mahal	revenue-paying unit, territorially defined right of a *zamindar* (q.v.)
mahalwari	settlement of land on the basis of *mahals* (q.v.)
mandal	circle, unit of district board administration.
nazrana	premium paid by a tenant to be admitted or re-admitted to a holding.
parchas	slips laying down rental agreements.
parganah	sub-division of a *tahsil* (q.v.) for revenue purposes.
pattidar	proprietary leaseholder, sharer in a coparcenary estate.
qasba	small town, production or distribution centre.

rabi	spring crop.
raris	notable,with inherited landed or commercial wealth.
sahukar	small scale banker, trader, money-lender.
sir	land held by a proprietor under title of personal cultivation.
sangathan	organization (in early 20th century north India, movement for the organization and protection of Hindus).
shuddhi	movement for the purification and reclamation of Hindus.
swadeshi	'of one's own land'; hence, movement for promotion of Indian-made goods.
swaraj	self-rule, independence.
tabligh	propagation (in early 20th century north India, movement for the propagation of the Muslim faith).
tahsil	administrative sub-division of a district.
taluqdar	proprietor of a *taluqa* or regional sub-division, usually comprising several *mahals* (q.v.) in Awadh.
tanzim	organization, movement for the organization and protection of Muslims.
ulema	Muslim learned men, theologians.
zamindar	holder of a right of property in land who engaged to pay revenue to the Government.

Notes

Chapter 1. Introduction

1. R C Majumdar, *History of the Freedom Movement in India*, Vol. I (Calcutta 1962), xii-xiv; J Nehru, *The Discovery of India* (London 1946; 3rd edn., 1951), 331; R P Dutt, *India Today* (London 1940; 2nd Indian edn., 1949), 312.
2. R C Majumdar, *et al.*, *An Advanced History of India* (London 1950), 984–8.
3. T G P Spear, 'British Historical Writing in the Era of the Nationalist Movements' in C H Philips (ed.), *Historians of India, Pakistan and Ceylon* (London 1961), 414.
4. Dutt, *India Today*, 296.
5. Majumdar, *History of the Freedom Movement*, I, xi.
6. For one of many classic statements, see R Craddock, *The Dilemma in India* (London 1929).
7. Majumdar, *History of the Freedom Movement*, I, xiv.
8. Nehru, *Discovery of India*, 336, 340.
9. P C Joshi, 'Development Perspectives in India: Some Reflections on Nehru and Gandhi', in B R Nanda and V C Joshi (eds), *Studies in Modern Indian History*, No. 1 (New Delhi 1972), 137–8; Bipan Chandra: 'Elements of Continuity and Change in Early Nationalist Activity', paper presented at Symposium on Continuity and Change in Indian National Movement, 33rd Session, Indian History Congress, (Muzaffarpur 1972), esp. fn 11.
10. V Chirol, *India* (London 1926), 213.
11. 'The politically-minded portion of the people of India…are intellectually our children,' Cd. 9109, *East India (Constitutional Reforms). Report on Indian Constitutional Reforms* (London 1918), 115. See also Lord Irwin, 'The Evolution of Political Life in India' in J Cumming (ed.), *Political India, 1832–1932* (Oxford 1932), and T G P Spear's review of A Basu, *The Growth of Education and Political Development in India*, in *The Indian Economic and Social History Review*, XII, 2 (April-June 1975), 196. For the significance of religion for Indian nationalist politics, see Earl of Ronaldshay. *The Heart of Aryavarta. A Study of the Psychology of Indian Unrest* (London 1925), 102–4; and (IOL) MSS. Eur. E. 220, Hailey Colln, 24A, Irwin's Massey Lecture at Toronto University (1932).
12. See, for example, D A Low, ed., *Soundings in Modern South Asian History* (London 1968); and J A Gallagher, *et al* (eds), *Locality, Province and Nation. Essays on Indian Politics, 1870 to 1940* (Cambridge 1973).
13. See A Seal, *The Emergence of Indian Nationalism. Competition and Collaboration in the later Nineteenth Century* (Cambridge 1968).

14. Gallagher, *et al* (eds), *Locality, Province and Nation*; C J Baker, 'Non-cooperation in South India' in Baker and D A Washbrook, *South India: Political Institutions and Political Change, 1880–1940* (Delhi 1975).

15. J H Broomfield, 'The Regional Elites: A Theory of Modern Indian History', *Indian Economic and Social History Review*, III, 3 (September 1966); E F Irschick, *Politics and Social Conflict in South India. The Non-Brahman Movement and Tamil Separatism, 1916–29.* (California 1969). Even C A Bayly: *The Local Roots of Indian Politics. Allahabad 1880–1920* (Oxford 1975), a perceptive study of politics in a limited area, refers only to the competence or otherwise of urban leaders to draw together local dissidences; see pp. 280, 282. There is no question of any initiative in 'local' quarters.

16. See, for example, Ranajit Guha, ed., *Subaltern Studies. Writings on South Asian History and Society*, Volumes I to VI (Delhi 1982–9) and the later volumes, VII-XI, in that series edited by other members of the Subaltern Studies collective; Sumit Sarkar, *Modern India, 1885–1947* (Delhi 1983; 2nd edn., London 1988); J Krishnamurty, ed., *Survival, Politics and Work. Indian Women, 1880–1980* (special issue of *Indian Economic and Social History Review*, XX, 1, March 1983); Kumkum Sangari and Sudesh Vaid, eds., *Recasting Women. Essays in Colonial History* (Delhi 1989); Tanika Sarkar, *Hindu Wife, Hindu Nation: Community, Religion and Cultural Nationalism* (Delhi 2001); and other books published by Kali for Women in the 1990s. Sarkar, *Modern India* (1988); Shahid Amin, 'Agrarian Bases of Nationalist Agitations in India. An Historiographical Survey', in D A Low ed., *The Indian National Congress. Centenary Hindsights* (Delhi 1988); Sugata Bose and Ayesha Jalal, *Modern South Asia. History, Culture, Political Economy* (Delhi 1997); and for UP, P D Reeves, *Landlords and Governments in Uttar Pradesh: A Study of their Relations until Zamindari Abolition* (Bombay 1991) provide useful bibliographies of relevant works.

17. The phrase is Gandhi's, referring to his incomprehension of the forces that lay behind the widespread and militant popular uprising against the Rowlatt Acts of 1919.

18. Hailey Colln, 51, Hailey-D A Low, 10 January 1961. See also ibid, 13B, Hailey-Irwin, 26 August 1928.

19. Sri Prakasa Colln (NML), File 'From G B Lambert', Lambert-Sri Prakasa, 12 December 1928 (emphasis added). Districts are sub-divided into *tahsils* and further into *parganahs* for administrative and revenue purposes.

20. The quotation comes from F Robinson, *Separatism among Indian Muslims. The Politics of the United Provinces Muslims, 1860–1923* (Cambridge 1974), 4. See also P R Brass, *Language, Religion and Politics in North India* (Cambridge 1974), 171; and Mushirul Hasan, *Nationalism and Communal Politics in India, 1916–28* (Delhi 1979).

21. Nehru, *Discovery of India*, 349.

22. *CWMG*, Volume XXIX (Ahmedabad 1967), 396.

Chapter 2. Uttar Pradesh After the First World War

1. See John R Mclane, *Indian Nationalism and the Early Congress* (Princeton, N.J., 1977); C A Bayly, *The Local Roots of Indian Politics*; Sudhir Chandra, *The Oppressive Present. Literature and Social Consciousness in Colonial India* (Delhi 1992).

2. *Census of India, 1921. United Provinces of Agra and Oudh. Volume XVI. Part I—Report* (Allahabad 1923), 38. The category 'urban' included 'any town, village,

suburb, bazaar or inhabited place' declared as a' town area' under the UP Town Areas Act of 1914; any 'local area' declared a municipality or a 'notified area' under the UP Municipalities Act of 1916 – a notified area being 'any local area, other than a municipality, town area or agricultural village' where it was considered desirable to make administrative provision for some or all the municipal functions, sanitation, public works, census operations, provision of basic medical facilities, etc.; any cantonment; and 'any other continuous group of houses permanently inhabited by not less than 5,000 persons which having regard to the character of the population, the relative density of the dwellings, the importance of the place as a centre of trade and its historic associations, the Provincial Census Superintendent decided to treat as a town'; *Census of India, 1931. United Provinces of Agra and Oudh. Vol. XVIII. Part I – Report*, 122.

3. *Doab*, the tract of country between two rivers, refers in this book to the land between the Ganga and Yamuna unless otherwise specified.

4. See J Krishnamurty, 'Changes in the Occupational Structure of the Indian Union, 1901–61' (typescript).

5. *Statistical Abstract for British India (Department of Commercial Intelligence and Statistics) (1916–17, 1926–7)*; See A K Bagchi, *Private Investment in India, 1900–39 (Cambridge 1972; Indian edition 1975)* for general picture.

6. *Upper India Chamber of Commerce, Cawnpore, 1888–1938 (n.p., n.d.)*, 29.

7. Hailey Colln, 51, P D Reeves's seminar paper (Australian National University, April 1960) on tenurial conditions in UP and Punjab; also B R Misra, *Land Revenue Policy in the United Provinces under British Rule* (Banaras 1942) and B H Baden-Powell, *Land Systems of British India*, Vol. II, Book III (Oxford 1892). For the special relationship between government and *taluqdars*, see Reeves, *Landlords and Governments in Uttar Pradesh*.

8 W and C Wiser, *Behind Mud Walls 1930–1960* (California 1967), 111.

9. K Nair, *Blossoms in the Dust* (London 1961), 75.

10. *UP Census, 1931. Part I*, 397. The census counted landowners who earned the major part of their income from land they held as tenants, or from other sources, in categories other than that of 'cultivating proprietors'. But it would be difficult to argue that men who earned most of their living as tenants or labourers were really peasant proprietors.

11. H R Nevill, *Rae Bareli: A Gazetteer. Being Volume XXXIX of the District Gazetteers of the United Provinces of Agra and Oudh* (Allahabad 1905), Appx., xxxvi; Robinson, *Separatism among Indian Muslims*, 61; E T Stokes; 'The Structure of Landholding in Uttar Pradesh, 1860–1948', *Indian Economic and Social History Review*, XII, 2 (April-June 1975), 119.

12. *Report of the United Provinces Zamindari Abolition Committee. Vol. II. Statistics* (Allahabad 1948), 12–17.

13. See D N Dhanagare, *Agrarian Movements and Gandhian Politics* (Agra 1975), 83–4 for a similar classification; also Stokes, 'Structure of Landholding...' for details of the pyramidal ownership structure. See chapter 6, section II below for an assessment of the situation in Agra and Rae Bareli districts.

14. *Report of the UP Zamindari Abolition Committee, II*, 6. In the *khatauni* or village accountant's register, Part I recorded the rights of those who held land as tenants or as their own *sir* or *khudkasht*, Part II the rights of sub-tenants and of tenants on *sir* and *khudkasht* land.

15. *Report of the United Provinces Provincial Banking Enquiry Committee, 1929–30, Volume I (Allahabad 1930)*, 25; see also E Whitcombe, *Agrarian Conditions in Northern India. Volume I. The United Provinces under British Rule, 1860–1900* (California 1971), 169, 173.

16. D M Stewart, *Gorakhpur (Western Portion) Settlement Report 1919*, 13, quoted in Stokes, 'Structure of Landholding...', 127.

17. *UP Census, 1931, Pt., I*, 396.

18. Idem.

19. P J Musgrave, 'Landlords and Lords of the Land: Estate Management and Social Control in Uttar Pradesh, 1860–1920', *Modern Asian Studies*, 6, 3, (July 1972), 274–5; and Musgrave, 'An Unseen Hand? Rural Credit and Rural Society in the United Provinces, 1860–1920,' Seminar paper, Institute of Commonwealth Studies, London (25 March 1975).

20. S S Nehru, *Caste and Credit in the Rural Area* (Calcutta 1932), 103.

21. *Final Report on the Settlement and Record Operations in District Agra* (Allahabad 1930), 'Note' by Settlement Commissioner, K N Knox, 5 April 1930, 1.

22. Whitcombe, *Agrarian Conditions in Northern India*, 119.

23. *Ibid.*, 166, 171–4; A Siddiqi, *Agrarian Change in Northern Indian State* (Oxford 1973), 133; Shahid Amin, *Sugarcane and Sugar in Gorakhpur* (Delhi 1984), 75–81.

24. Premchand, *Godan* (1936; new edn., Allahabad 1975).

25. National Council for Applied Economic Research, *Rehabilitation and Development of Basti District* (New Delhi 1959), 13, quoted in Nair, *Blossoms in the Dust*, 82–3. Cf. Nair's own description of the miserable conditions in the two Ballia villages she visited, ibid., 81–6.

26. Cf. T O Beidelman, *A Comparative Analysis of the Jajmani System* (New York 1959).

27. *Famine Inquiry Commission. Final Report* (Delhi 1945), 278. Emphasis added.

28. (IOL) MSS. Eur. F. 116, Harcourt Butler Colln, 80, 'Note on Amendment of Oudh Rent Act' enclosed with Letter no. 1/Camp, Secy Board of Revenue, UP-Chief Secy, UP, 1 February 1921.

29. ibid., D.O. No. 1336, Hailey-Hopkins, 19 January 1921. See also A A Waugh, *Rent and Revenue Policy in the United Provinces* (Lucknow 1932), 16.

30. ibid., 13–14; Misra, *Land Revenue Policy in UP*, 260–1.

31. Nehru, *Caste and Credit in the Rural Area*; Whitcombe, *Agrarian Conditions in Northern India*, 44. The factor of high caste appears to have been less significant than that of service/kinship links in the matter of rent reductions. See chapter 6, section II below for evidence of its further decline since the late nineteenth century.

32. *Report on the Revenue Administration of the United Provinces of Agra and Oudh, 1920–1*, 7, and *1922–3*, 'Government Resolution', 4; *Report on the Administration of the United Provinces of Agra and Oudh, 1920–1*, viii; P D Reeves, 'The Politics of Order. "Anti-non-cooperation" in the United Provinces, 1921', *Journal of Asian Studies*, XXV, 2 (February 1966), 262.

33. *Prices and Wages in India. 37th Issue* (Calcutta 1923), 154–5; *UP Administration Report, 1918–19*, ii and *1920–1*, ii.

34. The UP Government declared that two million people died of influenza in 1918. How it calculated this from the total number of deaths from fever is not known. The following table gives details of mortality in UP (plus birth rates) for 1916–9:

				Deaths from				
Year	Fever (including influenza)	Plague	Cholera	Smallpox	Gastric and Respiratory diseases	Total no. of deaths	Death rate per 1000	Birth rate per 1000
1916	997,496	49,368	33,300	1,515	43,694	1,381,299	29.5	43.09
1917	1,266,519	129,084	21,440	2,011	51,234	1,774,896	37.91	46.08
1918	3,217,678	174,805	119,746	2,908	53,276	3,856,762	82.37	39.89
1919	1,575,632	17,240	81,365	10,993	41,098	1,742,835	41.69	32.39

Source: **UP Administration Reports** (1916–17 to 1919–20).

35. For useful accounts of the agitation, see Reeves, 'The Politics of Order'; Dhanagare, *Agrarian Movements and Gandhian Politics*, 88–94; M H Siddiqi, *Agrarian Unrest in North India. The United Provinces, 1918–22* (New Delhi 1978); and Kapil Kumar, *Peasants in Revolt: Oudh, 1918–22* (Delhi 1984).
36. See Chapter 4 below.
37. *UP Census, 1921, I*, 60, 64; Brass, *Language, Religion and Politics*, 143.
38. Robinson, *Separatism among Indian Muslims*, 327–33; Bayly, *Local Roots of Indian Politics*, 255–6. See also the example of Azamgarh in chapter 3, section II below.
39. H Tinker, *The Foundations of Local Self-Government in India, Pakistan and Burma* (London 1954), 99.
40. P D Reeves, *et al, A Handbook to Elections in Uttar Pradesh, 1920–51* (Delhi 1975), xxxiv.
41. *Indian Statutory Commission. Volume IX. Memorandum submitted by the Government of the United Provinces to the Indian Statutory Commission* (London 1930), 481.
42. See D J H Page, *Prelude to Partition: The Indian Muslims and the Imperial System of Control, 1920–32.* (Delhi, 1982), 'Introduction' & Ch.1.
43. *UP Administration Report, 1927–8*, 90; Cmd. 3407, *Indian Statutory Commission. Interim Report of the Indian Statutory Commission. (Review of Growth of Education in British India by the Auxiliary Committee appointed by the Commission) Sept. 1929* (London 1929), 24–8, 121, 128.
44. *Statistical Abstract for British India* (1916–17 and 1926–7).
45. *UP Administration Report, 1927–8*, 90.
46. Ibid., 1928–9, 101.
47. *Mohalla* is a locality or ward of a town.
48. See *Aj, Abhyudaya, Pratap* and the large collection of Hindi journals held at KNPS, Banaras. Proscribed pamphlets (IOL, NAI) and interviews also indicate this clearly.
49. *Brahmana-sarvasva* (KNPS), Part 22 (January 1925).
50. There are echoes of this in Premchand's *Rangbhumi* in the characters of Vinay Singh and Sofia, who both turn revolutionary in the course of their public work.

Chapter 3. The Congress Organization, 1920–1940

1. Cd. 9109, *East India (Constitutional Reforms) (1918)*, 119–20.
2. See N V Rajkumar, *Development of the Congress Constitution* (New Delhi 1949).
3. Gopal Krishna, 'The Development of the Indian National Congress as a Mass Organisation, 1918–23', *Journal of Asian Studies*, XXV, 3 (May 1966).
4. AICC (NML) P24/1929, Sri Prakasa – JN, Banaras, 5 May 1929.
5. JN Colln (NML) Misc. Ps. 'A Report by a Congress Worker on his Tour in Karchana Tahsil, Dist. Allahabad, November 1933'.
6. Rajkumar, *Development of the Congress Constitution; Aj* (2–6 November 1934).
7. The argument is put forward in B R Tomlinson, *The Indian National Congress and the Raj, 1929–42* (London 1976).
8. J M Brown, *Gandhi's Rise to Power, Indian Politics, 1915–1922* (Cambridge 1972), 356; also R A Gordon, 'Aspects in the History of the Indian National Congress, with Special Reference to the Swarajya Party, 1919–1927', Oxford D Phil thesis (1970), 313–14.
9. The above is based on *Constitution and Rules of the United Provinces Congress Committee* (UP PCC, Allahabad 1921).
10. *The Leader* (4 May 1921); AICC 11/1926, for examples of the PCC Council membership.
11. Gopal Krishna, 'The Development of the INC'; AICC 3/1922, cited in J M Brown, *Gandhi's Rise to Power*, 355n.
12. GOI Home Poll, 1922, No. 741, quoted in Brown, *Gandhi's Rise to Power*, 320–1. Gopal Krishna, 'The Development of the INC' gives the smaller figure of Rs. 373,000 as UP's contribution between 1921 and 1923.
13. This account is based on UP GAD 604/1920 (SRR), Note on 'The Sewa Samiti movement in the United Provinces' by P Biggane, Asst to the DIG Police, CID, UP, 18 December 1919; 'Note on the Volunteer Movement in the United Provinces', P Biggane, 5 November 1920; 'Note on the Volunteer Movement in the United Provinces', S O'Connor, 27 May 1922.
14. Ibid, O'Connor's Note.
15. ibid (emphasis in original).
16. AICC 3/1922 Pt 2; O'Connor's Note, op. cit.
17. Cmd. 1586, *East India (Non-cooperation)*, 4; UP GAD 604/1920; Krishna Dutt Bajpayee: *Braj ka Itihas*, Pt. I (Mathura 1955); P D Tandon Colln (NAI), Grp K, File 2, S.n. 24, 'Servants of India Society. Report for 1932', Poona 12 June 1933.
18. See chapter 5 below.
19. C Brandt, *et al* (eds), *A Documentary History of Chinese Communism* (London 1952), 318. The communists claimed a membership of 50,000 for the former and 300,000 for the latter period.
20. M Fainsod, *How Russia is Ruled* (Harvard 1963), 249, gives a membership of 23,600 for 1917, 115,000 for 1918 and 251,000 for 1919.
21. For the electoral clash, see chapter 5, section II below.
22. AICC G1/1927, Report of Arbitration Board, Patna 19 April 1927. See also AICC 13/1926, Pt. II, Correspondence between MN and Sitla Sahai, 30 September and October 1926; AICC G74/1926; *The Leader* (5 and 15 December 1926).
23. AICC P24/1929, Sri Prakasa-JN, 15 March 1929; AICC 41/1929, Congress Bulletin No. 6. Other provinces were in no better shape at this time; MN Colln (NML) subject File 'INC', MN-J M Mehta, 20 June 1929.
24. *The Leader* (22 June, 4 and 14 September 1929).
25. AICC G-40 (i)/1929; *The Leader* (6 April and 13 December 1929); PAI (CID Office Lucknow), 6 April 1929 and 25 January 1930.

26. UP Police Dept 1077/1930 (SRR); (IOL), MSS. Eur. D. 724, Hume Colln, III, Pt. I, letter to his parents, Hardwar, 26 April 1930.

27. Govt of UP, 'Statement of Case Regarding No-Rent Campaign', copy in Hailey Colln, Vol. 22.

28. S Srivastava, *Uttar Pradesh ki Bardoli. Bakuliha, Zila Rae Bareli ka Itihas* (Rae Bareli 1967), 28; Rae Bareli Collectorate, Civil Disobedience Cases 1931, P S Sareni, Cases No. 84–5, date 5 February 1931.

29. Srivastava, *UP ki Bardoli*, 39.

30. PAI 28 March, 18 April, 2 May 1931, etc.

31. PAI 16 and 23 May 1931; UP Govt 'Statement of Case regarding No-Rent Campaign'.

32. See AICC G5 (Kw) (ii)/1931, Agra District Congress Conference, Address of Chandradhar Johri, Chairman Reception Committee; AICC G 140 (ii)/1931, Papers from DCC Mathura; AICC 63/1931, Kali Charan, Secy Kanauj Tahsil CC (Farrukhabad) – JN, Secy, AICC, 17 July 1931; and AICC 14/1931 Pt I, Memo submitted by the Executive Committee of the British Indian Association, Awadh, to H.E. the Governor; also Tandon Colln, File 69, Nos. 612 and 644; FR (NAI) May 1931, 1; and PAIs for 1931

33. See chapter 6 below.

34. AICC P 31/1935 and 22/1935–6; L Brennan, 'From one Raj to another: Congress Politics in Rohilkhand, 1930–50' in D A Low, ed., *Congress and the Raj. Facets of the Indian Struggle, 1917–47* (London 1977).

35. (IOL), MSS. Eur. E. 240, Templewood Colln, 12,725S (P & P), Viceroy-Secy of State for India, 23 November 1934.

36. (IOL), MSS. Eur. C. 152, Halifax Colln XVI, Viceroy-Secy of State, Home Dept, Teleg. P, 2 June 1930.

37. P D Reeves, *et al, Elections in Uttar Pradesh, 1920–51* (Delhi 1975), 33–4, 45–6.

38. AICC 12/1932, AICC Bulletin No. 2 (15 April 1932); J Nehru, *An Autobiography* (London 1936), 236.

39. Hailey Colln, 19B, Hailey-Crerar, 2 October 1930.

40. See chapter 6 below.

41. AICC 68/1931, Circular no. 17, PI/1615, Gen. Secy AICC – all PCCs, 16 July 1931.

42. ibid., CWC resolution, Bombay, 7–12 July 1931 on Hindustani Seva Dal; and 'Congress Seva Dal', undated circular (July 1931?); AICC 82/1931–8, CWC resolution, Bombay, 4–14 August 1931.

43. AICC P21/1931.

44. AICC P20/1934, Secy PCC-Secy AICC, 26 July and 2 August 1934; also AICC FD2/1935, letters no. 7 and 10 to Congress branches abroad, 28 February and 27 March 1935 respectively.

45. There were six presidents in this five-year span on account of the dispute in the provincial Congress in 1926, mentioned above.

46. There are biographies of some of the most prominent UP Congress leaders of the time, such as the Nehrus, Madan Mohan Malaviya, Pant and Rafi Ahmad Qidwai (see bibliography). But most of the biographical information used in this study has been collated from a variety of sources: newspapers, pamphlets, government reports, several *Who's Who*, biographies and commemoration (or congratulatory) volumes, and interviews.

47. *Abhyudaya* (2 October 1926).

48. JN Correspondence (NML) with G B Pant, Pant-JN, 10 September 1936. See also Tomlinson, *Indian National Congress and the Raj*, 65–112; Brennan, 'Political Change in Rohilkhand', 127, 411–12.

49. For a fuller account of these men, see G Pandey,' The Shastris of Kashi and Lahore:

the Making of Congress Leaders' in W H Morris-Jones (ed.), *The Making of Politicians: Studies from Asia and Africa* (London 1976).

50. Cf. Gopal Krishna, 'The Development of the INC', who observes that the Congress leadership in the Non-Cooperation period was 'selected by the test of sacrifice as well as by the criteria of education and social status'.

51. AICC 9/1925, MN-Pant, 15 August 1925. (I am indebted to David Page for this reference.)

52. Brennan, 'Political Change in Rohilkhand', 174, 182–3; Bayly, 'The Development of Political Organisation in the Allahabad Locality, 1880–1925', 325–32, 393.

53. *Peshkar* – clerk, court official; *munsif* – judge in subordinate civil court.

54. I am grateful to the late Th Shivmurti Singh, to Pt Rup Narain Tripathi (son of Pt Tikaram) and to Th Srinath Singh for much of my information on Allahabad district leaders.

55. *UP Banking Enquiry Committee*, Vol. II, 297.

56. Srivastava, *UP ki Bardoli*, 27.

57. Elections always produced a demand for larger funds than were available; see correspondence in AICC files for 1926, esp. AICC 13/1926, Pt. I and AICC 21/1926. The position grew worse in the mid-1930s when the Congress returned to the electoral arena and individual ambitions and factional rivalries made men hesitant to subscribe to any fund that would not be used in their own local area; see Tomlinson, *Indian National Congress and the Raj*, chapter 3.

58. Brennan, 'Political Change in Rohilkhand', 170; interview with Rup Narain Tripathi, Allahabad, 16 July 1972.

59. Hailey Colln, 27C, Srivastava-Hailey, 17 July 1934.

60. Sumit Sarkar, *The Swadeshi Movement in Bengal, 1903–8* (New Delhi 1973), esp. chapter III; Bagchi, *Private Investment in India*, 243.

61. Cf. NOP (IOL) 4 May 1929; AICC 4/1933; *The Leader* (14 October 1933).

62. *CWMG, XLI* (New Delhi 1970), 156–7.

63. D Rothermund, '*Nehru and Early Indian Socialism*' in S N Mukherjee (ed.), *Movement for National Freedom in India* (Oxford 1966), 108; Bipan Chandra, 'Elements of Continuity and Change in Early Nationalist Activity', 18; *Report of the 45th Indian National Congress, Karachi 1931* (Karachi 1931), 141.

64. AICC G-2/1931, Pt. I, 'Report on Civil Disobedience', Gen. Secies, AICC, October 1931, 10; JN Corresp. (NML), with L. Mulkraj Bhalla, JN – Bhalla, 8 March 1931; ibid., with Gandhi, Gandhi – Shantikumar, 31 March 1928.

65. ibid., MN-Gandhi, 25 April 1930; AICC P 24/1929, Sri Prakasa-JN, 5 May 1929.

66. Hailey Colln, 23A, Hailey-Willingdon 10 January 1932.

67. G D Birla, *In the Shadow of the Mahatma* (Calcutta 1953); AICC G—57 (ii)/1926, MN – Rangaswami Iyengar, 30 November 1926 and G-57 (iv)/1926, Raghupati Sahai-Iyengar, 16 September 1926; MN Colln. (NML) A-15, MN – Ansari, 9 January 1935; interview, M L Gautam, New Delhi 31 October 1972. See also Tandon Colln, Grp K, File 1, Tandon-Birla, 14 April 1930.

68. MN Colln, B-6, MN-Annie Besant, 30 September 1928; AICC P20/1936 JN-Pant 13 May 1936.

69. PAI 20 July 1929; JN Misc. Colln (NML), 'Report of the City sub-Committee on the Financial Condition of CCC, Allahabad (n.d., 1934/1935?); Nardeo Shastri (ed.), *Dehradun aur Garhwal Rajnaitik Andolan ka Itihas 1918–31* (n.p., 1932), 71, 112; also numerous interviews.

70. See G B Pant Colln (NAI) F4, Nos 14 and 118, and F6, no. 40, AICC 24/1934, incomplete list of UP delegates to the 1934 Congress; and *UP Political 'Who's Who'* (2nd edn., Allahabad 1936) indicate the large number of district Congress leaders working for insurance agencies.

71. MN Colln, Subject File 'Meerut Conspiracy Case', MN-Ansari, 21 April 1929; GOI Home Poll. (NAI) 443/1930, Extract from an Agent's report, 1 November 1930; *Navjivan* 9 April 1967, Anjani Kumar: 'Kunwar Brajesh Singh'; interviews.

72. AICC G139/1931, G N Singh, Secy Kanpur TCC-Gen Secy AICC, 1 July and 6 September 1931.

73. See chapter 6 below for the full implications of this position.

74. D Pandey, *The Arya Samaj and Indian Nationalism, 1875–1920* (New Delhi 1972), 103.

75. Hume Colln, III, Pt I, letters to his parents 26 April and 14 May 1930.

76. K D Bajpayee, *Braj ka Itihas, Pt. I.* (Mathura 1955); *Young India*, 31 January 1929 (in MN Colln, File G-1).

77. *The Progress of Education in India, 1917–22. Eighth Quinquennial Review*, Vol. I, (Calcutta 1923), 5.

78. Sri Prakasa, *Bharat Ratna Dr Bhagavan Das* (Meerut 1970), 78–9.

79. *Aj* (1–2 March 1929).

80. AICC G2/1931, Pt. I, 'Report on Civil Disobedience' by Gen Secies, AICC, October 1931, p. 57a.

81. UP Educ. (Confid.) Dept 127/1930 (SRR), 'Comment on Activities of the BHU', 14 June 1930.

82. UP GAD 241/1930 (SRR), Jagdish Prasad, Chief Secy, UP, 'Note' of 27 May 1930, with comment on it by Dy. Commissioner, Rae Bareli.

83. See n. 81 above; also FR September 1932, 1 and April 1933, 1; MN Colln, V-2, G S Vidyarthi-MN, 23 April 1930; PAIs for September 1930–January 1931 and for 1932.

84. Tandon Colln, File 35, Sn 1342, 'Report of Work during January 1930-December 1931 in the Meerut centre of SPS'.

85. UP Police Dept, 1504/1934 (SRR); 'Note on Subversive Movements and Organisations (other than Terrorist) in India, Director, Intelligence Bureau, GOI, September 1933.

86. UP Police Dept, op. cit. For an account of activities of LSM members in Civil Disobedience, see Tandon Colln, esp. File 52, Sn 321.

87. AICC P24/1929, Sri Prakasa-JN, 5 May 1929. For evidence of direct donations to the Congress, AICC G46/1931, Sitla Sahai, A-I Spinners' Assn-Secy AICC, 1 June 1927. Some UP Congressmen referred to the Khaddar Bhandars as *their* East India Co. (interview, M L Gautam, New Delhi 31 October 1972).

88. Local Intelligence Unit, Kotwali, Rae Bareli, *Confidential List of the more important Political & Quasi-Political Societies, Sabhas, and Anjumans in the United Provinces for the period ending 30 June 1933* (Allahabad 1933), 3. Madan Mohan Malaviya's Swadeshi Sanghas, established in many places in and after 1932, performed much the same kind of function, FR June 1932, 2 and February 1934, 2; PAI 10 December 1932.

89. AICC 24/1934, tentative list of delegates from UP to the Bombay Congress 1934; *The UP Political 'Who's Who'* (2nd edn., Allahabad 1936); interviews.

90. *The Leader* (16 December 1929).

91. Tandon Colln, File 141, Sn 277, printed appeal, 16 May 1931.

92. *Aj* (6 July 1931).

93. AICC P20/1934, Mohanlal Saxena, Secy PCC-Secy AICC, 5 June 1934; see also *The Leader* (14 September 1934).

94. Sarkar, *The Swadeshi Movement*, 148.

95. Cf. Hume Colln II, letter to his parents from Pachperwa, Gonda, 5 May 1929.

96. Zafar Imam, 'The Rise of Soviet Russia and Socialism in India, 1917–29' in B R Nanda (ed.), *Socialism in India* (New Delhi 1972), 62.

97. Zafar Imam, *op. cit.* refers to a UP branch of the Party, but AICC G52/1928, the relevant file in the Congress papers, does not contain a single reference to such a branch.

98. J Nehru, *A Bunch of Old Letters* (Bombay 1958), 70–1. Also JN Correspondence, with Narendra Deo, Deo-JN, 20 March 1929; AICC Suppl. (NML) 61/1924–30, Programme of UP Branch of Independence League, with circular letter from JN, 10 April 1929. *The Proceedings of the All Parties National Convention* (Allahabad 1929), Appendix A, gives a list of members of the League.

99. AICC G39/1928 and G39/1929; UP Educ. Dept. 127/1930; and FRs and PAIs for 1929.

100. AICC G39/1928 'Lucknow Youth League Constitution' (Lucknow 1929) and Circular letter from Gen. Secy, Lucknow Youth League, 24 June 1929; AICC G39/1929 'Leaflet No. 2' of Allahabad Youth League.

101. See the detailed account of the 1930 *satyagraha* in *Agra Satyagraha Sangram* (DCC, Agra 1931), P P Hin. B. 33 (IOL); Brennan, 'Political Change in Rohilkhand', 182–3.

102. AICC G39/1930, JN-Gen. Secy, All-India Students Federation, Karachi, 28 June 1931; AICC G/39/1928, Circular from J K Banerjea, Provincial Secy, Lucknow Youth League.

103. *The Pioneer* (9 October 1933), 'Whither India?' Pt I.

104. See especially AICC Suppl. 40/1926–39, correspondence and reports regarding the bitter and extended conflict over the composition of the Reception Committee for the Lucknow Congress; FR July 1934, 1ff. for intra-Congress quarrels in various UP districts. In the debate on the amendment of the 'manual labour' clause, Pattabhi Sitaramayya noted: 'There is no use disguising the fact that it has not been worked very honestly'; *Report of the 49th Session of the Indian National Congress, Lucknow, April 1936* (Allahabad, n.d.), 108.

105. AICC G14/1934–5, 'Annual Report of A-I Harijan Sevak Sangh, 1933–4'.

106. ibid., AICC F.D. 2/1935, letter no. 6 to Congress branches abroad, 21 February 1935; Leader (14 January and 1 April 1934).

107. See *Pioneer* (22–30 July 1934; 21 September 1934).

108. Cf. B R Ambedkar, *What Congress and Gandhi have done to the Untouchables* (Bombay 1945). The greatest condemnation of the Congress's Harijan movement is, of course, provided by the widespread politics of militant protest among Dalits today.

109. AICC G23/1934.

110. FR June 1934, 1 and 2, and September 1934, 1 and 2; *Abhyudaya* (11 June 1934); *Pioneer* (24 June 1934).

111. UP Congress Parliamentary Board pamphlet, *Congress and the Zamindar* (1934); GOI Home-Poll. 41/1/1934, Sampurnanand's 'A tentative Socialist programme for India', April 1934; *Congress Agrarian Enquiry Committee Report* (Bareilly 1936), 'Note' by Sampurnanand, xv-xvi; *Vidyapith* (KNPS), issues of *Ashvin, Paush* and *Chaitra* 1993 (1935 A.D.).

112. For the elaborate negotiations that preceded the passing of the measure, see Reeves, *Landlords and Governments in UP*, 230–7. For other CSP activities, see FR December 1934, 1 and 2; Brennan, 'Political Change in Rohilkhand', 243–6.

113. *Leader* (3, 4, and 25 October 1934); *Pioneer* (10 September 1934).

114. FRs for 1934–5; *Pioneer* (4 November 1935), statement issued by Sampurnanand and Narendra Deo on behalf of Congressmen who had just resigned from the PCC Council. See also Tomlinson, *Indian National Congress and the Raj*, ch.3.

Chapter 4. Spreading the Nationalist Message

1. Halifax Colln, IV, Wedgwood-Benn to Irwin, 19 July 1928 and XVI, Viceroy-Secy of State, Teleg. P. Home Dept, 2 June 1930; Hume Colln, III, Pt. I, Hume to his parents, Roorkee 20 July 1930; GOI Home-Poll 23/66/32, letters from Govts of UP, Bombay, CP, Bihar, etc., to Home Secy, GOI.
2. Literacy in UP was 5.5 per 1000 persons in 1931, 94 among men and only 11 among women; *UP Census 1931, Pt. I*, Chapter IX.
3. See chapter 2, sections II and III above.
4. Reeves, 'The Politics of Order', 262.
5. GOI Home-Poll. 1428/1932, D.O. No. 226/1932, from W C Dibble, 4 May 1932.
6. Halifax Colln, 25, Sapru-Irwin, 19 September 1930.
7. ibid., 19, Irwin-H. Spender-Clay, 4 October 1930; PAIs for 1930, 1932; Nehru, *Autobiography*, 236; interviews.
8. M Barns, *The Indian Press. A History of the Growth of Public Opinion in India* (London 1940), 373.
9. See Chapter 5 below.
10. *Report of the Indian Statutory Commission, Vol. I, Survey* (London 1930), 261.
11. 'Mobilisation in a Mass Movement: Congress "Propaganda" in the United Provinces (India), 1930–4', *Modern Asian Studies*, 9, 2 (1975).
12. PAI, 5 July 1930.
13. PP. Hin. B. 132 (IOL) and pamphlets no. 191, 203, 285, 831 (NAI).
14. JN correspondence, with Kesho Deo Malaviya, Malaviya – JN, 13 January 1934.
15. Pamphlet no. 457 (NAI).
16. Interview with Muzaffar Hasan, Allahabad, 3 January 1973.
17. Pamphlet no. 1175 (NAI).
18. e.g. PAI, 21 September 1929.
19. *CWMG, XXI* (Delhi 1966), 75.
20. NOP, 9 March 1929. See PAI, 20 April and 19 October 1929 and UP Police Dept 202/1930 (SRR) for other examples of such propaganda.
21. *Agra Satyagraha Sangram, passim.; Shult par kaisi biti* (Ranikhet Tahsil Congress Committee, Almora 1932), PP. Hin. B. 126 (IOL), p. 10; *Abhyudaya* (18 November 1931); *Pratap* (11 August 1929); interviews, especially with Jagan Prasad Rawat, Lucknow, 15–16 January 1973 and Radhe Shyam Sharma, Banaras, 16 February 1973. For *satyagraha* in the Kumaun hills, see Ramchandra Guha, *The Unquiet Woods: Ecological Change and Peasant Resistance in the Himalaya* (Berkeley 1989).
22. Nehru, *Autobiography*, 237.
23. AICC P20/1929, 'Reports on Visits to Aligarh, Muttra and Hathras' from JN-Secy PCC, 22 July 1929.
24. FR September 1936, 1; November 1936, 2 and February 1937, 1. Cf S Gopal, *Jawaharlal Nehru. A Bibliography. Volume One. 1889–1947* (Bombay 1976), pp. 215–17.
25. Nehru, *Autobiography*, 171.
26. NOPs June–August 1928; PAI 30 June, 4 August 1928; FR August 1928, 1; GOI Home Poll. 197/1928.
27. Halifax Colln., VI, Hailey-Irwin, 13 May 1930 (enclosed with Irwin-Wedgwood Benn, 22 May 1930) and XIX, Irwin – G R Lane-Fox, 31 March 1930; Hailey Colln., 17B, Hailey – Hirtzel, 4 April 1930. For escalation of nationalist agitation on account of subsequent arrests, ibid., telegram Hailey-Viceroy (in reply to Viceroy's telegram of 22 April 1930).
28. FR February 1928, 1; PAI 11 February 1928.
29. FR February 1928, 2.

30. GOI Home Poll, 130, 1929, DO. 1840–C R., G W Gwynne, D.C. Lucknow-Commissioner, Lucknow, 5 December 1928 (hereafter, Gwynne's letter, 5 December 1928). The reference to 'the Hindu community' was an example of the Government's peculiar way of describing the state of political feelings, as the following account should show.

31. PAIs 1–15 December 1928; NOPs 24 November and 1 December 1928: FR November 1928, 2.

32. *Abhyudaya* (24 November 1928).

33. idem.; PAI, 8 December 1928.

34. GOI Home Poll. 130/1929, D.O. No. D/300/28, Commissioner Agra-Chiel Secy, UP, 13 December 1928; PAI 8 December 1928.

35. The following account is based on GOI Home Poll. 130/1928; *Pioneer* (2 December 1928), JN's statement to the press; *Abhyudaya* (1 and 8 December 1928).

36. At the time, the exact date of the Commission's arrival had not been made public.

37. FR November 1928, 2.

38. GOI Home Poll. 130/1929, Annexure 'A' to Gwynne's letter, 5 December 1928.

39. Cf 'Appeal to Lucknow University Students' (n.d. but issued 30 November 1928, judging by the reference to the *taluqdars'* garden party), *ibid.*

40. GOI Home Poll. 130/1929, Gwynne's letter, 5 December 1928.

41. JN estimated the distance to be 1/4 mile; *Pioneer* (2 December 1928).

42. Hailey Colln, 14B, Hailey – Crerar, Lucknow 6 December 1929.

43. *Pioneer* (2 December 1928).

44. NOP, 8 December 1928.

45. NOP, 22 December 1928; *Pioneer* (2 December 1928).

46. *Pioneer* (6 December 1928).

47. GOI Home Poll 130/1929, Chief Secy UP-Secy, Home Dept 20 December 1928.

48. *Pioneer* (7 December 1928, 16 and 23 January 1929).

49. Nehru, *Autobiography*, 176. Gaol lists at Agra, Allahabad, Azamgarh and Rae Bareli contain numerous entries such as the following: Name: *Gandhi-bhakt* (follower of Gandhi); Address: India; Occupation: Freedom-fighter. This form of propaganda was reputedly first used by Chandrashekhar Azad – whose adopted surname means 'free'.

50. UP Judicial (Crim.) Dept 1210/1929 (SRR), extracts from *Aj, Indian Daily Telegraph, Leader, Republic* (Kanpur), *Pratap, Sainik*; and interviews, Vijay Kumar Sinha, New Delhi, 31 October 1972, Manmathnath Gupta, New Delhi, 1 November 1972, Chandra Bhanu Gupta, Lucknow, 17 November 1972, Rup Narain Tripathi, Allahabad, 16 July 1972.

51. UP Judicial (Crim.) Dept 1210/1926.

52. Manmathnath Gupta, *Bharat ke Krantikari* (Delhi 1969) and *Ve Amar Krantikari* (Delhi 1970); Bhagwandas Mahaur and others, *Yash ki Dharohar* (Delhi 1968) and other publications in the series 'Shaheed Granth Mala' brought out by Atma Ram & Sons, Delhi, in the 1960s. Interviews as in n.50 above.

53. Halifax Colln, V, Peel-Irwin, 14 March 1929, and X, Telegram, Viceroy-Secy of State, 10 March 1929.

54. FR March 1929, 2.

55. FR September 1929, 1 and 2; Hailey Colln, 16A, Hailey-Irwin, 16 October 1929.

56. Hailey Colln, 16A, Hailey – O'Dwyer, 4 October 1929.

57. See chapter 6 below.

58. Hailey Colln, 15B, note by D Petrie, enclosed with Crerar-Hailey, 3 July 1929.

59. See UP GAD 241/1930 (SRR). A very large number of Congressmen who became important public figures later had left their careers or schools in 1920–1. The biographical data available have far fewer references to such sacrifices in the early 1930s.

60. See UP Educ. Dept 53/1930 (UPSA); and UP Police Dept 1672/1930 (SRR), D.O. 786, Commissioner Allahabad-all Collectors, 26 November 1930. Old teachers in Jamunipur, Kotwa and Leelapur villages in Allahabad district recalled that in the years 1930–2, the Government adopted the policy of posting rural school-teachers away from their home areas in order to reduce their influence.

61. Cf. Hailey Colln, 19B, Hailey – de Montmorency, 16 September 1930; also Hailey – Irwin, 3 October 1930 and ibid., 19A, Minutes of Conference held at Viceregal Lodge on 23 July 1930.

62. UP GAD 283/1930 (SRR), D.O. No. 157, D M Etah – Chief Secy UP, 12 June 1932.

63. Cf. Hailey Colln, 17B, telegram, Hailey-Viceroy (reply to telegram of 22 April 1930); PAI 1 February 1930; *Agra Satyagraha Sangram*.

64. See, for example, UP Police Dept 1504/1934 (SRR) 'A Note on Terrorism in India (except Bengal)' by H Williamson, with additional notes by local governments, (Simla, GOI Press 1933); and G Pandey, ed., *The Indian Nation in 1942* (Calcutta, 1988), *passim*.

65. P P Hin. B. 179 and 395 (IOL); See also Pamphlets No. 112, 553, 1031, 1141, 1151, 1156, 1163, 1186, 1284, etc. (NAI).

66. See G Pandey, 'Mobilisation in a Mass Movement: Congress "Propaganda" in the United Provinces'.

67. AICC G-140/1931, Part V, printed Hindi leaflet signed by Narmada Prasad, Shiv Murti and Lal Bahadur, secretaries of the DCC, Allahabad (n.d.).

68. A copy of the leaflet is found in *Abhyudaya* (18 November 1931), Pamphlet No. 990 (NAI). There is a translation of it in GOI, Home Poll. 33/36/1931.

69. This translation of a 'specimen leaflet' is given in FR February 1932, 1.

70. A A Waugh, *Rent and Revenue Policy in the United Provinces*, 10 and 25. He gives the year 1929–30 for the Rs. 60 lakhs remission, but *UP Revenue Administration Report*, 1928–9 and 1929–30 indicates that this is a mistake. See chapter 6, section III below for remissions in later years.

71. Hailey Colln, 29C, A A Waugh, 'Rent and Revenue problems' (1934), 4. The total number of districts affected thus was 19.

72. In the *kharif* 1338 F. remission on canal dues was Rs. 5¾ lakhs, much of it in Meerut division, and on *taqavi* Rs. 3½ lakhs, much of this in Mathura district.

73. Cf. Whitcombe, *Agrarian Relations in Northern India. Vol. I*, 194, 273; J Rosselli, 'Theory and Practice in Northern India: The Background to the Land "Settlement" of 1833', *Indian Economic and Social History Review*, 8, 2 (1971); Siddiqi, *Agrarian Change in a Northern Indian State*, 126–7, 130–3.

74. Waugh, 'Rent and Revenue Problems' (1934), 5 (emphasis added).

75. Hailey Colln, 20, Hailey de – de Montmorency, 7 May 1931, and Hailey-Crerar, 8 May 1931.

76. ibid., 25 C, Hailey – Richard Burn, 8 March 1933.

77. Hume Colln, III, Pt. 2, Hume to his parents, Rae Bareli 18 December 1931. Hailey also noted the need to use force to collect landlord and government dues; left to themselves, 'practically they [the landlords] would collect nothing', Hailey Colln, 22, Hailey – Crerar, 9 November 1931.

78. See chapter 2, section II above.

79. NOP 1 September 1928.

80. NOP 29 September 1928. Hundreds of letters giving accounts of the peasants' suffering were published in the Congress papers, NOPs 12 and 26 May, 2, 9 and 16 June 1928, etc.

81. *Abhyudaya* (10 November 1928); FR January 1928, 1 and 2, June 1929, 1, February 1930, 1; and PAIs for 1928–30.

82. Hailey Colln, 29 C, 'Report on the Present Economic Situation in UP' (by E A H Blunt, 1932), 17, and Waugh, 'Rent and Revenue Problems' (1934), 8; *Agrarian Distress in the United Provinces. Being the Report of the Committee appointed by the Council of the UP Provincial Congress Committee to enquire into the Agrarian Situation in the Province* (Allahabad 1931), 116.

83. Hailey Colln, 22, Hailey – Chhatari 30 October 1931. For details of negotiations, GOI Home-Poll 33/36/1931 and 54/1931; AICC G-25/1931; *Pioneer* and *Leader* (October 1931).

84. Cmd. 3997, *Indian Round Table Conference (Second Session) 7 Sept. 1931–1 Dec. 1931. Proceedings* (London 1932), 390.

85. Syed Mahmud Colln. (NAI) File 'From JN-1930', Notes in JN's hand (n.d., but evidently written in October 1930). See also JN Misc. Ps., 'The Programme (of Congress)', V N Tewari – JN, Allahabad 28 December 1930.

86. AICC G-140 (kw)(i)/1931, JN-Altafur Rahman, 30 July 1931.

87. See Ch. 6 below.

88. Hindu, Sikh and Muslim greetings. pamphlet No. 255 (NAI).

89. In the *Azad Bharat Tract*, Pamphlet No. 576 (NAI), the song mentions Shivaji, Maharana Pratap, Abbas Tyabji, Tara Singh and numerous others.

90. Pamphlet No. 316 (NAI).

91. Pamphlet No. 285 (NAI).

92. *Satyagraha Samachar* (23 April 1930), leader, in UP Police Dept 106/1930 (UPSA).

93. *Agrarian Distress in the United Provinces*, Appendix XIV. The amount of 8 or 12 annas refers to the proportion of the rupee (16 annas) to be paid.

94. AICC 14/1931, Pt. I, Mushir Husain Kidwai – Gandhi, Lucknow, 9 July 1931; GOI Home Poll. 33/24/31, statements regarding events in Rae Bareli, Bara Banki, Allahabad and other districts in May – June 1931; also Govt's 'Statement of Case Regarding No-Rent Campaign'.

95. Cf. Nehru, *Autobiography*, 237.

96. Halifax Colln, 22, Lambert – Irwin, 4 February 1929.

97. See chapter 6 below.

98. Hailey Colln, 19A, Hailey – Verney Lovett, 3 July 1930 (emphasis added).

99. Hume Colln, III, Pt I, Hume to his parents, 6 and 24 May 1930.

100. FR March 1932, 2.

101. Gaol records of 1930–3 at Agra, Allahabad, Azamgarh and Rae Bareli Collectorates; *Svatantrata Sangram ke Sainik* (volumes for all districts published by the UP Govt in connection with the celebration of the Silver Jubilee of Indian independence).

102. Interview with C B Gupta, Lucknow, 17 and 24 November 1972; M L Gautam, New Delhi, 31 October 1972; Santoshanand, Azamgarh, 20 February 1973. Professor Irfan Habib of Aligarh recalled that even in the 1946 elections in UP, large numbers of Muslim weavers voted for the Congress.

103. *UP Census 1931, Pt. I*, 417.

104. MN Ps., T-1, MN – Tandon, 18 May 1930.

105. R C Majumdar (ed.), *Struggle for Freedom*, 527, fn 15; Nehru, *Autobiography*, 344; *CWMG, XXII* (Delhi 1966), 253, 303; Srivastava: *UP ki Bardoli*, 48; and interviews.

106. For the examples of the Rajas of Samastipur and Kalakankar, see PAI 23 November 1929.

107. GOI Home Poll. 130/1929; FR July 1928, 2; Hailey Colln, 19B, Hailey-de Montmorency, 16 September 1930, and Hailey – Irwin, 3 October 1930; ibid., 28A, Hailey-Willingdon, 18 September 1934.

108. *Satyagraha Samachar* (5 and 10 May 1930); *Abhyudaya* (3 May 1930).

109. *Satyagraha Samachar* (21 April 1930).

110. *The Pioneer* (17 April 1929).
111. H N Kunzru, for example, became president of the UP Board of the All India
     Servants of Untouchables Society (later the Harijan Sevak Sangh) in 1932. Earlier
     he had resigned his seat in the central Legislative Assembly as a protest against
     the Government's action against *satyagrahis*.
112. AICC 17/1930, 'The Week out of Jail', Circular P1/3009 to all PCCs, 14 October 1930.
113. *Agra Satyagraha Sangram*, 6, 47.
114. MN Colln R-8, MN – Rao Krishnapal Singh, Allahabad, 1 May 1930.
115. The rest of this paragraph is based on *Agra Satyagraha Sangram, passim*, and
     interviews with Achal Singh, Jagan Prasad Rawat, Radhe Shyam Sharma and
     Vidyavati Rathore.
116. FR October 1930, 1; see also Sir Sita Ram Colln (NAI) F. 29, No. 84, Munshi Lal
     Agrawal – Sita Ram, Meerut 19 September 1930, for the impact in Meerut; and
     Hailey Colln, 19B, Hailey – Malcolm Seton, 6 October 1930.
117. Interview with Brahmachari of Gorakhpur, Allahabad, 21 July 1972.
118. FR August 1930, 1.
119. See *Svatantrata Sangram ke Sainik*, volumes for the UP districts.
120. *Svatantrata Sangram ke Sainik*, Allahabad Division, and 'Malaka Gaol Records'
     (Collectorate, Allahabad) respectively. The discrepancy in the totals arises partly
     because the former source contains in it the names of all political prisoners of
     Allahabad, whether gaoled in Malaka Gaol, the Naini Central Gaol (where promi-
     nent leaders were sent) or elsewhere.
121. GOI Home-Poll. 23/66/1932, J R W Bennett – Secy, GOI, 2 December 1932.
122. GOI Home-Poll. 23/66/1932.

Chapter 5. The Alienation of the Muslims

 1. Bayly, *Local Roots of Indian Politics*, 111–13; Rafiuddin Ahmed, *The Bengal Mus-
    lims, 1871–1906: A Quest for Identity* (Delhi 1981); Sandria Frietag, *Collective
    Action and Community. Public Arenas and the Emergence of Communalism in
    North India* (Berkeley and Los Angeles, 1989); Anand Yang, *The Limited Raj:
    Agrarian Relations in Colonial India. Saran District, 1793–1920* (Berkeley and Los
    Angeles, 1989); G Pandey, *The Construction of Communalism in Colonial North
    India* (Delhi 1990).
 2. *Brass, Language, Religion and Politics in North India*, chapter 3; Robinson, 'Mu-
    nicipal Government and Muslim Separatism in the United Provinces, 1883–1926'
    in Gallagher et al (eds), *Locality, Province and Nation*.
 3. D J H Page, *Prelude to Partition*.
 4. See chapter 3; section II above.
 5. R A Gordon, 'The Hindu Mahasabha and the Indian National Congress, 1915–26',
    Modern Asian Studies, 9, 2 (1975).
 6. UP Govt. 'A' Progs. (IOL) No. 71, 'Communal Friction in the UP, 1924', No. 6522,
    Chief Secy UP – Home Secy GOI, 2 January 1925.
 7. PAI 27 February 1926; PAIs for January–June 1928.
 8. See chapter 3, section IV above.
 9. J Nehru, *A Bunch of Old Letters* (Bombay 1958), 6–7.
10. *The Leader* (5 April 1930), Malaviya's letter of resignation from the Legislative
    Assembly.
11. Striking evidence of this is provided by the attitude of Hasrat Mohani. This leading
    'no-changer' supported the establishment of the ICP which would accept ministerial

office in any province given the right conditions; he felt that, after all the compromises made by the Swarajists, the pretence at 'Non-Cooperation inside the Councils' should be dropped; *Abhyudaya* (2 October 1926).

12. For the moves leading up to the establishment of the ICP, see *The Leader* (28 February, 24 and 27 March, 7 April, 9 and 12 May, 28 August 1926); MN-JN Correspondence, Vol. XII, MN's letters to JN, March–September 1926; AICC G-57 (iv) Pt. I/1926, MN's correspondence with Rangaswami Iyengar, Gen. Secy AICC, September 1926.

13. This account is based on UP GAD 246/1926 and 613/1926 (SRR), PAIs 1925–7 and newspaper reports. See also Page, *Prelude to Partition*, 80–84.

14. PAI, 27 March and 15 May 1926.

15. UP GAD 246/1926, Note on music in front of mosques by H S Crosthwaite, D M Allahabad, 23 May 1926.

16. UP GAD 680/1925, Commissioner Allahabad-Chief Secy UP, 14 September 1925, cited in Page, *Prelude to Partition*, 84.

17. UP GAD 613/1926, telegram, Malaviya – P. S. to Governor, 5 October 1926.

18. Nehru, *A Bunch of Old Letters*, 49–50.

19. *ibid.*

20. PAI 1 May 1926.

21. *The Leader* (11 and 25 August 1926); *Abhyudaya* (31 July 1926); PAI 14 and 21 August 1926. See also *Aj* (2 October 1926), report of Awadh Hindu Sabha sanctioning support to specified candidates.

22. PAI 28 August 1926.

23. PAI 9 October 1926; Aj (4 and 8 October 1926). Both estimated the attendance at the meeting to be about 5000, a remarkable figure in a town with 12,000 Hindu inhabitants in 1931.

24. MN Colln, 'Statements', statement to press, 10 December 1926.

25. PAI 27 March; *Abhyudaya* (13 and 20 March 1926).

26. AICC Suppl. 36/1926.

27. AICC 13/1926, Pt. I, MN-Sri Prakasa correspondence of July 1926, and Pt. II, Sitla Sahai's letters of July 1926; AICC 57 (ii) 1926, MN-Rangaswami Iyengar, 25 June 1926; *Abhyudaya* (21 August 1926).

28. AICC 13/1926, Pt. II, Sitla Sahai-MN, 2 August 1926 (also his letters of 13 and 21 July 1926); *Abhyudaya* (31 July 1926); *The Leader* (11 August 1926).

29. AICC 13/1926 Pt I, telegrams between Raghupati Sahai, Sitla Sahai and MN, October and November 1926; and AICC 10/1926, telegram MN-manager, *Aj* Press (26 November 1926).

30. PAI 25 September 1926.

31. Halifax Colln. II, Irwin – Birkenhead, 23 September 1926.

32. The following account of the Pratapgarh meeting is based on MN Colln 'Miscellaneous', speech at Pratapgarh, 23 November 1926.

33. The resolution called for an enquiry into what was the 'established local custom' at different places.

34. *Abhyudaya* (23 November 1929).

35. See chapters 2 and 3 above.

36. PAI 1 February 1930.

37. E.g., PAI 17 August 1929.

38. *Abhyudaya* (19 January, 9 February, 20 July 1929); PAI 12 and 19 October and 2 November 1929.

39. *Abhyudaya* (31 August and 14 September 1929).

40. Hailey Colln, 13B and C, Hailey's correspondence of August and September 1928.

41. ibid., 13B, Hailey – Fazl-i-Hussain, 25 August 1928. Even without the Nehru Report,

something could be done. As the Viceroy put it, 'It seems an unnatural and an unnecessary state of things for many of the principal representatives of the landed interest to have drifted away from Government, and I should suppose that, with a little attention and encouragement, they might be persuaded to drift back again', ibid., 13B, Irwin-Hailey, 22 August 1928.

42. Halifax Colln, 23, Chhatari-Irwin, 18 November 1929; 24, Hailey – Cunningham, 26 April 1920; Hailey Colln. 18A, Hailey-Chhatari, 1 May 1930 and Hailey – Haig, 10 May 1930.

43. ibid.

44. UP GAD 241/1930 (SRR), D.O. No. 199, Commissioner Allahabad-Chief Secy, UP, 9 May 1930.

45. Hailey Colln, 18B, unaddressed note signed Hailey, 2 June 1930. See also ibid., 18B, Hailey – de Montmorency, 5 June 1930 and ibid., 23A, Hailey – de Montmorency, 31 January 1932, which shows the Government's concern at the slightest sign of a Muslim 'drift towards Congress polities'.

46. Hailey Colln 19B, Hailey-Crerar, 25 September 1930; PAI 6 and 13 September 1930.

47. As in n. 44 above.

48. AICC 68/1931, typescript of 'Report of Cawnpore Riots Enquiry Committee' (hereafter 'Congress Kanpur Enquiry, 1931'), 180. This report has been reprinted, minus certain appendices, in N G Barrier, ed., *Roots of Communal Politics* (Delhi 1976).

49. Halifax Colln, 26, Hidayat Husain-Lambert, 5 March 1931 (enclosed with Lambert-Irwin, 16 March 1931).

50. Cmd. 3891, *East India Cawnpore Riots. Report of the Commission of Inquiry and Resolution of the Government of the United Provinces* (London 1931), 9. This paragraph, and the following two, are based on this report, and on *Aj* (February 1931), *The Leader* (21 March 1931), *Abhyudaya* (25 March 1931), and *All-India Reporter, 1933. Allahabad Section* (Nagpur 1933), 315–16.

51. Cmd. 3883, *Report of the Royal Commission on Labour in India* (London 1931), 275. In 1918, the average population per acre for the city area alone, i.e. minus the civil lines and cantonment, was 57.8, but in areas like Butcher Khana Khurd and Coolie Bazaar it was as high as 532 and 562; *Royal Commission on Labour in India. Evidence. Vol. III. Part I* (London 1931), 281.

52. *East India Cawnpore Riots*, 8.

53. *UP Administration Report, 1921–2*, 47.

54. *UP Census, 1931*, I, 142.

55. 'Congress Kanpur Enquiry 1931', 178; Robinson, *Separatism among Indian Muslims*, 15. In the 1930s Hindu firms like Jhuggilal Kamlapat Singhania expanded rapidly, adding to the cotton gins, oil and flour mills which they had earlier established by setting up cotton and sugar mills and extending their activities to several other fields; Bagchi, *Private Investment in India*, 209.

56. *UP Revenue Administration Report, 1920–1*, 1 and *1922–3*, 'Govt. Resolution', 4; *UP Administration Report, 1920–1*, viii.

57. See Pandey, *Construction of Communalism*, ch. 3; *UP Banking Enquiry Committee*, I, 255; V B Singh (ed.), *The Economic History of India, 1857–1956* (Bombay 1965), 286, 296; Bagchi, *Private Investment in India*, 228–9 and Nair, *Blossoms in the Dust*, 85–6, for decline in weavers' conditions; P C Joshi, 'The Decline of Indigenous Handicrafts in Uttar Pradesh', *Indian Economic and Social History Review*, I, 1 (July-September 1963) for the traditional view.

58. H R Nevill, *Cawnpore: a Gazetteer. Being Vol. XIX of the District Gazetteers of the United Provinces of Agra and Oudh* (Allahabad 1909), 124; *District Gazetteers. Supplementary Notes and Statistics, Vol. XIX* (Allahabad 1916), 5.

59. UP Police Dept File 1504/1934 (SRR).
60. UP Police Dept 1263/1931 (SRR), Sale's 'Report on Cawnpore Communal Riots,' 16 April 1931; Hailey Colln, 19A, 'Note' by R J S Dodd, 25 August 1930.
61. Congress Kanpur Enquiry, 1931', 172.
62. *East India Cawnpore Riots, 9.*
63. 'Congress Kanpur Enquiry, 1931', 170–1.
64. GOI Home-Poll. 150/1934, S N A Jafri, 'Statement on Muslim Organisations in India'; *Abhyudaya* (2 November 1929).
65. UP GAD 241/1930 (SRR), D.O. 199, Commissioner Allahabad-Chief Secy UP, 9 May 1930; FR April 1930, 2; *East India Cawnpore Riots*, 6.
66. ibid., 4; PAI 17 January and 14 February 1931.
67. Robinson, *Separatism among Indian Muslims*, 212–4; *East India Cawnpore Riots*, 8.
68. ibid.; pamphlets such as H P Dwivedi, *Kanpur ka Katl-i-Am, urf Nadir Shahi Loot* (Kanpur 1931). Cf. K McPherson, 'The Muslims of Calcutta, 1918 to 1935,' ANU PhD thesis (1972), 165, 326, 339, and P Woodruff, *The Men Who Ruled India, The Guardians* (London 1954), 257–8, for the participation of such elements in other communal riots.
69. The District Magistrate reported after the riots that of the 965 wounded, 368 were classified Hindus, 292 Muslims and 305 could not be classified. At an earlier stage, of 148, 48 were said to be Hindus, 100 Muslims; UP Police Dept 1263/1931.
70. *Royal Commission on Labour in India, III, Part 1*, 281.
71. *East India Cawnpore Riots*, 59, gives the following figures for crimes in Coolie Bazaar *mohalla* during the first four days of the riot: 5 murders, 7 attempted murders, 9 dacoities with murders, 156 dacoities, 3 robberies, 16 riots, 8 cases of arson, 9 'miscellaneous' crimes.
72. ibid., 23, 27–9.
73. Ibid., 4.
74. ibid., 40; 'Congress Kanpur Enquiry, 1931'; *Pratap* (12 and 19 April 1931); UP Police Dept 1263/1931, telegram of 5 April 1931.
75. *East India Cawnpore Riots*, 32–3.
76. UP Police Dept 1263/1931, 'Notes' by Jagdish Prasad, 6 April 1931 and G B Lambert, 10 April 1931; interview Jagan Prasad Rawat, Lucknow, 15 January 1973.
77. *Najat* (Bijnor) asked in 1926, for example, 'Where is Aman Sabha?... the non-existence of the Aman Sabhas is a living proof of the fact that Government does not regard the Hindu-Muslim quarrels to be subversive of peace and that from its point of view patriotism is the only unpardonable offence.' The Government too admitted its reluctance to intervene in such disputes; UP GAD 246/1926.
78. *East India Cawnpore Riots*, 40; *Pioneer* (29 March 1931).
79. UP Police Dept 1263/1931, telegram 92/Z, UPAO – India Home, 14 April 1931; (*East India Cawnpore Riots*, 53, gave a figure of 294 dead); 'Congress Kanpur Enquiry, 1931', 312.
80. *East India Cawnpore Riots*, 30.
81. 'The arrival of fugitives, some wounded, from Kanpur caused alarm in several places, and most local authorities have had considerable difficulty in restoring confidence and maintaining the peace;' PAI 11 April 1931.
82. UP Police Dept 1263/1931, 'Note' by Jagdish Prasad, 6 April 1931, and 'Note' accompanying Hidayat Husain-Fazl-i-Husain, 16 April 1931.
83. *ibid.*
84. *Pratap* (21 June 1931).
85. Officials observed at the time of the 1942 revolt that Hindu clerks preferred to go through Muslim quarters where for the last ten years they had been 'afraid to show their faces'. L/P and J/5/271 (IOL), D.O.No. F. 2/8/42-C.X. 19 August 1942.

86. *Pratap* (1 June and 9 August 1931).
87. Replicas of the mausoleum of Husain which are taken out in procession during the Muharram and buried (or immersed in water) on the tenth and last day of the observance. Chehlum is the fortieth day after the death of a person, observed particularly in memory of Husain.
88. *Pratap* (7 and 21 June, 5 and 12 July 1931); PAIs 6 June, 11, 18, 25 July 1931. Orders under Sec. 144 remained in force until the end of September, while the Gandhi signboard was reluctantly taken down by the Hindus concerned on 3 September.
89. L/P and J/5/270 (IOL), D.O. No. F2/1/41-C.X., 3 February 1941, and D.O. No. F2/3/41-C.X., 5 April 1941.
90. *The Leader* (19 April 1926).
91. JN correspondence, with Govind Malaviya, Malaviya-JN 26 June 1926 (JN was then in Europe).
92. PAI 8 May 1926. See Section II above for the abandoning of the 1925 Dasehra celebrations.
93. MN Colln, 'Statements', statement to press, 10 December 1926; Nehru, *A Bunch of Old Letters*, 49–50.
94. FR December 1925-February 1926; *The Leader* (16 December 1925 and 18 February 1926) for local election results; Reeves *et al.*, *Elections in UP*, 101–21 and 126–48 for UPLC results. (I have added one to their total of Swarajists elected in 1923 – for Mohanlal Saxena, a prominent Non-Cooperator in 1920–1 and chief whip of the UP Swaraj Party in 1924–6).
95. *Aj* (5 April 1926).
96. Reeves, *et al*, *Elections in UP*, 138, do not give Tiloi the ICP label, but *Abhyudaya* (2 October 1926) does. Ganga Prasad Pandey (Shukla?) listed among the Swarajist candidates announced in August and again in November 1926 appears not to have contested in the end. In general the situation regarding party affiliations was so confused that three different government authorities gave three different versions of 'final results' in the 1926 elections to the UPLC! (See table below.)

	FR I December 1926	PAI 18 December 1926	Halifax Colln II Irwin-Wedgwood Benn 30 December 1926
Swaraj Party	21	19	21
ICP	6	11	9
Liberals	5	12	0
Hindu Sabha	—	2	—
Landlords	16	46	21
Independents	51	—	50
Independent Muslim Party	—	10	—
Total	99	100	101

97. AICC 13/1926, Pt II, Sahai-MN, 27 July 1926 and MN-Sahai, 24 July 1926. See also MN-Sahai, 11 July and Sahai-MN, 13 July.
98. AICC 13/1926, Pt I, MN-Rananjay Singh (*alias* Daddan Saheb), 26 July 1926 and replies, telegram of 6 August and letter of 7 August 1926; Reeves, *et al.*, *Elections in UP*, 34.

99. UP GAD 246/1926, note by D M. Allahabad, 23 May 1926.
100. MN Colln, Miscellaneous, Subject file, 'MN's message to Brelvi on the occasion of the formation of the Muslim Congress Party' (1929).
101. Khaliquzzaman, *Pathway to Pakistan*, 129.
102. N N Mitra, *The Indian Quarterly Register* (July-December 1927), Vol. II, 16; NOP 4 February and 22 December 1928; *Pioneer* (1 September 1928).
103. *Abhyudaya* (2 November 1929).
104. PAI 26 October and 7 December 1929, 1 February 1930.
105. PAI 4 October 1930; Rae Bareli, Local Intelligence Unit, record of Riyasat Husain's political activities.
106. Private Colln held at Shibli Manzil, Azamgarh, MN – Sulaiman Nadvi, 16 October 1928; Halifax Colln, 24, Hailey – Cunningham, 26 April 1930. A *fatwa* is a formal opinion on a point of Islamic law.
107. Khaliquzzaman, *Pathway to Pakistan*, 129.
108. *National Herald* (2 November 1972) (part of a serial 'Life and Times of a Gadfly. Story of Rafi Ahmed Kidwai', by 'Rafian', a man closely associated with Qidwai for most of his public life). *Aj* (22 November 1934), leader, also expressed the feeling that Muslim voters would heed Muslim leaders alone.
109. Reeves, *et al., Elections in UP*, 35, 304.
110. Many Congressmen who were concurrently members of the Hindu Sabha were allowed to hold office in Congress organizations despite a stipulation to the contrary in the 1934 Congress constitution. Again, in Agra at the time of the 1934 elections, Congressmen propagated the story that Hriday Nath Kunzru, the Malaviya candidate, was a Kunjru and not a Hindu at all; *The Leader* (11 November 1934).
111. MN-JN Correspondence (NML), Vol. XV, MN-JN, 10 May 1930; FR May 1932, 2.
112. *East India Cawnpore Riots*, 7; 'Congress Kanpur Enquiry, 1931,' 178. FR May 1933, 1 also notes the opposition of an important section of Congress leaders to the publication of the latter report for fear that it might further inflame communal ill-will.
113. Bayly, 'The Development of Political Organisation in the Allahabad Locality,' 151–2, 360.
114. From newspapers and other sources, I have checked reports of twenty-three official meetings of provincial Congress leaders during this period.
115. *Abhyudaya* (17 and 24 September and 8 October 1934); *The Leader* (24 September and 11 October 1934); FR July 1934, 2, August 1934, 1 and September 1934, 2. These indicate that the situation was in many ways reminiscent of 1926. But much had changed in the intervening years. The Civil Disobedience and the 'no-tax' campaigns, with their populist appeal, had left their mark. The prestige of the Congress was now greater than in 1926 and so was central control of its organization. Altogether there were fewer 'defections' from the party, and in the elections that followed, the official Congress easily triumphed over the breakaway group.
116. *The Leader* (7 January 1934).
117. See Mushirul Hasan, 'The Muslim Mass Contacts Campaign: Analysis of a Strategy of Political Mobilization', in Mushirul Hasan, ed., *India's Partition. Process, Strategy and Mobilization* (Delhi 1993); and Salil Misra, *A Narrative of Communal Politics. Uttar Pradesh, 1937–9* (New Delhi 2001), pp. 229ff.
118. Abul Kalam Azad's well-known comments constitute one of the best known articulations of this view; see A K Azad, *India Wins Freedom: The Complete Version* (Delhi 1988).
119. Cf. Hasan, ed., *India's Partition*, 'Introduction', pp. 23–5; Sumit Sarkar, *Modern India, 1885–1947* (Delhi 1983), pp. 355–6.

120. In addition to the references cited in the previous three footnotes, see Khaliquzzaman, *Pathway to Pakistan*, 175; Hardy, *The Muslims of British India*, 227–8; 'Report of the Committee appointed by the Council of the All-India Muslim League to Inquire into Muslim Grievances in the Congress Governed Provinces' in Jamil-ud-din Ahmad (comp.) *Historic Documents of the Muslim Freedom Movement* (Lahore 1970), esp. 278–80.

121. Hasan, ed., *India's Partition*, 'Introduction', p. 24. For Nehru's view, see Uma Kaura, *Muslims and Indian Nationalism* (Delhi 1977), p. 123.

122. Sarkar, *Modern India*, p. 349; Reeves, *Landlords and Governments in UP*, p. 229.

123. Reeves *et al*, eds., *Handbook to Elections in UP*, p. 311.

124. Interviews with Ali Sardar Jafri and others who were students of Aligarh University in the 1930s and '40s. Cf. Hasan, 'Muslim Mass Contacts Campaign', pp. 143–4, 150.

125. 'Congress Kanpur Enquiry, 1931', 327–33.

126. Hasan, 'Muslim Mass Contacts Campaign', p. 156.

127. Cmd. 3997. *Indian Round Table Conference (Second Session)*, 360; *NOP* 20 and 27 June, 5 December 1931; Hasan, ed., *India's Partition*, 'Introduction', p. 20.

Chapter 6. Mass Mobilization

1. Nehru, *Autobiography*, 238; Sumit Sarkar: 'The Logic of Gandhian Nationalism: Civil Disobedience and the Gandhi-Irwin Pact', *Indian Historical Review*, III, 1 (July 1976).

2. See chapter 3, section III above.

3. Nehru, *Autobiography*, 282.

4. See chapter 4 above.

5. Hume Colln, IV, Hume to his parents, 27 January 1932.

6. For Butler of Awadh, see Reeves, *Landlords and Governments in UP*, 47 and *passim*.

7. See P D Reeves, 'The Politics of Order'; W F Crawley, 'Kisan Sabhas and Agrarian Revolt in the United Provinces, 1920 to 1921', *Modern Asian Studies*, 5, 2, April 1971; Dhanagare, *Agrarian Movements and Gandhian Politics*, 88–94; M H Siddiqi, *Agrarian Unrest in North India. The United Provinces, 1918–22* (New Delhi 1978); and Kapil Kumar, *Peasants in Revolt: Oudh, 1918–22* (Delhi 1984).

8. Nehru, *Autobiography*, p. 51.

9. Ibid., pp. 49, 51, 54–5.

10. Ibid., p. 54.

11. Ibid., p. 53; emphasis added.

12. *The Independent*, 13 Jan 1921, cited in P D Reeves, 'The Landlords' Response to Political Change in the United Provinces of Agra and Oudh, India, 1921–37', ANU Ph.D. thesis, 1963, p. 117.

13. This account of social and physical conditions in Agra and Rae Bareli is based on the *District Gazetteers* of Agra and Rae Bareli (by H R Nevill, 1905), *Final Report on the Third Regular Settlement of the Rae Bareli District* (Allahabad 1929), *Final Report on the Settlement and Record Operations in District Agra* (Allahabad 1930), R F Mudie, *Cultivators' Debt in the Agra District* (Allahabad 1931), S S Nehru *Caste and Credit in the Rural Area*, and Hailey Colln, Vol. 29.

14. Except for Mathura, a district very like Agra, which had a still lighter average rainfall and sparser rural population.

15. *Final Settlement Report of Agra* (1930), 12.
16. ibid., Knox's 'Note', 2–3.
17. See chapter 2, section II above.
18. *Season & Crop Report for the United Provinces* (annual) for 1905–6 to 1933–4. (I am grateful to Elizabeth Whitcombe for allowing me to use the data she had tabulated for this period).
19. Special categories of under-proprietors and sub-settlement holders arose in Awadh after the 1857 uprising when the Government, while granting *sanads* to the *taluqdars*, decided to recognize and record the traditional rights of inferior holders and to limit the demands of the *taluqdars* against such persons.
20. S H Fremantle, *Report on the 2nd Settlement of the Rae Bareli District, Oudh, 1897* (Allahabad 1898), 25, 36–7.
21. ibid., 45; *Collection of Papers Relating to the Condition of the Tenantry and the Working of the Present Rent-Law in Oudh, Vol. I* (Allahabad 1883), 135, 145, 147–9.
22. (IOL) MSS. Eur. F. 116, Harcourt Butler Colln, 80, Hailey-Hopkins, 19 January 1921.
23. *Ibid; Papers Relating to the Condition of the Tenantry, Vol. I*, 256–7 and *Vol. II* (1883), 161.
24. J F Macandrew, *Report of the Settlement Operations of the Rae Bareli District* (Lucknow 1872), Government Resolution, 3.
25. Hailey Colln, 21A, Hailey-Crerar, 24 July 1931.
26. *Final Settlement Report of Rae Bareli* (1929), Knox's 'Note', 2–3.
27. *UP Zamindari Abolition Committee, II*, 46–7.
28. *Report on the 2nd Settlement of Rae Bareli, 1897*, 32, and Settlement Commissioner's letter, 3; *Rae Bareli District Gazetteer*, (1905), 114.
29. Musgrave, 'Landlords and Lords of the Land', argues this case for UP; D Washbrook, 'Country Politics, Madras 1880 to 1930' in Gallagher, *et al* (eds), *Locality, Province and Nation*, 210, generalizes the argument for the country as a whole.
30. See R Guha, 'Neel Darpan: the Image of a Peasant Revolt in a Liberal Mirror', *Journal of Peasant Studies*, 2, 1 (October 1975) for an analysis of such a struggle for initiative in another peasant struggle; and for a far more wide-ranging analysis, R Guha, *Elementary Aspects of Peasant Insurgency in Colonial India* (Delhi 1983).
31. Waugh, *Rent and Revenue Policy*, (1932), 17.
32. Hailey Colln, 29B, 'Agricultural Prices in the United Provinces' (n.d., but covers the period up to August 1932).
33. ibid., 29C, 'Report on the present Economic Situation in the United Provinces' by E A H Blunt (n.d., but evidently written in 1933), 15.
34. Waugh, *Rent and Revenue Policy*, 27; S C Chaturvedi, *Rural Wages in the United Provinces* (Govt of UP, Dept of Economics and Statistics, Allahabad 1947), 510–17.
35. *UP Census, 1931, I*, 395–7. For relinquishment of land, see *UP Revenue Administration Report*, 1928–9 to 1931–2; Waugh, *Rent and Revenue Policy* (1932), 32; GOI Home-Poll. 33/36/31, D.O.1385-S. Jagdish Prasad-Emerson, 26 October 1931, also Hailey-Crerar 9 November 1931.
36. Hailey Colln, 29C, Blunt's 'Report on the Present Economic Situation', 12.
37. See *Season and Crop Report of UP*, 1927–8 to 1933–4; and *Agricultural Statistics of India*, 1930–1 to 1933–4.
38. *UP Administration Report 1929–30*, xix, and *1930–1*, xv.
39. Hailey Colln, 29A, 'Note for Rent and Revenue Committee' (n.d.).
40. Nehru, *Autobiography*, 171.
41. Waugh, 'Rent and Revenue Problems' (1934), 5. The following discussion of the remissions question is based on this report.

42. Hailey Colln, 20, Hailey-Lord Peel, 25 May 1931.

43. Cf. Blunt, 'Report on the Present Economic Situation', 18.

44. Waugh, *Rent and Revenue Policy* (1932), 18.

45. This was the proportion to be taken as land revenue under the UP Land Revenue (Amendment) Act of 1929.

46. Hailey Colln, 21B, Hailey-Willingdon, 12 August 1931; Hume Colln, IV, Hume to his parents, 14 August 1932.

47. Waugh, 'Rent and Revenue Problems' (1934), 10.

48. *UP Revenue Administration Report, 1928–9*, Appx. B, 2.

49. See e.g. *Pratap* (15 September 1929).

50. *Confidential List of the More Important Political and Quasi-Political Organisations* (1930; 2nd edn 1933), copy at Local Intelligence Unit, Kotwali, Rae Bareli; for renewed Congress propaganda, see chapter 4, section V above.

51. FR, March 1930, 2; PAI 22 March 1930; Halifax Colln, 19, Irwin – G R Lane-Fox, 31 March 1930. The following account of political activities in Agra and Rae Bareli is based on PAIs, contemporary pamphlets and leaflets, especially *Agra Satyagraha Sangram*, and interviews. Congress and government files and newspaper reports provided supplementary information.

52. See PAIs 11 January, 1 and 8 March 1930.

53. e.g., see PAI 24 January 1931; *Agrarian Distress in UP*, 208; and *Agra Satyagraha Sangram*, 53–4. Congress leaders working in the Agra rural areas in the mid-1920s had also sought to associate landowners with their village organization efforts; *Aj* (15 March 1926), letter from Deokinandan Vibhav, organizer, Kisan-Mazdur Ashram, Agra, 19 February 1926.

54. AICC G-59/1930, correspondence between JN and Sitla Sahai, 9–11 April 1930.

55. PAIs 26 April and 24 May 1930, noticed the distribution of 'no-rent' leaflets. See also PAIs 14 and 21 June 1930.

56. PAI 5 July 1930.

57. PAI 30 August 1930.

58. *Agra Satyagraha Sangram*, 89–90, notes that 10,000 leaflets containing the PCC council resolution on non-payment of taxes were distributed in the district in the last three months of 1930; see also NOPs, December 1930 and January 1931.

59. *Agra Satyagraha Sangram*, 98–9; *Pratap* (18 January 1931). I have rendered *lagan* (literally, rent) as tax; it is clear from the context that this is what is meant.

60. *Agra Satyagraha Sangram*, 66–70.

61. ibid., 90; FR, December 1930, 2.

62. *Agra Satyagraha Sangram*, 90–4. (*Prasad* is an offering of sweetmeats or fruit made to a deity and later distributed among devotees).

63. See UP Police Dept 1568/1934 (SRR), extracts from *Sainik*, December 1930 and January 1931, for examples of police brutality. Of course, these were not the only villages where men were forced to leave their homes and holdings. Throughout the province there was a large number of formal (i.e. legal) relinquishments of holdings, apart from temporary retirements. In Agra province, legal relinquishments had been high since the mid-1920s, averaging about 20,000 annually. In 1931–2 the figure shot up to 71,430. In Awadh the figure was 5204 in 1930–1 and 17,609 in 1931–2; *UP Revenue Administration Reports*, for relevant years.

64. *Agra Satyagraha Sangram*, 95–6; *Pratap* (18 and 25 January 1931); interviews with Jagan Prasad Rawat, Lucknow, 15–16 January 1973.

65. *Agra Satyagraha Sangram*, 96.

66. Rai Sahib Chaudhri Surajpal Singh, a landlord of the village (in Tahsil Bah), objected — allegedly at government instigation — to the setting up of a Congress camp on his lands. The result was an armed clash between the landlord's men and police, on

the one hand, and Congressmen and their supporters on the other. Local traders manned the Congress organization in the area, and it was said that there was a longstanding enmity between them and the Chaudhri. This may have been partly responsible for the clash. A detailed account is given in ibid., 29–35.

67. PAIs April-May 1931; AICC G-5/(Kw) (ii)/1931.
68. NOP 28 March 1931.
69. See, e.g., PAI 4 April and 9 May 1931.
70. PAI 28 March 1931. Significantly enough, less than six months earlier, JN had strongly opposed the idea of peasants asking the Government for greater remissions, Syed Mahmud Colln., File 'From JN-1930', Note (in JN's hand, evidently written in October 1930).
71. *Agrarian Distress in UP*, 212; AICC G-5 (Kw) (ii)/1931, 'Agra District Congress Conference. Address of Shri Chandradhar Johri, Chairman Reception Committee'.
72. AICC P-21/1931, 'Achal Gram Seva Sangh' and 'Achal Gram Sevak Sangh – Constitution and Rules' (both Hindi); and PAI 18 July 1931. Achal Singh himself described the Sangh's work as chiefly that of 'medicine and propaganda'; interview, New Delhi, 8 March 1973.
73. PAI 17 October 1931.
74. PAI 25 July 1931.
75. PAI 19 September 1931.
76. PAI 9 May 1931.
77. PAI 11 July 1931.
78. *The Pioneer* (1 and 15 July 1931); PAI 11 July 1931; *Agrarian Distress in UP*, 206–25.
79. ibid., 274; and above example of Shahjagarhi.
80. Interview, Jagan Prasad Rawat, Lucknow, 15 January 1973.
81. Gaol lists indicate a far smaller number of rural arrests than in 1930.
82. PAI 14 May 1932.
83. FR April 1932, 2, May 1932, 1, October 1932, 1; PAIs, 9 April 1932ff.; UP Police Dept 1890/1932, D.O. 435-S, Collector Agra-Chief Secy UP, 14 July 1932; UP Congress bulletins for 1932–3 among proscribed pamphlets held at NAI.
84. PAI 5 April 1930.
85. PAI 5 July 1930.
86. Hailey Colln, 22, Government's 'Statement of Case Regarding the No-Rent Campaign'; NOP 18 April 1931, quoting *Pathik*.
87. See chapter 3, section III above.
88. PAI 13 June, 9 and 2 May 1931 respectively.
89. Chapter 3, section III.
90. GOI Home-Poll. 33/23/1931, Note on events in Rae Bareli enclosed with D.O. No. 707, Jagdish Prasad-Emerson, 16 July 1931.
91. Standard *bigha* under Mughal rule equalled 5/8 acre, but the measure varied from region to region in UP.
92. See 'Village Crime Registers' in Local Intelligence Unit, Rae Bareli Kotwali, and Rae Bareli Collectorate files of court cases and judgments for the years 1930–3.
93. *Abhyudaya* (18 November 1931).
94. PAI 28 February, 14 March and 8 August 1931; *Pratap* (6 September and 18 October 1931); and *Agrarian Distress in UP*, 119–21, 'Report on the Firing in Panwari' by Rafi Ahmad Kidwai.
95. GOI Home-Poll. 33/XVI and Kw/1931, D.O. 600/Z, Jagdish Prasad-Emerson, 30 June 1931.
96. PAI 27 June 1931.
97. PAI 25 October 1930 and 10 January 1931.

98. See UP Police Dept 1077/1930 (SRR), Commissioner, Lucknow Divn-Jagdish Prasad, 15 January 1931.
99. e.g., PAI 10 January 1931.
100. *Agrarian Distress in UP*, 115.
101. PAI 28 March 1931.
102. *Agrarian Distress in UP*, 121–4; AICC G-140/1931, Pt IV, Sitla Sahai-JN, 13 September 1931.
103. Hailey Colln, 20, Hailey-Irwin, 9 May 1931.
104. As in n.95 above.
105. *The Pioneer* (8 July 1931) (emphasis added).
106. Government's 'Statement of Case Regarding "No-Rent" Campaign'.
107. PAI 16 May 1931, Maharajganj meeting, 8 May, for instance.
108. GOI Home Poll. 33/24/31, note on Rae Bareli events; also PAIs, April–June 1931. For similar exhortations by Congress leaders of other districts, see e.g. *The Leader* (19, 26 and 27 June 1931), Tandon's Press Note, and Raghubir Sahai and Uma Shankar's letters.
109. PAI 8 August 1931, meeting of 19 July.
110. PAI 11 April 1931; *Agrarian Distress in UP*, 113; Hailey Colln, 20, Madan Mohan Malaviya-Emerson, 15 April 1931, notes the efforts of the Allahabad and Rae Bareli DCCs to bring about settlements with *zamindars*. For other Congress-landlord agreements, see GOI Home Poll. 33/XVI and Kw/1931, JN-Jagdish Prasad, Allahabad, 11 March 1931; and *Abhyudaya* (13 May 1931).
111. *Pratap* (13 January 1921), in Rae Bareli Collectorate Records, file on 'Munshiganj Firing, 1921'.
112. *Agrarian Distress in UP*, 122.
113. ibid., 113.
114. AICC G-140/1931, Pt II, English translation of the agreement signed on 25 October 1931 by Sitla Sahai and the *zamindar*, Arkha, at the residence of the Sub-divisional Officer, Salon, Rae Bareli.
115. PAI 9 May 1931.
116. PAI 9 July 1931.
117. GOI Home Poll. 33/XVI and Kw/1931, Letter No. 45-P/7, Dy. Commissioner, Rae Bareli-Chief Secy UP, 22 July 1931.
118. AICC G-59/1931, JN-Rana Umanath Bux Singh of Khajurgaon, Rae Bareli (n.d.); PAI 8 August 1931.
119. PAI 26 September 1931.
120. PAI 9 May 1931; AICC G-59/1931, letters from Anjani Kumar and Mata Prasad Misra-JN, June 1931 and JN-Misra, 1 July 1931.
121. PAI 4 July and 8 August 1931. Damodar Swarup Seth, the Bareilly Congress leader, constituted the one-man committee.
122. PAI 9 May 1931.
123. e.g. *Pratap* (2 and 9 August 1931); NOP 22 August 1931.
124. *Agrarian Distress in UP*, 113–29 and 272–3; AICC G-59/1931, Sitla Sahai-JN, 20 July 1931; also PAI 25 July 1931 and NOP 30 May, 4 and 11 July 1931.
125. AICC G-140 (kw) (i)/1931, JN-Altafur Rahman, 30 July 1931.
126. PAI 24 October 1931.
127. Hume Colln, IV, Hume to his parents, 3 March, 3 April, 14 and 26 July 1932.
128. ibid., IV, letters of 3 March, 10 July 1932; PAI 11 June, 2 July 1932.
129. ibid; III, Pt 2, Hume to his parents, 18 December 1931, and IV, letters of 29 May and 10 July 1932.
130. Raja Awadesh Singh of Kalakankar gave a Ford car, petrol and a driver for the use of the Bachhrawan (Rae Bareli) Congress in 1931; *Navajivan* (9 April 1967). The

taluqdar of Semri passed on to the Rae Bareli Congress leadership the two circulars issued by the District Magistrate in 1931, calling for joint Government-landlord action against the Congress and unruly peasants; Satya Narain Srivastava: '*Svargiya Lokpriya Pt. Jawahar Lal Nehru ke Puneet tatha Madhur Sansmaran*' (Ms., which was in Sri Srivastava's possession, Bakuliha, Rae Bareli). See also chapter 4, section VII above.

131. *Abhyudaya* (5 April 1930). See also AICC P20/1929, JN-Chandrabhal Johri and JN-Sri Prakasa, both dated 12 July 1929.
132. PAI 6 July and 3 August 1929.
133. PAI 15 March 1930.
134. PAI 3 August 1929, 29 March and 5 April 1930.
135. See chapter 3, section IV above.
136. Interview, Allahabad, 3 January 1973.
137. *Abhyudaya* (8 December 1930).
138. PAI 9 December 1933.
139. PAI 3 February and 19 May 1934.
140. PAI 14 November 1931; *Abhyudaya* (25 November 1931).
141. GOI Home-Poll. 33/XVI and Kw/1931, Confidl D.O. 663/S, Jagdish Prasad-Emerson, 9 July 1931; PAI 20 June 1931.
142. PAI 11 and 25 April, 9 May, 13 and 20 June 1931.
143. *Abhyudaya* (18 November 1931).
144. See chapter 5, section VI above.
145. PAI 20 June 1931.
146. PAI 16, 23 and 30 May 1931.
147. AICC G-140 (Kw) (i)/1931 JN-Altafur Rahman, 30 July 1931. In this last respect, at any rate, the Congress and the Government had a common object; the Allahabad authorities posted additional police to Manjhanpur to maintain the peace. *All-India Reporter. 1934. Allahabad Section* (Nagpur 1934), 'Ramhit and others v. Emperor', 776–9; PAI 20 June 1931 and interviews with Babu Mangla Prasad, one of the Congress leaders involved in this case (Allahabad, 22 June 1971, 29–30 June 1972), for information on the Bhatwaria Case.
148. *Abhyudaya* (11 and 18 February 1931).
149. UP Police Dept 202/1931 (SRR); *Aj* (17 May, 27 June, 6 July 1931); NOP 30 May, 20 and 27 June, 18 July 1931; PAI 4 July 1931; GOI Home Poll. 33/XVI and Kw/1931, D.O. 600/Z, Jagdish Prasad-Emerson, 30 June 1931, and Confidl D.O. No. 752-D, Jagdish Prasad-Emerson, 25 July 1931; GOI Home Poll. 33/24/31, D.O. No. 707 – [illegible], Prasad-Emerson, 16 July 1931.
150. Hailey Colln, 23 A, Hailey-Findlater Stewart, 19 January 1932, and Hailey-de Montmorency, 31 January 1932; also Templewood Colln, 15, Hailey-Samuel Hoare, 28 February 1932.
151. Waugh, 'Rent and Revenue Problems' (1934), 7.
152. See chapter 3, section IV above.
153. *Svatantrata Sangram ke Sainik. Rae Bareli*, 'Introduction'; *Agrarian Distress in UP*, 125–7; NOP 22 August 1931, report on Rae Bareli from *Pratap*; Local Intelligence Unit records, Kotwali, Rae Bareli.
154. *Final Settlement Report of Rae Bareli* (1929), 13; *UP Banking Enquiry Committee*, I, 96.
155. See chapter 3, section V above.
156. *UP Government Gazette* (10 September 1932), Pt. VIII, 257
157. *Congress Agrarian Enquiry Committee Report* (1936), 68–9 and 72.
158. PAI 1 September 1928, and 14 and 21 December 1929; B.N. Datar (ed.), *Harihar Nath Shastri, Life and Work* (Bombay 1968), 18–19. Cf. JN's exhortation to the

All-India Trade Union Congress to agitate on precisely these issues, *Indian Quarterly Register*, 1929, Vol. II, 427.

159. Datar (ed.), *Harihar Nath Shastri*, 21; PAI 12, 19, 26 December 1931.
160. See chapter 4, section VI above.
161. K M Panikkar and A Pershad (eds.), *The Voice of Freedom. Selected Speeches of Pandit Motilal Nehru* (London 1961), 512 (emphasis added).
162. *Proceedings of the Legislative Council of the United Provinces. Official Report.* XXIX, 355, cited in Reeves, 'The Landlords' Response to Political Change', 197.
163. *The Leader* (11 July 1926), 'Why this compromise?'.
164. Halifax Colln, 20, Marris-Irwin, 2 July 1926. See Reeves, *Landlords and Governments in UP*, 126–36, for an excellent account of the proceedings in the legislature.
165. AICC G-140 (Kw) (i)/1931, JN-Altafur Rahman, 30 July 1931; also cited in ch. 4 above.
166. See Conrad Brandt, *et al.* (eds), *A Documentary History of Chinese Communism*; Stuart R Schram, 'Mao Tse-Tung and the Role of the Various Classes in the Chinese Revolution, 1923–7', in 'The Polity and Economy of China' (typescript).
167. *The Leader* (23–4 September and 13 October 1933, 10 January and 18 April 1934); GOI Home-Poll 4/7/34.
168. *Aj* (10 June 1934).
169. *Aj* (22 September 1934); also chapter 3, section VII above.
170. PAI 31 October 1931.
171. n. 114 above.
172. Like many others, he dropped the surname once he had joined the nationalist agitation in an attempt to refuse caste distinctions; interview, Rae Bareli, 14 January 1973.
173. GOI Home Poll. 33/24/31, D.O. 17/6, D C , Rae Bareli-Commissioner, Lucknow, 30 June 1931; also 'Statement of Case Regarding "No-Rent" Campaign'.
174. AICC G-59/1931, JN-Secy PCC, 2 July 1931, enclosing complaints from Sitla Sahai.
175. *Agrarian Distress in UP*, 113; GOI Home Poll. 33/24/31 D. O. 17/6, D C Rae Bareli-Commissioner, Lucknow, 30 June 1931, indicates that the Raja had also started a Khadi Vidyala Vidyalaya in which Sitla Sahai's wife taught spinning.
176. *Agrarian Distress in UP*, 124–8.
177. See NOP 24 and 31 October, 7 November 1931.
178. *Aj* (5 December 1931); UP Govt's 'Statement of Case Regarding No-Rent Campaign', extracts from JN's cable to Gandhi on 16 October 1931, Gandhi's reply, and the All-India Congress President Vallabhbhai Patel's letter of 10 November 1931 to the President of the UP PCC, saying that since collections began in mid-November they could not await Gandhi's return and 'he saw no alternative before the Provincial Committee but ... [that of] advising peasants to refuse voluntarily to pay any rent or revenue till adequate relief was secured'.
179. NOP 15 August, 19 September 1929.
180. See chapter 3, section VII above.
181. *Agrarian Distress in UP, passim.*
182. *Congress Agrarian Enquiry Committee Report*, chapter on 'Recommendations'.
183. The Lucknow Congress leader, Gopi Nath Srivastava, admitted this openly: 'The role of the landless....in the determination of the Congress policy is not yet active,' he wrote; *When Congress Ruled (A Close-Range Survey of the Congress Administration during the Twenty-Eight Months of 1937–9 in the United Provinces)* (Lucknow, n.d.), 18.
184. See P D Reeves, *Landlords and Governments in UP*, pp. 230–47, for a full discussion of this measure.

185. Nehru, *Autobiography*, 58.
186. See chapter 5, section V above.

Chapter 7. Conclusion

1. *UP Administration Report, 1921–2*, xviii. Bayly, 'The Development of Political Organisation in the Allahabad Locality', 369–71 and 382, describes a similar development in northern Allahabad.
2. See M H Siddiqi, *Agrarian Unrest in North India*; Kapil Kumar, *Peasants in Revolt*; Reeves, 'The Politics of Order'; W F Crawley, 'Kisan Sabhas and Agrarian Revolt'; G Pandey, 'Peasant Revolt and Indian Nationalism. The Peasant Movement in Awadh, 1919–22', in R Guha, ed., *Subaltern Studies. Writings on South Asian Society and History*, Volume I (Delhi 1982).
3. For an elaboration of this argument, see my 'Congress and the Nation, 1917–1947', in Richard Sisson and Stanley Wolpert, eds., *Congress and Indian Nationalism. The Pre-Independence Phase* (Berkeley and Los Angeles, 1988).
4. *SWJN*, 7:93, 97, 108.
5. *SWJN*, 7:190.
6. Durga Das, ed., *Sardar Patel's Correspondence, 1945–50*, Volume 3 (Ahmedabad, 1971), 168.
7. Partha Chatterji, *Nationalist Thought and the Colonial World. A Derivative Discourse?* (Delhi 1986), ch. 5.
8. CWMG, XXXXVIII:242–3.
9. SWJN, 17:510 (emphasis added).
10. S. Gopal, *Jawaharlal Nehru: A Biography*, Volume I (London, 1975), 56. Cf. also Ranajit Guha, 'Discipline and Mobilize' in Partha Chatterjee and Gyanendra Pandey, eds., *Subaltern Studies. Writings on South Asian Society and History. Volume VII* (Delhi 1992).
11. Headman or chief, in this instance of one caste in a village.
12. Premchand, *Godan*, 177.
13. See chapter 3, section III.
14. See D E U Baker, 'The Changing Leadership of the Congress in the Central Provinces and Berar, 1919–39', in D A Low (ed.), *Congress and the Raj* (London 1977).
15. I owe this formulation to the late Professor Ravinder Kumar.
16. S N Sen Gupta, 'The Depression' in Radhakamal Mukerjee (ed.), *Economic Problems of Modern India*, Vol. I (London 1939), 339; *Abhyudaya* ('Kisan Number') (18 November 1931), p. 32.
17. There was no longer any talk of '*Swaraj* in one year' and senior Congress leaders did their best to restrain followers who promised the abolition of all rents under *swaraj*.
18. The powerful communist movement in Kerala, for example, absorbed many groups of Congressmen who had begun their radical political work in the CSP; see Dilip Menon, *Caste, Nationalism, and Communism in South India: Malabar, 1900–48* (Cambridge 1994); and A K Gopalan, *Kerala, Past and Present* (London 1959), 50ff.
19. See chapter 3, section VII above.
20. This sentence was written in response to the extraordinary explanatory status accorded to the constitutional structure by a group of Cambridge historians writing on Indian nationalism in the 1970s; see especially the volume edited by Gallagher, *et al*, *Locality, Province and Nation*. I allow it to stand here as a reminder of the narrowness of some of the debates of that time.

21. A powerful illustration of this for one phase of the nationalist struggle is now available in Shahid Amin, *Event, Metaphor, Memory. Chauri-Chaura, 1922–92* (Berkeley and Los Angeles, 1995).
22. Chapter 6, section VI.
23. *Agrarian Distress in UP*, 86–7.
24. ibid. 82 (emphasis added).
25. See *Svatantrata Sangram ke Sainik* (Allahabad Division), 193; and for details of the Bhatwaria riot, *All India Reporter 1934 (Allahabad Section)*, 776–9.
26. This account is based *on All India Reporter 1924 (Allahabad Section)*,' Abdullah & others v. King-Emperor', 233–51, and Judgement of Sessions Judge H E Holmes in 'King-Emperor v. Nazar Ali & others', Trial no. 44 & 45 of 1922 (Gorakhpur Collectorate records). Shahid Amin drew my attention to the latter. His book, *Event, Metaphor, Memor*, now provides the best starting point for any understanding of Chauri Chaura.
27. The organizers named in the judgements cited above, except for the two Muslims, were all identified by single names, very probably a pointer to low caste. And the low status of two of them – the carpenter (*barhai*) and milkman (*ahir*) – was directly indicated.
28. D Hardiman, *Peasant Nationalists of Gujarat. Kheda District, 1917–34* (Delhi 1981).
29. J Pouchepadass, 'Local Leaders and the Intelligentsia in the Champaran Satyagraha (1917): A Study in Peasant Mobilisation', *Contributions to Indian Sociology*, NS, no. 8, 1974; Arvind Das, *Agrarian Unrest and Socio-Economic Change in Bihar, 1900–80* (New Delhi 1983). See also B B Misra, *Selected Documents on Mahatma Gandhis Movement in Champaran, 1917–18* (Patna, 1963), pp. 9ff; and Stephen Henningham, *Peasant Movements in Colonial India: North Bihar, 1917–42* (Canberra 1982).
30. This paragraph owed much to discussions I had with Ranajit Guha and David Hardiman. Consider in this context what Baba Ramchandra, the leader of the Awadh Kisan Sabha movement, had to say in notes that he made in 1939: "It was felt that if we could link our Kisan movement with some established organization, or gain the support of well-to-do (privileged?) groups and lawyers, then this movement would become the future of India"; Ramchandra Collection I, subject file 1 (NML).
31. See R Kumar (ed.), *Essays on Gandhian Politics. The Rowlatt Satyagraha of 1919* (Oxford 1971); M Venkatarangaiya (ed.), *The Freedom Struggle in Andhra Pradesh. Vol. III (1921–31)* (Hyderabad 1965), 79–93, 365–407; D Arnold, 'Rebellious Hillmen: the Gudem-Rampa Risings, 1839–1924' in Guha, ed., *Subaltern Studies*, Volume I; D Baker, 'The Changing Leadership of the Congress in the Central Provinces and Berar, 1919–39'; and C Bates, 'Congress and the Tribals', in M Shepperdson and C Simmons, eds., *The Indian National Congress and the Political Economy of India, 1885–1985* (Aldershot 1988).
32. *The Swadeshi Movement in Bengal*, 515–6.
33. H Sanyal, 'Nationalist Movement in Arambagh, 1921–42' (*Anya Artha*, nos. 6–8, Sept. 1974–May 1975). I am grateful to Tanika Sarkar for translating from the Bengali.
34. See Partha Chatterjee, Bengal 1920-47: The Land Question (Calcutta 1984).
35. *Congress Government in UP, July 1937–October 1938: An Authoritative Record of Legislative and Administrative Activities of the Congress Ministry in the UP*, (Allahabad: n.p., n.d.), pp. viii–ix.

Select Bibliography

MANUSCRIPT SOURCES

1. *Official*

   India Office Records, London
   'A' Proceedings of the Government of the United Provinces of Agra and Oudh [Awadh]
   Public and Judicial Papers
   Notes on the Press of the United Provinces of Agra and Oudh (weekly, by the Government Reporter)

   National Archives of India, New Delhi
   Proceedings and files of the Government of India, Home Department, Political Branch. (These include the 'Fortnightly Reports for the United Provinces of Agra and Oudh')

   UP Secretariat Record Room, Lucknow, and UP State Archives, Lucknow
   Proceedings and files of the Government of the United Provinces of Agra and Oudh, Agriculture, Appointments, Confidential, Education, Finance, General Administration, Judicial (Civil), Judicial (Criminal), Police and Reform Departments

   Criminal Investigation Department Office, Lucknow
   'Police Abstracts of Intelligence for the United Provinces of Agra and Oudh' (weekly)

   Collectorate Record Rooms, Agra, Allahabad, Azamgarh and Rae Bareli
   Gaol records and court cases relating to political agitation

   Kotwali, Rae Bareli

Local intelligence records of political and criminal activities in the district

2. *Unofficial*
All India Congress Committee Papers (NML)
All India Congress Committee Supplementary Papers (NML)
Butler, Spencer Harcourt. Papers (IOL, Mss. Eur. F. 116)
Chaturvedi, Banarasidas. Papers (NAI)
Haig, Harry Graham. Papers (IOL, Mss. Eur. F. 115)
Hailey, William Malcolm. Papers (IOL, Mss. Eur. E. 220)
Halifax, First Earl of. First Baron Irwin. Wood, Edward Frederick Lindley. Papers (IOL, Mss. Eur. C. 152)
Hindu Mahasabha Papers (NML)
Hume, Andrew Parke. Papers (IOL, Mss. Eur. D. 724)
Nehru, Jawaharlal. Correspondence (NML)
Nehru, Jawaharlal. Papers (NML)
Nehru, Motilal. Papers (NML)
Nehru, Motilal and Jawaharlal. Correspondence between them (NML)
Paliwal, Sri Krishna Dutt. Gaol Diary, unfinished autobiography and other papers (Allahabad Museum)
Pant, Govind Ballabh. Papers (NAI)
Sampurnanand Papers (NAI)
Satya Bhakta Papers (NAI)
Shibli Manzil. Collection of Papers including correspondence of Masud Ali and Suleiman Nadvi (Shibli Manzil, Azamgarh)
Sita Ram Papers (NAI)
Sri Prakasa Papers (NML)
Srivastava, Satya Narain. Papers (Bakuliha village, Rae Bareli)
Sunderlal Papers (NML)
Syed Mahmud Papers (NML)
Tandon, Purushottam Das. Papers (NAI)
Templewood, First Viscount. Hoare, Samuel John Gurney. Papers (IOL, Mss. Eur. E. 240)

PRINTED SOURCES

1. *Official Publications*
All-India Reporter. Allahabad Section (annual).

Census of India, 1921. United Provinces of Agra and Oudh. Volume XVI (Allahabad 1923).

Census of India, 1931. United Provinces of Agra and Oudh. Volume XVIII (Allahabad 1933).

Census of India, 1951. Volume II. Uttar Pradesh (Allahabad 1951).

Confidential List of the more important Political and Quasi-Political Societies, Sabhas and Anjumans in the United Provinces for the period ending 30 June 1933 (Allahabad 1933).

Collection of Papers Relating to the Condition of the Tenantry and the Working of the Present Rent-Law in Oudh, 2 vols (Allahabad 1883).

East India (Cawnpore Riots). Report of the Committee of Inquiry and Resolution of the Government of the United Provinces, Cmd 3891 (London 1931).

East India (Constitutional Reforms). Report on Indian Constitutional Reforms, Cmd 9109 (London 1918).

East India (Emergency Measures). Action taken to counteract the Civil Disobedience Movement, Cmd 4014 (London 1932).

East India (Non-Cooperation) Telegraphic Correspondence Regarding the Situation in India, Cmd 1586 (London 1922).

Famine Inquiry Commission. Final Report (Delhi 1945).

Final Report on the Settlement and Record Operations in District Agra by R F Mudie (Allahabad 1930).

Report on the Settlement Operations of the Rae Bareli District by J F McAndrew (Lucknow 1872).

Report on the 2nd Settlement of the Rae Bareli District, Oudh, 1897 by S H Fremantle (Allahabad 1898).

Final Report on the Third Regular Settlement of the Rae Bareli District by A C Turner (Allahabad 1929).

Indian Round Table Conference Proceedings (First, Second and Third Sessions) (London 1931–32).

Indian Statutory Commission. Interim Report of the Indian Statutory Commission (Review of Growth of Education in British India by the Auxiliary Committee appointed by the Commission), September 1929, Cmd 3407 (London 1929).

Indian Statutory Commission. Volume I: Survey (London 1930).

Indian Statutory Commission. Volume IX. Memorandum submitted by the Government of the United Provinces to the Indian Statutory Commission (London 1930).

Report of the United Provinces Provincial Banking Enquiry Committee 1929–1930, 4 volumes (Allahabad 1930–1).

Report of the United Provinces Zamindari Abolition Committee (Allahabad 1948).

Report on Agriculture in the United Provinces, prepared under the orders of the Government of UP for the Royal Commission on Agriculture in India (Naini Tal 1926).

Report of the Royal Commission on Labour in India, Cmd 3883 (London 1931).

Royal Commission on Labour in India - Evidence. Vol III (London 1931).

Rural Wages in the United Provinces by S C Chaturvedi (Allahabad 1947).

2. *Reports of political organizations and other associations*

   All Parties Conference, 1928 – *Report of the Committee appointed by the Conference to determine the Principles of the Constitution for India. Together with a summary of the Proceedings of the Conference held at Lucknow* (Allahabad 1928).

   – *Supplementary Report of the Committee* (Allahabad 1928).
   – *Proceedings of the All Parties' National Convention* (Allahabad 1929).

   UP Provincial Congress Committee – *Agrarian Distress in the United Provinces. Being the report of the Committee appointed by the Council of the UP Provincial Congress Committee to enquire into the Agrarian situation in the Province* (Bareilly 1936).

   – *Constitution and Rules of the United Provinces Congress Committee* (Allahabad 1921).

   Upper India Chamber of Commerce – *Upper India Chamber of Commerce Cawnpore, 1888–1938* (n.p., n.d.)

3. *Newspapers and Journals*

   Abhyudaya (Allahabad)
   Aj (Banaras)
   Bharat (Allahabad)
   Brahmana-sarvasva (Etawah)
   Chand (Allahabad)
   The Indian Annual Register (Calcutta), published as *The Indian Quarterly Register* from 1924 to 1929
   Kalyan (Gorakhpur)
   Kisanopkarak (Pratapgarh)
   The Leader (Allahabad)
   Madhuri (Lucknow)

Maya (Allahabad)
The Pioneer (Allahabad)
Pratap (Kanpur)
Prem (Brindaban, Mathura)
Vidyapith (Banaras)

4. Selected Secondary Works

Ahmed, J, 1970, *Historic Documents of the Muslim Freedom Movement*, Lahore.

Ahmed, R, 1981, *The Bengal Muslims, 1871–1906. A Quest for Identity*, Delhi.

Amin, S, 1988, 'Agrarian Bases of Nationalist Agitations in India. An Historiographical Survey', in DA Low ed., *The Indian National Congress. Centenary Hindsights*, Delhi.

Amin, S, 1995, *Event, Metaphor, Memory: Chauri Chaura, 1922–1992*, Berkeley and Los Angeles.

Azad, Abul Kalam, 1988, *India Wins Freedom: The Complete Version*, Delhi.

Baker, C J and Washbrook, D A, 1975, *South India: Political Institutions and Political Change 1880–1940*, Delhi.

Barrier, N G, 1976, *Roots of Communal Politics*, ed., Delhi.

Bayly, C A, 1970, 'The Development of Political Organisation in the Allahabad Locality, 1880–1925', Oxford, D. Phil. Thesis.

Bayly, C A, 1975, *The Local Roots of Indian Politics. Allahabad, 1880–1920*, Oxford.

Birla, G D, 1953, *In the Shadow of the Mahatma*, Calcutta.

Bose, S and Jalal, A, 1997, *Modern South Asia. History, Culture, Political Economy*, London and New York.

Brass, P R, 1974, *Language, Religion and Politics in North India*, Cambridge.

Brennan, L, 1972, 'Political Change in Rohilkhand, 1932–52', Sussex Ph.D. thesis.

Brown, J M, 1972, *Gandhi's Rise to Power. Indian Politics, 1915–22*, Cambridge.

Chakrabarty, D, 1989, *Rethinking Working Class History: Bengal, 1890–1940*, Princeton, N.J.

Chandra, B, 1972, 'Elements of Continuity and Change in Early Nationalist Activity', paper presented at Symposium on Continuity and Change in Indian National Movement, 33rd session, Indian History Congress, Muzaffarpur.

Chandra, S, 1992, *The Oppressive Present. Literature and Social Consciousness in Colonial India*, Delhi.

Chatterjee, P, 1986, *Nationalist Thought and the Colonial World. A Derivative Discourse?* New Delhi.

Chatterjee, P, 1994, *The Nation and its Fragments. Colonial and Postcolonial Histories*, Princeton, N.J.

Chatterjee, P and Pandey, G, 1992, *Subaltern Studies. Writings on South Asian Society and History, VII*, eds., Delhi.

Chaturvedi, S, 1972, *Madan Mohan Malaviya*, New Delhi.

Chopra, P N, 1960, *Rafi Ahmad Kidwai*, Agra.

Crawley, W F, 1971, 'Kisan Sabhas and Agrarian Revolt in the United Provinces', *Modern Asian Studies*, 5, 2.

Das, A N, 1983, *Agrarian Unrest and Socio-Economic Change in Bihar, 1900–80*, New Delhi.

Dhanagare, D N, 1975, *Agrarian Movements and Gandhian Politics*, Agra.

Dutt, R P, 1940, *India Today*, London; 2nd Indian edn., 1949.

Frietag, S, 1989, *Collective Action and Community. Public Arenas and the Emergence of Communalism in North India*, Berkeley and Los Angeles.

Gallagher, J A, et al., 1970, *Locality, Province and Nation. Essays on Indian Politics, 1870–1940*, eds., Cambridge.

Gandhi, M K, 1960–75, *Collected Works of Mahatma Gandhi*, Ahmedabad.

Gopal, S, 1975, *Jawaharlal Nehru. A Political Biography, Volume I*, London.

Gopal, Krishna, 3 May 1966, 'The Development of the Indian National Congress as a Mass Organization, 1918–23', *Journal of Asian Studies*, XXV.

Gopalan, A K, 1959, *Kerala, Past and Present*, London.

Gordon, R A, 1975, 'The Hindu Mahasabha and the Indian National Congress, 1915–26', *Modern Asian Studies*, 9, 2.

Guha, Ranajit, 1983, *Elementary Aspects of Peasant Insurgency in Colonial India*, Delhi.

Guha, Ranajit, 1982–9, *Subaltern Studies. Writings on South Asian Society and History, I–VI*, ed., Delhi.

Guha, Ramchandra, 1989, *The Unquiet Woods: Ecological Change and Peasant Resistance in the Himalaya*, Berkeley and Los Angeles.

Gupta, M, 1969, *Bharat ke Krantikari*, Delhi.

Hardiman, D, 1981, *Peasant Nationalists of Gujarat. Kheda District, 1917–34*, Delhi.

Hardy, P, 1972, *The Muslims of British India*, Cambridge.

Hasan, M, 1993, *India's Partition: Process, Strategy and Mobilization*, ed., Delhi.

Hasan, M, 1979, *Nationalism and Communal Politics in India, 1916–28*, Delhi.

Henningham, S, 1982, *Peasant Movements in Colonial India: North Bihar, 191–42*, Canberra.

Irschick, E F, 1969, *Politics and Social Conflict in South India. The Non-Brahman Movement and Tamil Separatism, 1916–29*, California.

Jain, A P, 1965, *Rafi Ahmad Kidwai*, Bombay.

Joshi, P C, July–September 1963, 'The Decline of Indigenous Handicrafts in Uttar Pradesh', *Indian Economic and Social History Review*, I.

Kaura, Uma, 1977, *Muslims and Indian Nationalism*, Delhi.

Khaliquzzaman, Choudhary, 1961, *Pathway to Pakistan*, Lahore.

Krishnamurthy, J, March 1983, *Survival Politics and Work. Indian Women, 1880–1980*, Special issue of *Indian Economic and Social History Review*, XX ed.

Kumar, K, 1984, *Peasants in Revolt: Oudh, 1918–22*, Delhi.

Kumar, R, 1971, *Essays on Gandhian Politics. The Rowlatt Satyagraha of 1919*, ed., Oxford.

Low, D A, 1968, *Soundings in Modern South Asian History*, ed., London.

Low, D A, 1977, *Congress and the Raj. Facets of the Indian Struggle, 1917–47*, ed., London.

Mahaur, B, et al., 1968, *Yash Ki Dharohar*, Delhi.

McLane, J, 1977, *Indian Nationalism and the Early Congress*, Princeton, N.J.

Menon, D, 1994, *Caste, Nationalism and Communism in South India: Malabar, 1900–48*, Cambridge.

Minault, G, 1982, *The Khilafat Movement: Religious Symbolism and Political Mobilization in India*, Delhi.

Misra, B R, 1942, *Land Revenue Policy in the United Provinces under British Rule*, Banaras.

Misra, S, 2001, *A Narrative of Communal Politics: Uttar Pradesh, 1937–39*, New Delhi.

Morris-Jones, W H, 1976, *The Making of Politicians: Studies from Asia and Africa*, ed., London.

Musgrave, P J, July 1972, 'Landlords and Lords of the Land: Estate Management and Social Control in Uttar Pradesh, 1860–1920', *Modern Asian Studies*, 6, 3.

Nair, K, 1961, *Blossoms in the Dust*, London.

Nanda, B R, 1962, *The Nehrus, Motilal and Jawaharlal*, London.

Nanda, B R and Joshi, V C, 1972, *Studies in Modern Indian History, No. 1*, ed., New Delhi.

Nehru, J, 1936, *An Autobiography*, London.

Nehru, J, 1958, *A Bunch of Old Letters*, Bombay.

Nehru, J, 1946, *The Discovery of India*, London; 3rd edn., 1951.

Page, D J H, 1982, *Prelude to Partition. The Indian Muslims and the Imperial System of Control, 1920–1932*, Delhi.

Pandey, D, 1972, *The Arya Samaj and Indian Nationalism, 1875–1920*, New Delhi.

Pandey, G, 1990, *The Construction of Communalism in Colonial North India*, Delhi.

Pandey, G, 1988, *The Indian Nation in 1942*, ed., Calcutta.

Pandey, G, 1975, 'Mobilisation in a Mass Movement: Congress "Propaganda" in the United Provinces (India), 1930–34', *Modern Asian Studies*, 9, 2.

Panikkar, K M and Pershad, A, 1961, *The Voice of Freedom. Selected Speeches of Pandit Motilal Nehru*, eds., London.

Pouchepadass, J, 1974, 'Local Leaders and the Intelligentsia in the Champaran Satyagraha, (1917): A study in Peasant Mobilisation', *Contributions to Indian Sociology*, NS, No. 8.

Premchand, 1936, *Godan*; new edn Allahabad, 1975.

Premchand, 1971, *Mansarovar, Part I*, Allahabad.

Rajkumar, N V, 1949, *Development of the Congress Constitution*, New Delhi.

Reeves, P D, et al., 1975, *A Handbook to Elections in Uttar Pradesh 1920–51*, Delhi.

Reeves, P D, 1991, *Landlords and Governments in Uttar Pradesh: A Study of their Relations until Zamindari Abolition*, Bombay.

Reeves, P D, February 1966, 'The Politics of Order. "Anti-non-cooperation" in the United Provinces, 1921', *Journal of Asian Studies*, XXV.

Robinson, F, 1974, *Separatism Among Indian Muslims. The Politics of the United Provinces Muslims, 1860–1923*, Cambridge.

Ronaldshay, Earl of, 1925, *The Heart of Aryavarta. A Study of the Psychology of Indian Unrest*, London.

Sampurnanand, 1962, *Memories and Reflections*, Bombay.

Sanyal, H, September 1974–May 1975, 'Nationalist Movement in Arambagh, 1921–42' *Anya Artha*, nos 6–8.

Sangari, K and Vaid, S, 1989, *Recasting Women. Essays in Colonial History*, eds., Delhi.

Sarkar, S, 1 July 1976, 'The Logic of Gandhian Nationalism: Civil Disobedience and the Gandhi–Irwin Pact', *Indian Historical Review*, III.

Sarkar, S, 1983, *Modern India, 1885–1947*, Delhi; 2nd edn., London, 1988.

Sarkar, S, 1973, *The Swadeshi Movement in Bengal, 1903–8*, New Delhi.

Sarkar, T, 2001, *Hindu Wife, Hindu Nation: Community, Religion and Cultural Nationalism*, Delhi.

Seal, A, 1968, *The Emergence of Indian Nationalism. Competition and Collaboration in the later Nineteenth Century*, Cambridge.

Shepperdson, M and C Simmons, 1988, *The Indian National Congress and the Political Economy of India, 1885–1985*, eds., Aldershot.

Shyam, Sunder and Savitri Shyam, 1960, *The Political Life of Pandit Govind Ballabh Pant*, Lucknow.

Siddiqi, A, 1973, *Agrarian Change in a Northern Indian State*, Oxford.

Siddiqi, M H, 1978, *Agrarian Unrest in North India. United Provinces, 1918–22*, New Delhi.

Sisson, R and Wolpert, S, 1988, *Congress and Indian Nationalism. The Pre-Independence Phase*, eds., Berkeley and Los Angeles.

Sri Prakasa, 1970, *Bharat Ratna Dr Bhagavan Das*, Meerut.

Srivastava, G N, n.d., *When Congress Ruled (A Close-Range Survey of the Congress Administration during the Twenty-eight months of 1937–39 in the United Provinces)*, Lucknow.

Tomlinson, B R, 1976, *The Indian National Congress and the Raj, 1929–42*, London.

Venkatarangaiya, M, 1965, *The Freedom Struggle in Andhra Pradesh. Vol III (1921–1931)*, Hyderabad.

Waugh, A A, 1932, *Rent and Revenue Policy in the United Provinces*, Lucknow.

Whitcombe, E, 1971, *Agrarian Conditions in Northern India, Vol. I. The United Provinces Under British Rule, 1860–1900*, Berkeley and Los Angeles.

Wiser, W and C, 1967, *Behind Mud Walls 1930–1960*, Berkeley and Los Angeles.

Yadav, J N S, 1971, *Lal Bahadur Shastri*, Delhi.

Yang, A, 1989, *The Limited Raj: Agrarian Relations in Colonial India. Saran District, 1793–1920*, Berkeley and Los Angeles.

Index